THE JEWISH PEOPLE, THE HOLY LAND,
AND THE STATE OF ISRAEL

Studies in
Judaism and Christianity

*Exploration of Issues in the
Contemporary Dialogue Between
Christians and Jews*

Editors
Lawrence Boadt, CSP
Kevin A. Lynch, CSP
Yehezkel Landau
Dr. Peter Pettit
Dr. Elena Procario-Foley
Dr. Ann Riggs
Michael Kerrigan, CSP

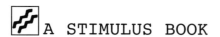 A STIMULUS BOOK

THE JEWISH PEOPLE, THE HOLY LAND, AND THE STATE OF ISRAEL

A Catholic View

Richard C. Lux

A STIMULUS BOOK

PAULIST PRESS ◆ NEW YORK ◆ MAHWAH, NJ

Chapter 3, "The Holy Land," was previously published as "The Land of Israel (*Eretz Yisra'el*) in Jewish and Christian Understanding," in *Studies in Christian-Jewish Relations* 3 (2008) and is included here with permission of that journal's editoral board.

Cover design by Sharyn Banks
Book design by Lynn Else and Theresa M. Sparacio

Library of Congress Cataloging-in-Publication Data

Lux, Richard C.
    The Jewish people, the Holy Land, and the state of Israel : a Catholic view / Richard C. Lux.
        p. cm.
    "A Stimulus book."
    Includes bibliographical references (p.   ) and index.
    ISBN 978-0-8091-4632-1 (alk. paper)
    1. Judaism (Christian theology) 2. Israel (Christian theology) 3. Catholic Church—Doctrines. 4. Palestine in Christianity. I. Title.
    BM535.L795 2010
    261.2′6—dc22

                                                                            2009029064

Published by Paulist Press
997 Macarthur Boulevard
Mahwah, New Jersey 07430

www.paulistpress.com

Printed and bound in the
United States of America

Contents

Foreword

Modern political states struggle regularly with the proper relationship of religious faith and civil government. Are they rightly kept separate, or should there be a close and intertwined linkage between the two? Western secular democracies generally maintain some level of separation of the two, and the trend is growing stronger yearly, especially in the traditionally Christian-dominated nations of Europe. The model often cited has been the experience of the United States of America, where separation of church and state has been accompanied by a strong religious energy alongside relative peace between, and tolerance of, different religious traditions and faiths. Yet many religious people worry that this same environment of tolerance is undermining the religious principles and values that form the foundations of civil government; they also worry that the secular principle accepts no moral norms or religious beliefs as fundamental, but works from a relativity to all beliefs and morals, while forming the ideal citizen as a person of loyalty to the civil laws of the state, regardless of their religious convictions, and generally overriding them.

The struggle is even fiercer in other parts of the world where religion and civil government are strongly linked in the consciousness of the great majority of people. Nowhere is this more true than in nations with majority Muslim populations, where it is generally understood that the national identity is closely tied to Islam as a ruling principle for government. This close unity of faith and political rule is not an absolute necessity in Islamic belief—the faith can flourish in any place—but is an ideal to strive for. Such religious-political tensions have flared up in Nigeria, Iraq, Turkey, Egypt, and many other places, but nowhere so acutely as in the territory we call Palestine.

We can trace the intense modern conflict to the rise of the Zionist movement in England and Western Europe during the 1890s, especially after the Balfour Declaration of November 2, 1917, that granted Jews the right of return to the area of Palestine under Jewish mandate to be a *national* homeland, as long as it was *clearly understood that nothing shall be done which may prejudice the civil and religious rights of existing non-Jewish communities in Palestine.* Despite such lofty language, there was no way to prevent anger, resentment, violence, and injustice, as floods of Jewish immigrants — a new people — sought to claim land which had already been settled and claimed by Arab Christians and Muslims. Terrible battles followed throughout the 1920s and 1930s, but no one was prepared for the full revelation of the horrors of the Holocaust, which led to the United Nations declaration in November 1947 of a State of Israel, independent of the Arab nation of Jordan. But the conflict did not end there. It has continued as the single most difficult international issue ever since. No solution is really in sight, although hopefully political leaders will continue to urgently seek a workable and acceptable answer. However, there is also the religious urgency that is intrinsically bound up with any political discussion because of the status of this land as the "Holy Land" to Jews, Christians, and Muslims.

The Stimulus Books series provides thoughtful reflections on critical questions of Jewish-Christian dialogue, but always includes sensitivity to Muslim concerns when the topic demands it. Richard Lux, an eminently qualified specialist in dialogue issues, has provided an excellent guide to why the Holy Land is sacred and of vital importance to Christians as well as Jews. Most Jews highly value the importance of Israel as both a political and a religious reality, but they often think that Christians don't value their claims and only want to save their own shrines marking the events of the life of Jesus.

In this book, Professor Lux leads us through the deep religious connections between Christians and Jews through their common belief in God's covenant, described in the Hebrew and Christian Scriptures. He leads us through the transforming movement among Christian churches, especially Catholicism, to rid their teachings of all traces of anti-Semitism and to form a positive covenant theology and spirituality that unites Christians and Jews. He guides us carefully through the New Testament understanding of this relationship — even in St. Paul! At the same time, he discusses the sensitive rights of Arab Muslims and Christians, as well as the issues that have to be faced and solved if a truly religious covenant understanding that remains faithful to God, the common father of all three monotheistic faiths, is to be achieved. He pictures for us a new relationship between Catholicism and the State of Israel that invites further reflection on the challenges and the conclusions he has drawn.

This is a wonderful introduction to the positive religious aspects of Jewish-Christian understanding of the State of Israel as a Holy Land for Jews in particular, but which must also be sacred in the thinking of Christians and Muslims alike. It will not be the answer to the political problems that must be solved, but it will educate us in how deeply religious faith must inform the relationship of Jews and Christians with one another, and in how our bond in covenant faith calls for new imagination in seeking a solution of the land and state, a solution that does not leave out the religious dimension central to Jewish identity, nor forgets the sensitivities and rights of Christians and Muslims who also live there.

Lawrence Boadt, CSP
Professor Emeritus of Sacred Scripture
Washington Theological Union
Publisher, Paulist Press

Preface

Why write a book about the people, land, and State of Israel? It is highly unlikely that this book will make the *New York Times* best-seller list, bring personal financial gain, movie rights, or a syndicated series.

To fulfill the "publish or perish" dictum in academia? I already have tenure, am nearing retirement, and, since traditionally Catholic seminaries usually do not place pressure on their faculty to publish, this dictum is not applicable. So why publish?

Perhaps the prophet Jeremiah said it best when complaining to the LORD about his vocation, his call to be a spokesperson for God: He tells God that he is fed up and has decided to keep quiet. "But then it becomes like fire burning in my heart, imprisoned in my bones; I grow weary holding it in, I cannot endure it" (Jer 20:9).

The odyssey of this book began innocently enough with an invitation in spring 1975 to be a charter member of a new Catholic-Jewish dialogue group in Milwaukee, Wisconsin. My flippant reply to the priest ecumenical director was "Why not, I teach about dead Jews all the time (the "Old Testament"), it would be nice to talk to some live Jews." I tell this true story with some embarrassment as interfaith dialogue with the Jewish community—locally, nationally, and internationally—has become the passion and focus of my life since that day.

I have been to Israel many times leading study tours, engaging in research there, traveling on fact-finding missions with both Christian and Jewish groups. In 1982, I co-chaired the Sixth National Workshop on Christian-Jewish Relations in Milwaukee along with a Lutheran pastor and an Orthodox rabbi, served on the Advisory Committee on Catholic-Jewish Relations of the U.S. Bishops Conference, and talked myself hoarse on too many lectures to mention on Christian-Jewish topics.

Authors often feel obligated to give long accounts of all those that contributed in any way to their publication, and I will not violate that convention.

It begins first (*and not last*) with my wife of over forty years, Mary, who always supported and encouraged me in this dialogue engagement that often took as much time as my full-time position teaching scripture at Sacred Heart School of Theology.

Secondly, I owe a great debt of gratitude to my seminary, which has always been totally supportive of my involvement in interfaith relations. During the course of many years and through many different administrators, I never heard of word of disapproval or suggestion that I was spending too much time in "extracurricular" activities not directly related to the seminary. On the contrary, the seminary gave wonderful financial support on many occasions, including paying all the costs for our seminarians and faculty to attend the Sixth National Workshop on Christian-Jewish Relations.

Next, I would like to thank Archbishop Emeritus Rembert J. Weakland, OSB, of Milwaukee for his enduring support of the dialogue in his diocese and pressing me to think critically about covenant in a dialogue with an Orthodox rabbi at a religious leaders conference he gathered together in 1983.

Gratitude is also due to Father Larry Boadt, CSP, then editor of *The Catholic World*, who asked me to write about the Holy Land. These ideas continued to germinate until 1987, when an NCCJ Fellowship brought me to the Shalom Hartman Institute in Jerusalem where dialogue with David Hartman, Paul van Buren, and Krister Stendahl, along with eighteen other participants (Catholic, Protestant, and Jewish), helped further develop my ideas.

In spring 1997, I spent a very happy and fruitful four months at the Tantur Ecumenical Institute in Jerusalem as a Fellow with Rev. Thomas Stransky, CSP, a pioneer in Catholic-Jewish relations during and after the Second Vatican Council. I thank him for his encouragement, challenges, and insights.

Finally, my last sabbatical in fall 2005 was spent at the Collegeville Ecumenical Institute where Benedictine hospitality and scholarly support is peerless. I finished the complete draft of this book there.

While no book's preface would be complete without a long list of people to be thanked, many will remain nameless. They themselves know, however, how they have supported, encouraged, challenged, dialogued, and been there for me when it counted:

Of blessed memory: Rabbi Harry Pastor; Rabbi David S. Shapiro; Saul Sorrin; Sylvia Weber; Ateret Cohen; Rev. Dr. David Lewis; Sr. Rose Thering, OP; Rev. Edward Flannery; Fr. Tom Garvey, SCJ; and Rabbi Leon Klenicki.

There are also friends, colleagues, and dialogue partners: Judith Cohen; Bob Peterman; Kathy Heilbronner; Judi Longdin; Elliot Bernstein; Rev. Laurin Wenig; Rev. David Cooper; Florence and Leslie Bern; Michael Weber; John Gallam; Rev. Vince McNally; Rev. Richard Schlenker; Rev. Jerry Clifford; Rev. Bill Harter; David Blewitt; Sr. Maureen Hopkins, SDS; Rev. Joseph Dean, SCJ; Rabbi Ron Shapiro; Rabbi Marc Berkson; Rabbi Barry Silberg; Sandy Hoffman; Israel Wolnerman; John Claubaux; Phil Cunningham; Eugene Fisher; Rabbi James A. Rudin; Judith Banki; Rev. Michael McGarry, CSP; Rev. John T. Pawlikowski, OSM; Amy-Jill Levine; Rev. Petra Heldt; Rabbi Ron Kronish; past and present members of the National Christian Leadership Conference for Israel; the 1987 fellows at Tantur, especially the late Michael Prior, CM, with whom I disagreed on almost every issue, and Coos Schoenfeld, with whom I agreed; and the Collegeville Ecumenical Institute fellows in fall 2005.

Without helpful, efficient, and hard-working librarians, most scholars would be fatally handicapped, and so, last but not least, my enduring gratitude goes to the librarians of Tantur Ecumenical Institute, St. John's University Library, Dehon Library of the Sacred Heart School of Theology, and Marquette University Library.

My heartfelt gratitude also goes to Father Larry Boadt, CSP, who for years patiently listened to my theories and my promises of finishing a book on the Jewish people and Israel and then—when the book was finally finished—submitted it to the Stimulus board for consideration with his support. Fr. Michael Kerrigan, CSP, has expertly edited and reformatted the manuscript and footnotes, which were incompatible with Paulist Press guidelines—thank you for your kind and patient work! Any errors in the text are solely mine, not Paulist Press's.

To guide the reader through this book, here is a short summary of each chapter with the theses I've tried to demonstrate:

1. "Present Catholic Church Teaching on Jews and Judaism" traces the history of the development of church teaching from supersessionism to post–Second Vatican Council and beyond.

2. "The Jewish People" traces the paradigm shift in Pauline studies, two-covenant versus one-covenant theories, and my one-covenant model with a new image and modality.

3. "The Holy Land" discusses how the Hebrew Scriptures and Christian Scriptures treat the land, postbiblical Christian relationship with the land, and my new model for understanding and experiencing the Holy Land.

4. "Between Land and State: Palestinian Perspectives" looks at the significance of, and attachment to, the land and to Jerusalem, of Palestinian Christians and Palestinian Muslims.

5. "The State of Israel" covers the relationship of the church to Zionism (since 1897); relations between the Vatican and the State of Israel, culminating in the Fundamental Agreement in 1993, with some subsequent developments; Christian theological approaches to the State of Israel (Catholic, Jewish, and Protestant); messianic understandings; and a new view of Zionism and the State of Israel in parallel with a new imaging of the Catholic Church.

6. "Issues, Reflections, and Conclusions" summarizes the six propositions in the book, then discusses a number of consequences and challenges to these new images/models of the relationship to the Jewish people, the Holy Land, and the State of Israel.

I dedicate this book to all those, named and unnamed, who are working to make the future relationship between Christians and Jews a positive and supporting relationship. We can't change the past, but we Christians can take responsibility for the past and work to make the future different.

May this book contribute toward that future.

1
Present Catholic Church Teaching on Jews and Judaism

INTRODUCTION

The long history of the relationship between Christians and Jews is generally not well known by most Roman Catholics. This relationship, one of anti-Judaism and anti-Semitism,[1] includes most of Jewish history since the time of Jesus.[2] In 1965, Father Edward Flannery wrote one of the first comprehensive histories of anti-Semitism, *The Anguish of the Jews*, in which he said:

> The vast majority of Christians, even well educated, are all but totally ignorant of what happened to Jews in history and of the culpable involvement of the Church. They are ignorant of this because, except for a few recent inclusions, the antisemitic record does not appear in Christian history books or social studies, and because Christians are not inclined to read histories of antisemitism. Jews on the other hand are by and large acutely aware of this page of history if for no other reason than that it is so extensively and intimately intermingled with the history of the Jews and Judaism. It is little exaggeration to state that those pages of history Jews have committed to memory are the very ones that have been torn from Christian (and secular) history books. This [book is a contribution]…toward the reinsertion of those pages.[3]

The Second Vatican Council (1962–65) brought about a dramatic change in Catholic teaching about the relationship between Catholics and Jews. In order to appreciate how far we Catholics of the

1

Western Church have come since the end of the Second Vatican Council in 1965, the work of the late professor Jules Isaac is particularly illuminating. Alone among his family to escape the Nazis in France, he published in 1947 the book *Jesus and Israel*, which aimed at dispelling myths and hatred about the Jewish people relative to Jesus. In 1948, he created l'Amitié Judéo-Chrétienne, "a French interfaith group which was to work not only for the complete eradication of false notions in regard to the beliefs of Jews and Christians, but also for a positive appreciation of each other's heritage."[4] Isaac met with Pius XII in 1949, but it was his meeting in 1960 with John XXIII that produced concrete results. John XXIII ordered the creation of a subcommittee of the Vatican Council to study the issue of the Christian-Jewish relationship. The work of this committee ultimately resulted in the Vatican Council's *Declaration on the Relationship of the Church to Non-Christian Religions* (*Nostra Aetate*). Its statement (paragraph 4) on the Jewish people was a revolutionary change in church teaching.[5]

In his book, *The Teaching of Contempt*, Jules Isaac sketched out the Christian theological anti-Judaism that had been an integral part of Christian teaching. He showed that this teaching began in the second century, reached its full maturation in the early Middle Ages, and continued to the present.

Although much of this teaching has been eradicated from the faith life of the ordinary Catholic, some of it remains in popular Catholicism and in religious-education textbooks.[6] The teaching of contempt expresses itself in ten doctrines:

1. Promulgates an erroneous, univocal, and stereotypical view of the religious and ethical world of the Hebrew scriptures (the Old Testament)
2. Denies the indebtedness of Christianity to the religious genius of Judaism
3. Denigrates first-century Palestinian Judaism
4. Teaches that the dispersion of the Jews from the land of Israel was a divine punishment for their rejection of Jesus
5. Fails to educate Christian people about the polemical (and intra-Jewish) character of certain texts of the Christian scripture, including the pejorative invoking of "the Jews," and caricatures of the Pharisees

6. Characterizes Jesus in ways that reject his Jewishness and his fidelity to his Jewish tradition
7. Conveys the erroneous impression of universal antipathy toward Jesus by Jews of his time
8. Employs a singular, messianic interpretation of the religious motives of the Jews of Jesus' time (that is, that only the messianic expectation was prominent in the religious imaginations of the people and that only one particular understanding of messianism prevailed)
9. Stereotypes Jewish leadership and exonerates the Roman officials
10. Charges the Jews with deicide,[7] a charge "murderous...," as Isaac wrote, "in its generation of hatred and crime but also...radically false."[8]

Padraic O'Hare rightly observes that "taken together, these attitudes and teachings, these errors and prejudices constitute the foundation of Christian theological anti-Judaism,"[9] which eventually developed into the hatred of Jews simply because they are Jews, (anti-Semitism).

It is important to distinguish anti-Judaism from anti-Semitism. Pope John Paul II, in his address to the Vatican symposium on "The Roots of Anti-Judaism in the Christian Milieu," describes anti-Judaism as the "erroneous and unjust interpretations of the New Testament relative to the Jewish people and their presumed guilt circulat[ing] for too long, engendering sentiments of hostility toward this people."[10] On the other hand, *anti-Semitism* is a term that "was first used in 1880 by the German writer Wilhelm Marr to distinguish modern European secular antipathy to Jews from hostility to the Jewish religion. In recent usage, the term has come to denote hatred of Jews and Judaism in all forms."[11] While these two terms signify two different rationales for malevolence toward the Jewish people, they are almost inextricably linked together. Anti-Judaism is the theological foundation for attitudes against the Jewish religion, anti-Semitism is the proposition that the Jews are an inferior race of people. As Sidney Hall has rightly observed:

[T]wo thousand years of Christian anti-Jewish theology contributed to the crimes of the Nazis, through both theological justification and silence. The logical progression of anti-Jewish theology among Gentiles in the first century to the oven chambers of Auschwitz was from the Christian protest, "you have no right to live among us *as Jews*," to "You have no right to live *among us*," to "You have no right *to live*."[12]

This progression of action from conversion to expulsion to annihilation was initially motivated by the theological doctrine of supersessionism that took root very early in the life of the church. By the third century CE (if not earlier), the church's prevailing view of the Jews was a *theological* anti-Judaism. Into the core of the nascent church were planted the inner, psychological roots of Christian self-understanding grounded in the belief in the replacement of the Jews in divine affection by Christians, and the perfection of a corrupt, "carnal" Judaism in a "spiritual" Christianity. In one word, this is the theological doctrine of *supersessionism*, "that idea that Christianity has perfected and replaced Judaism. Supersessionism is the ideology of contempt."[13] This doctrine has been the consistent common teaching of the Catholic Church until the Second Vatican Council. How can we identify the content of this teaching?

The principal tenets of supersessionism are "(1) God's revelation in Jesus Christ supersedes the revelation to Israel, (2) The New Testament [completely] fulfills the Old Testament, (3) The Church replaces the Jews as God's people, (4) Judaism is obsolete, its covenant abrogated, (5) Post-exilic Judaism was legalistic, (6) The Jews did not heed the warning of the prophets, (7) The Jews did not understand the prophecies about Jesus, (8) The Jews were Christ-killers."[14] Thus, we have the theological foundation for many centuries of church teaching on the Jews.

SECOND VATICAN COUNCIL AND SUBSEQUENT DEVELOPMENTS

It is hard to appreciate what a revolutionary change in direction occurred as a result of the Second Vatican Council and subsequent developments in postconciliar documents in the more than forty years since the conclusion of the council. The continued development of

this change is due especially to the bold leadership and encouragement of Pope John Paul II.[15]

Pope Benedict XVI, who met with the delegates of the
International Jewish Committee on Interreligious Consultations on
June 9, 2005, has continued this positive direction and commitment.
Noting that 2005 marked the fortieth anniversary of the declaration
Nostra Aetate of the Second Vatican Council, he said:

> At the very beginning of my Pontificate, I wish to assure
> you that the Church remains firmly committed, in her cate-
> chesis and in every aspect of her life, to implementing this
> decisive teaching.
>
> In the years following the Council, my predecessors
> Pope Paul VI and, in a particular way. Pope John Paul II,
> took significant steps towards improving relations with the
> Jewish people. *It is my intention to continue on this path*
> [emphasis in the original].[16]

He goes on to acknowledge an important unfinished agenda:
"Of its very nature this imperative must include a continued reflection
on the profound historical, moral and theological questions presented
by the experience of the Shoah."[17]

Three principal documents set out the new directions of
Catholic teaching on Jews and Judaism. They are (1) the Second
Vatican Council's *Declaration on the Relationship of the Church to
Non-Christian Religions*, 1965, and known by the Latin title *Nostra
Aetate*, (2) the document issued by the Commission for Religious
Relations with the Jews, *Guidelines and Suggestions for Implementing the Conciliar Declaration "Nostra Aetate,"* 1975, and usually abbreviated as just the *Guidelines*. This Vatican Commission for
Religious Relations with the Jews was set up to implement the decree
of the Vatican Council on Catholic-Jewish relations and was part of
the overall mandate of the council to set up postconciliar commis-
sions to ensure that the council documents did not merely become
interesting historical material shelved in a library.[18] And (3), also
issued by the Vatican's Commission for Religious Relations with the
Jews, was the 1985 document, *Notes on the Correct Way to Present
Jews and Judaism in Preaching and Catechesis in the Roman*

Catholic Church. This document is usually referred to simply as the *Notes*.

The two documents following the Vatican II declaration, namely, the *Guidelines* in 1975 and the *Notes* in 1985, were themselves the result of years of positively developing relations between the Catholic and Jewish communities and especially statements made by national bishops' conferences, including the landmark statement of the American Catholic bishops in 1975 entitled, "Statement on Catholic-Jewish Relations." This document is the only episcopal conference document explicitly quoted in the Vatican *Notes*.

In general we can say that *Nostra Aetate* was the Magna Carta for a dramatic reversal and new direction in the church's teaching and relations with the Jewish people.[19] Subsequently, the Vatican *Guidelines* of 1975 charted ways in which these new directions should apply; namely, they described the general areas in need of dialogue and the approach to be taken in an encounter with another religious tradition. Diverse areas treated were: liturgical applications, including the commentaries on the biblical texts; the areas of teaching and education, including catechisms, religious textbooks, history books, and the mass media; and lastly, guidelines for joint social action. These 1975 *Guidelines* also go on to say that

> the problem of Jewish-Christian relations concerns the Church as such, since it is when "pondering her own mystery" that she comes up against the mystery of Israel. Therefore, even in areas where no Jewish communities exist, this remains an important problem. There is also an ecumenical aspect to the question: The very return of Christians to the sources and origins of their faith, grafted onto the earlier covenant, helps the search for unity in Christ, the cornerstone.[20]

Given the long history of our poisonous relationship, this is an astounding statement. It means that the agenda for Catholic-Jewish relations deals with the very self-identity of the church and Christianity and that therefore we must take this agenda seriously, even if we live in an area where there is no significant Jewish community present. While Jews do not need Christians for an understanding of their own identity and rationale for their existence as a religious people,

Christians do. This should be obvious because of the historical origins of Christianity.

The third document issued by the Vatican, the 1985 *Notes*, spells out in considerable detail the content to be embodied in preaching and catechesis. This document is one of the fruits of twenty years of Catholic-Jewish dialogue. It is an important landmark, but is certainly not the final word.

OVERVIEW OF CURRENT CHURCH TEACHING

The content of the church's present teaching can be summarized in fourteen elaborated statements:[21]

1. The church decries and rejects any kind of **anti-Semitism** and in the 1985 *Notes* mandates the importance of an accurate teaching on Judaism in order to counteract any anti-Semitic teaching.
2. The church also goes on to develop and acknowledge that following the biblical period the Jewish people went on to develop a rich and diverse religious tradition of **Judaism**. The church acknowledges that this is a sign of God's plan and that Judaism has been a continuously rich tradition from the early rabbinical period through the Middle Ages and on to modern times.
3. The Second Vatican Council first acknowledged that there is a **spiritual bond** between the church and Judaism. The *Notes* describes this bond as a unique relationship that links Jews and Christians at "the very level of their identity" and is "founded on the design of the God of the Covenant." Therefore, the topic of "Jews and Judaism should not occupy an occasional or marginal place in catechesis; their presence there is essential and should be organically integrated." This means that it is no longer sufficient to make simply passing reference to Jews and the "Old Testament" as a preparation for Christianity, but rather, the relation between Jews and Christians must occupy a central and integral place in our catechesis and the discussion of our identity as Christians.

4. The **Pharisees** have been traditionally identified in the New Testament as hypocritical evildoers. This centuries-long vilification has finally been formally rejected. Beginning in the *Guidelines* of 1975 and now spelled out in great detail in the *Notes* (and also discussed in great detail in the *US Bishops 1975 Statement*), the Pharisees are finally given their rightful place and interpretation in Judaism and in Christianity. The *Notes* acknowledges that Jesus shared "with the majority of Palestinian Jews of that time" central elements of Pharisaic doctrine (n. 17), including the resurrection of the body, forms of piety like almsgiving, prayer, fasting (see Matthew 6:1–18), the liturgical practice of addressing God as "Father," and the priority of the commandment to love God and our neighbor (see Deuteronomy 6:5, Leviticus 19:18, and Mark 12:28–34). This positive relationship with the Pharisees is also true for Paul (see Acts 23:8), who always considered that his membership with the Pharisees was a title of honor (Acts 23:6; 26:5, and Philippians 3:5). It is noteworthy, too, that the Pharisees are not mentioned in accounts of the passion. In addition, in Luke's work, the Pharisee Rabbi Gamaliel (Acts 5:34–39) defends the apostles in a meeting of the Sanhedrin. Thus, as the *Notes* says, "an exclusively negative picture of the Pharisees is likely to be inaccurate and unjust.... If in the Gospels and elsewhere in the NT there are all sorts of unfavorable references to the Pharisees, they should be seen against the background of a complex and diversified movement. Criticisms of various types of Pharisees are moreover not lacking in rabbinical sources."

5. In attempting to understand how to **define the Jews**, *Nostra Aetate* defines them solely in biblical terms, whereas the *Guidelines* of 1975 and the *Notes* of 1985 (as well as the American Bishops Statement of 1975) say that Christians should learn "by what essential traits the Jews define themselves in the light of their own religious tradition." Moreover, the *Notes* cites John Paul II, who calls upon catechists and preachers "to assess Judaism carefully and with due awareness of the faith and religious life of the Jewish people as they are professed and practiced still today." Therefore, in this context,

mentions of the "Holocaust and the State of Israel are proper subjects for affirmative Catholic teaching."

6. Concerning the **Holocaust**, the *Notes* "mandates the development of Holocaust curricula in religious education programming: 'catechesis should…help in understanding the meaning for Jews of the extermination (Shoah) during the years 1939–1945, and its consequences.'" The church took a further step in 1998 with the promulgation of "We Remember: A Reflection on the 'Shoah.'"[22] Its twin focus is repentance (*tushuva*) and hope for the future. Catholics are called upon to renew their awareness of their Hebrew roots, commit themselves to building a different future with the Jewish people, and "to reflect deeply on the significance of the Shoah."[23]

7. Regarding the **State of Israel**: The Vatican Council and the *Guidelines* make no mention of it, although the *1975 American Catholic Bishop's Statement* says that

> in dialogue with Christians, Jews have explained that they do not consider themselves as a church, a sect, or a denomination, as is the case among Christian communities, but rather as a peoplehood that is not solely racial, ethnic or religious, but in a sense a composite of all these. It is for such reasons that an overwhelming majority of Jews see themselves bound in one way or another to the Land of Israel. Most Jews see this tie to the land as essential to their Jewishness. Whatever difficulties Christians may experience in sharing this view they should strive to understand the link between land and people, which Jews have expressed in their writings and worship throughout two millennia as a longing for the homeland, holy Zion.[24]

The Vatican *Notes* speaks of the religious attachment between the "Jewish people and the Land of Israel as one that finds its roots in the Biblical tradition and as an essential aspect of Jewish covenantal fidelity to the one God." It also affirms the "existence of the State of Israel on the basis of the common principles of international law," while warning against a biblical fundamentalist approach to contemporary political options in the Middle East.[25]

8. Regarding the **crucifixion** of Jesus, the church utterly rejects the charge of deicide or "Christ-killers" and in the Second Vatican Council declaration says that Christ underwent his passion and death because of the sins of all, and the *Notes* adds that "the catechism of the Council of Trent teaches that Christian sinners are more to blame for the death of Christ than those few Jews who brought it about.... In the same way and for the same reason, the Jews should not be presented as repudiated or cursed by God, as if such views followed from the Holy Scriptures." We ought then to ask, Why are there hostile references to the Jews (and Pharisees) in the gospels? The *Notes* acknowledges the three stages in the development of the writing of the gospels; namely, the original life situation of the historical Jesus, then the reinterpretation of the words and deeds of Jesus in light of the resurrection experience, and finally the life situation of the particular theology of each evangelist as he composed each gospel.[26] Thus, the *Notes* says that

   it cannot be ruled out that some references hostile or less than favorable to the Jews have their historical context in conflicts between the nascent Church and the Jewish community. Certain controversies reflect Christian-Jewish relations long after the time of Jesus. (par. 21)

9. For the first time, the 1985 *Notes* begins to struggle with the meaning for Christians of the **Jewish "no" to Christian claims**. As a key to this struggle, it looks to chapters 9—11 of Paul's Letter to the Romans and hints that a positive response to the permanence of Israel and therefore to the Jewish "no" to Christian claims is to be understood as a "sign to be interpreted within God's design."

10. The Vatican documents present the church as the new people of God, yet they say that does not imply that the **people of God** (the Jews) of the Old Covenant have been in any way superseded by or rejected by God. The *Guidelines* also cautions against setting the New Testament tradition against the Old Testament in such a way as would make the religion of the Old Testament to be one only of "justice, fear and legalism with no appeal to the love of God and neighbor." This is another

explicit rejection of the teaching of the second-century heretic Marcion,[27] a teaching that has inhered in popular Catholicism for many centuries.

11. The *Guidelines* also acknowledges, when referring to the categories of **promise and fulfillment**, that both Jews and Christians are eschatologically driven people hoping for a future end-time of peace and justice; it acknowledges that each starts from a different point of view—the Jews with the hope of the coming Messiah and Christians with the return of the Messiah; yet both are a people who wait in hope.

12. The **typological model of biblical interpretation** has been a problem in the Jewish-Christian relationship from at least the patristic period to the present. The *Notes* attempts to deal with typology but, in my view and that of many others, does not deal with it very successfully. The *Notes* correctly describes typology as an "interpretation [that] consists in reading the Old Testament as preparation and, in certain aspects, outline and foreshadowing of the New (cf., e.g. Heb 5:5–10)."[28] In sum, Christ is the key and reference point for an understanding of the Hebrew scriptures. This interpretative principle is justified by a comment Paul makes to the Corinthian community warning them of overconfidence (1 Cor 10:1–13).[29] At best, the *Notes* acknowledges that there can be

> a Christian reading of the Old Testament that does not necessarily coincide with the Jewish reading. Thus Christian identity and Jewish identity should be carefully distinguished in their respective reading of the Bible. But this detracts nothing from the value of the Old Testament in the Church and does nothing to hinder Christians from profiting discerningly from the traditions of Jewish reading. (II.6)[30]

13. Each of the three documents reaffirms the importance of **joint social action** and the *Notes* says that "we must also accept our responsibility to prepare the world for the coming of the Messiah [by implication either his first or second coming] by working together for social justice.… To this we are driven… by a common hope for the Kingdom of God" (n. 11).

14. The *Notes* acknowledges that there has been a **Jewish witness to the world** of "its often heroic fidelity to God and to exalt him in the presence of all the living"; it also "affirms that Christian catechesis cannot adequately convey the Christian message without taking into account past and present Jewish tradition."

Concluding this overview of Vatican II's *Nostra Aetate* and the subsequent documents, the *Guidelines* and the *Notes*, it is not possible for a Catholic to say that a knowledge of Judaism along with a positive working relationship with Jews and the Jewish community is simply the domain of a few church professionals or ecumenical "fanatics." It is the responsibility of all Christians, because it involves our very self-identity.

CATECHISM OF THE CATHOLIC CHURCH

The danger with all church documents is that they are either not taken seriously or that they are ignored in subsequent teaching. Have these new directions and teachings found their way into mainline church teaching? To test and see, let us examine the present *Catechism of the Catholic Church*.[31]

An analysis of this catechism shows that it does not lend itself to a neat and orderly treatment of, or encapsulation of, Vatican II and post-Vatican II documents on the relation of Catholic Christians to the Jewish people. This is because the *Catechism* is intended to present a comprehensive overview of Catholic doctrine and practice and not to focus on the relationship with the Jewish people with which some of our other documents are primarily concerned. The purpose of the *Catechism*, as enunciated by John Paul II in the Introduction, is not "to replace the local catechisms duly approved by the ecclesiastical authorities, the diocesan Bishops and the Episcopal Conferences.... It is meant to encourage and assist in the writing of new local catechisms, which take into account various situations and cultures, while carefully preserving the unity of faith and fidelity to catholic doctrine" (p. 6).

The *Catechism* has both the strengths and weaknesses of a work put together by a large committee.[32] Its strength lies in the process of broad consultation and emendation underlying it, which considered many divergent viewpoints. In fact, the *Catechism* is already in an official second edition, having incorporated many modifications into the original 1992 text.[33] Its principal weakness is that some teachings of the Second Vatican Council and subsequent ecclesial documents on Jews and Judaism are implicitly brought into question by some sections of the *Catechism*.[34] Yet Rabbi Jack Bemporad finds the *Catechism* to be devoid of all those statements in the Christian scriptures and in the Catholic tradition that were hostile to Jews and used as a basis for the teaching of contempt as enunciated by Jules Isaac. Even in the use of "fulfillment theology" in the *Catechism*, he notes that this type of language is used by all universal religions, including Judaism. What is significant is whether this terminology can lead to the condemnation and vilification of other religions. Though this kind of language led that way in the past, the new *Catechism* does not draw these conclusions as the old *Baltimore Catechism* did.[35]

The *Catechism* is divided into four parts:

Part I: "The Profession of Faith," which speaks of the divine/human encounter and how we come to faith (nos. 1–184), and then treats in detail the Apostles' Creed (nos. 185–1065)

Part II: "The Celebration of the Christian Mystery," beginning with the liturgy and the paschal mystery (nos. 1066–1206) and a detailed treatment of each of the seven sacraments (Nos. 1210–1690)

Part III: "Life in Christ," devoted to the moral/ethical issues of human life including conscience, virtue, sin, social issues, social justice, and a detailed treatment of the Ten Commandments (nos. 1691–2557)

Part IV: "Christian Prayer," which contains a general discussion of prayer and then a detailed examination of the Lord's Prayer, the Our Father (nos. 2558–2865).

On the one hand, there is in it no special section concerning the Jewish people except for paragraphs 839–40, which occur in the context of the general treatment of non-Christian religions as a subsection of a discussion of the phrase "one, holy, catholic, and apostolic" church in the Apostles' Creed.

On the other hand, "the *Catechism* reflects rather well the present state of Catholic teaching on Jews and Judaism. It does not in any sense seek to 'back away' from the Second Vatican Council, but rather to consolidate post-Conciliar official teaching to date. It attempts to integrate into its approach the teachings of the Holy See's Commission for Religious Relations with the Jews of 1974 and 1985."[36] Yet it does not move "forward the discussion beyond the present state of the official documentation." In this regard it "does not always live up to the fullness of the vision of Pope John Paul II on Catholic-Jewish relations, but is rather more cautious in some areas than is the Pope."[37]

We could summarize eight basic catechetical principles enunciated by the *Catechism* on the Jews:

1. *The church's understanding of God's people, the Jews, is stated in the present tense, not the past tense.*[38] Article 63 says, "Israel is the priestly people of God, 'called by the name of the LORD,' (Deut 28:10) and 'the first to hear the word of God,' the people of 'elder brethren' in the faith of Abraham."

2. "Whatever the historical involvement of individuals, *Jews as such are not collectively responsible for Jesus' death.*" As article 597 states: "The historical complexity of Jesus' trial is apparent in the Gospel accounts. God alone knows the personal sin of the participants (Judas, the Sanhedrin, and Pilate). Hence we cannot lay responsibility for the trial on the Jews in Jerusalem as a whole, despite the outcry of a manipulated crowd and the global reproaches contained in the apostles' calls to conversion after Pentecost [in Acts].… Still less can we extend responsibility to other Jews of different times and places, based merely on the crowd's cry: 'His blood be on us and on our children!' a formula for ratifying a judicial sentence [Mt 27:25]. As the Church declared at the Second Vatican Council: …[N]either all Jews indiscriminately at that time, nor Jews today, can be charged with the crimes committed during his Passion.…[T]he Jews should not be spoken of as rejected or accursed as if this followed from holy Scripture."

3. *"God's Covenant with the Jewish people is 'irrevocable'"* (839–40, 2173). "The New Covenant has neither abrogated nor superseded 'the First Covenant' (522). The *Catechism* is very explicit: *"The Old Covenant has never been revoked"* (121) [emphasis added].

4. *"The Hebrew Scriptures are to be presented 'as the true Word of God' with their own permanent integrity and dignity"* (123). As the 1975 Vatican *Guidelines* makes clear, "The Hebrew

Bible and the Jewish tradition founded on it must not be set against the New Testament in such a way that the former seems to constitute a religion of only retributive justice, fear, and legalism, with no appeal to love of God and neighbor."[39]

5. "While Christians validly see in the Hebrew Scriptures 'prefigurations of what God accomplished in the fullness of time in the person of his incarnate Son' (128), *typology and fulfillment are not the only valid approaches to interpreting the Hebrew Bible*."[40] As article 129 says, "Such typological reading discloses the inexhaustible content of the Old Testament, but it must not make us forget that the Old Testament retains its own intrinsic value as revelation reaffirmed by Our Lord himself."

6. In two paragraphs (839–40) the *Catechism* points out what is considered essential to an understanding of *"the relationship of the Church with the Jewish people."* The first echoes the Second Vatican Council's statement in *Nostra Aetate*, as well as the pope's 1986 address at the Rome synagogue[41] and the prayer 'for the Jewish People' from the revised Good Friday liturgy:[42] "When she delves into her own mystery, the Church, the People of God in the new Covenant, discovers her link with the Jewish People, 'the first to hear the Word of God.' The Jewish faith, unlike other non-Christian religions, is already a response to God's revelation in the old Covenant"(839). Then the *Catechism* cites Romans 9:4–5 and 11:29 as did the Vatican Council document. Herein the "validity not only of the 'first covenant' but of present day Jewish belief and practice as a faithful 'response to God's revelation' is affirmed."[43]

7. *The shared eschatological urgency of Christians and Jews is recognized, yet differences are also clearly acknowledged.* Article 840 says, "When one considers the future, God's People of the old Covenant and the new People of God tend towards similar goals: expectation of the coming (or the return) of the Messiah. But one awaits the return of the Messiah who died and rose from the dead and is recognized as Lord and Son of God; the other awaits the coming of a Messiah, whose features remain hidden till the end of time.…"

8. Lastly, the *Catechism* declares that "*a better knowledge of the Jewish people's faith and religious life as professed and lived even now can help our better understanding of certain aspects*

of Christian liturgy" (1096). This section then spells out the Jewish roots of Christian liturgical practices and great feasts of the church, especially Passover, which "both celebrate." As the *Catechism* notes in affirming both commonality and differences: "For Jews it is the Passover of history, tending toward the future; for Christians it is the Passover fulfilled in the death and Resurrection of Christ, though always in expectation of its definitive consummation" (1096). This celebratory event calls Jews and Christians to work together to prepare the world for God's reign.

Conclusion on the *Catechism*

This list by no means exhausts what the *Catechism* has to say about Jews and Judaism, but it is indicative of the core of the new teachings of the Second Vatican Council being incorporated into official catechetical teaching. All the hates enunciated earlier, namely, the teaching of contempt and the theological doctrine of supersessionism, have been utterly and totally rejected by today's church. Although the *Catechism* stills falls short of some of the teachings of the *Notes* and the *Guidelines*, it is nonetheless a remarkable step forward in church teaching. Rabbi Jack Bemporad says it best:

> …to Jews, it would be an understatement to say that this Catechism is "new." It is not merely "new." From Jewish perspective, it is revolutionary. A revolutionary assertion by the Church of brotherhood and love towards the Jewish people. Being taught upon its principles, no Catholic child could ever confront a Jewish child with contempt and condemnation, no Catholic community could ever make a Jewish family feel unwelcome — without violating the very innate bond between the Church and God's Covenant.[44]

THE JEWISH PEOPLE AND THEIR SACRED SCRIPTURES IN THE CHRISTIAN BIBLE

In 2001, the Pontifical Biblical Commission issued the document "The Jewish People and Their Sacred Scriptures in the Christian Bible." This publication has sparked many commentaries, both Catholic and

Jewish,[45] which have been generally positive although some serious questions still remain with positions taken in the document.

Its positive contributions as summarized by Sister Joan E. Cook[46] include:

1. a clear articulation of the development of Christian-Jewish relations since Vatican II founded on a "rejection of all kinds of anti-Semitism and...remembrance of the Jewish roots of Christianity"[47]
2. in the relationship between the Testaments, "it highlights the inseparability between Christianity and its Bible and Judaism and its Scriptures...[by delineating the] three-fold paradigm of continuity, discontinuity and progression within the Old Testament itself and between the two testaments"[48]
3. the ultimate result is to confirm and extend the theology of the ongoing Jewish covenantal relationship.

The most frequently commented-upon sections of the commission's document are paragraphs 21, 22, and 65.[49] These paragraphs have elicited the most discussion because they concern the understanding of fulfillment, Jewish and Christian interpretation of the Old Testament, and the relationship of the church with Israel. The PBC stresses that "Christian faith recognizes the fulfillment, in Christ, of the Scriptures and the hopes of Israel, but it does not understand this fulfillment as a literal one."[50] This means that texts of the Old Testament read as messianic prophecies had a meaning and interpretation for the contemporary hearers of the word, whereas the "messiahship of Jesus has a meaning that is new and original."[51] The completion of the work of Christ will not take place until the end-time so that "Jewish messianic expectation is not in vain";[52] Jewish expectation is a stimulant to keep the eschatological expectation of our faith alive because both Jews and Christians live in expectation. We are both messianic people, but "[t]he difference is that for us the One who is to come will have the traits of the Jesus who has already come and is already present and active among us."[53] This leaves ambiguous the personage of the future Jewish Messiah who is to come. As Christians, we believe that the movement of the Old Testament was toward Christ, but the PBC notes the important distinction that this is "a retrospective perception whose point of departure is not in the text as such, but in the events of the New Testament proclaimed by the apostolic preaching."[54] Thus, this is a theological interpretation whose foundation must begin with an historical-critical exegesis. The question then arises whether Christians should read the Bible as the Jews do. The answer is a positive yes, but with a caution. As Christians, we

> can and ought to admit that the Jewish reading of the Bible is a possible one, in continuity with the Jewish Sacred Scriptures from the Second Temple period, a reading analogous to the Christian reading that developed in parallel fashion. Each of these two readings is part of the vision of each respective faith of which it is a product and an expression. Consequently, they cannot be reduced one into the other.[55]

The PBC cautions that Christians cannot consent to the totality of a Jewish interpretation of the Hebrew scriptures because that would "exclude faith in Jesus as Messiah and Son of God." Nevertheless, Christians can "learn much from Jewish exegesis practiced for more than two thousand years, and, in fact, they have learned much in the course of history."[56]

Paragraph 65 speaks of the development between the Old Testament and the New Testament that brings to fulfillment the person of Jesus in his mission. The notion of new covenant and peoplehood is given a continuity with the original peoplehood of Israel. Paragraph 65 says:

> Far from being a substitution for Israel, the Church is in solidarity with it. To the Christians who have come from the nations, the apostle Paul declares that they are grafted to the good olive tree which is Israel (Rom 11:16, 17). That said, the Church is conscious of being given a universal horizon by Christ, in conformity with Abraham's vocation.... The reign of God is no longer confined to [historical] Israel alone, but is open to all, including the pagans.... The hope placed in the royal house of David, although defunct for six centuries, becomes a key for the reading of history: it is concentrated from now on in Jesus Christ, a humble and distant descendant.[57]

Thus, the church does not replace Israel, but is joined in solidarity with historical Israel, and Jesus as a Davidic Messiah is a key, but not the only key for the reading of history.[58]

Other frequently commented-upon sections of the PBC document are paragraphs 66, 67, and 69.[59] These paragraphs offer a clear articulation of the different groups within postexilic Judaism; namely, the Samaritans, the Pharisees, the Sadducees, and the Essenes. This is well done except that the description of the Pharisees' controversies with Jesus and the early Christian community does not always make clear the later development and reinterpretation of the three stages in the development of the writing of the gospels as they were made clear in the 1964 declaration of the PBC on the "Historicity of the Gospels."[60]

The conclusion of the document (paragraphs 84–87) draws together its contributions on the enduring value and importance of the Old Testament, the value of the Jewish interpretation of these texts, and the important interrelationship between Jews and Christians. Pastorally, the document hopes that it will be a positive contribution toward ongoing biblical and theological study between Jews and Christians and an encouragement to the church toward that love of the Jewish people as emphasized by Paul VI and John Paul II. In spite of the fact "that the new Testament is essentially a proclamation of the fulfillment of God's plan in Jesus Christ [which] puts it in serious disagreement with the vast majority of the Jewish people who do not accept this fulfillment,"[61] this should not lead to "anti-Jewish sentiment" nor rupture our two faith communities. Citing the example of Paul in Romans 9—11, the document affirms that "an attitude of respect, esteem and love for the Jewish people is the only truly Christian attitude in a situation which is mysteriously part of the beneficent and positive plan of God."[62] It ends affirming dialogue based on what we share together and encouraging the strengthening of the bonds between us.

In light of the general overwhelmingly positive response of Catholic and Protestant scholars on the PBC document, it may come as a surprise to read the insightful and often sharply worded critique of this document by the esteemed Jewish New Testament scholar Amy-Jill Levine.[63] A brief selection of her comments indicates that from the Jewish perspective there are still some serious and erroneous

understandings of Second Temple Judaism and subsequent developments. She complains that

> the authors are not informed by Jewish scholarship: the
> PBC affirms that "Christians can…learn much from
> Jewish exegesis practiced for more than two thousand
> years"; the problem is that it fails to show how.… [Another
> serious failing is] the PBC's lack of sustained engagement
> with ancient Jewish sources, especially those preserved by
> the Synagogue [which accounts for some of their erro-
> neous ideas].[64]

Levine cuts to the heart of the issue when she says that the PBC

> confidently identifies the *Sitz im Leben* of each gospel,
> describes the composition of Second-Temple Judaism and
> the Jewish practices of expelling and then killing Chris-
> tians, and even delineates Jesus' intent. Each case offers
> what for the Church would be the most generous, most
> benevolent reading: Judaism appears generally xenopho-
> bic while the church is universal; Judaism's prophets
> engage in more castigation of the covenant community
> than does the (more forgiving) New Testament; there is no
> "anti-Judaism" in the canon, etc. Missing is the explicit
> recognition that the history it proffers is subjective; miss-
> ing is the awareness that its historical-critical observations
> can serve as apologia for theological agendas; missing is
> the sensitivity needed to hear how the numerous comments
> both in the New Testament and from the PBC on Judaism
> would sound to Jewish ears. This last matter has the
> gravest value, since the Document's initial concern is anti-
> Semitism.[65]

She further adds that the

> PBC leaves its readers with an image of an Old Testament
> and a Judaism with "restrictive" and "imperfect" and "cul-
> tic" (the term codes negatively) concerns that are "of great
> importance." It offers no indication of how these Old
> Testament concerns are interpreted by the Jewish commu-

nity from the Second Temple to today or of any compara-
ble Catholic concerns. The "discontinuity" has become
supersessionism.[66]

Given the improved relations since Vatican II and the expanding
collaboration and dialogue between Catholic and Jewish scholars, it is
surprising that apparently no Jewish scholars were involved in any
way in this project. As Levine points out: "Had the committee worked
directly with Jewish biblical scholars, potentially damaging comments or phrasings might have been eliminated."[67] She has made
many detailed and perceptive observations on the lacunae, misinter-
pretations, and errors in the document, although she expresses the
belief that

> [b]oth Catholic scholar and Catholic Document have
> opened the way to better interfaith relations and to better
> understandings of the Bible of the Church. To read one
> Testament in light of the other will enhance appreciation of
> both; for Catholics to read the two Testaments together with
> Jews will do the same. To notice both continuity and discon-
> tinuity between the texts establishes a model by which con-
> tinuity and discontinuity between past and future can be
> recognized, and when necessary encouraged.[68]

Some serious points have been made here. It would appear that
the church needs to extend to church documents an actual working
collaboration between Catholic and Jewish scholars in areas touching
upon the Christian-Jewish relationship.

Nevertheless, the change in the church's teaching and activities
since Vatican II indicates that we are at last well on the way toward
establishing a new positive relationship with the people of the First
Testament, the Jewish people.

2
The Jewish People

Given the church's developments in recent teachings on our relationship to the Jewish people, that is, that the covenant of God with this people has never been broken, abolished, or superseded, how might we reimage our relationship to them? The Vatican Council speaks of our bond with the Jewish people and that it is when the church ponders her own mystery, that is, engages in self-reflection and searches for her own identity that she encounters Israel.

At the beginning of his pontificate, John Paul II said, in addressing representatives of Jewish organizations in Rome on March 12, 1979, for a meeting of the International Jewish Liaison Committee (the official dialogue group between the Jews and the Vatican) that

> the Council made very clear that, "while searching into the mystery of the Church," it recalled "the spiritual bond linking the people of the New Covenant with Abraham's stock" [*Nostra Aetate*, 4]. Thus it understood that our two religious communities are connected and closely related at the very level of their respective religious identities.[1]

He continued to stress and develop this understanding in 1980 when he addressed the Jewish community in Mainz, Germany, and noted that in

> the Declaration on the Relationship of the Church with Judaism in April of this year, the bishops of the Federal Republic of Germany put this sentence at the beginning: *"Whoever meets Jesus Christ, meets Judaism." I would like to make these words mine, too* [emphasis added]. The faith of the Church in Jesus Christ, the son of David and the son of Abraham [cf. Matt. 1:1], actually contains what

the bishops call in that declaration "the spiritual heritage of Israel for the Church" [11], a living heritage, which must be understood and preserved in its depth and richness by us Catholic Christians.... The first dimension of this dialogue, that is, the meeting between the people of God of the Old Covenant, never revoked by God [cf. Rom. 11:29], and that of the New Covenant, *is at the same time a dialogue within our Church* [emphasis added].²

Two years later in an address to delegates at a meeting of representatives of Episcopal Conferences, representatives of the Orthodox Churches, of the Anglican Communion, of the Lutheran World Federation, the World Council of Churches, and experts in Catholic-Jewish relations who were from the Vatican Commission for Religious Relations with the Jews, he stresses even more forcefully than earlier, the bonding between Christians and Jews:³

[Regarding *Nostra Aetate* and my Address of March 12, 1979, it] means that the links between the Church and the Jewish people are founded on the design of the God of the Covenant...[and] since the appearance, two thousand years ago, *of a new branch from the common root* [emphasis added], relations between our two communities have been marked by the misunderstandings and resentments with which we are familiar.... The terrible persecutions suffered by the Jews in different periods of history have finally opened the eyes of many and appalled many people's hearts. Christians have taken the right path, that of justice and brotherhood, in seeking to come together with their Semitic brethren, respectfully and perseveringly, in the common heritage that all value so highly. Should it not be pointed out, especially to those who remain skeptical, even hostile, that this reconciliation should not be confused with a sort of religious relativism, less still with a loss of identity?... Finally, our common spiritual patrimony is particularly important when we turn to our belief in only one God, good and merciful, who loves men and is loved by them [cf. Wisd. of Sol. 24:26], Lord of history and of the destinies of men, who is our Father and who chose Israel, "the good olive tree onto which have been grafted the wild olive branches, those of the gentiles" [*Nostra Aetate*, 4; cf. also Rom 11:17–24].[4]

John Paul uses the familial language of brotherhood (and sister-hood), pointing to our common roots, as he indicates in quoting St. Paul, our common destinies, and an understanding of Jesus and our self-identity, which leads us to the mystery of Israel.

How might one further develop his thought? To appropriate the title of a popular movie of a few years ago we should go "Back to the Future" to discover some creative possibilities.

PAUL, THE JEWISH APOSTLE TO THE GENTILES

As Gentile (non-Jewish) Christians, we ought to look to that great apostle who lived daily with the problem of the relation of his Gentile converts to the Jewish people, the people of the God of the covenant of Sinai—namely, Paul! We need first to clear away many misunderstandings, caricatures, and distorted views of Paul—his person and his theology. There has been a virtual revolution in Pauline studies in the last thirty years.

The Jesuit New Testament scholar Daniel Harrington called it a "paradigm shift,"[5] by which he means the infusion of new life into these studies from revolutionary insights and a rediscovery of "old" material from a fresh perspective. This reexamination of Paul first began with the seminal essay by Krister Stendahl, "The Apostle Paul and the Introspective Conscience of the West," published in English in 1963,[6] in which he said:

> Western interpreters have found the common denominator between Paul and the experience of man, since Paul's statements about "justification by faith" have been hailed as the answer to the problem which faces the ruthlessly honest man in his practice of introspection. Especially in Protestant Christianity—which, however, at this point has its roots in Augustine and in the piety of the Middle Ages—the Pauline awareness of sin has been interpreted in the light of Luther's struggle with his conscience. But it is exactly at that point that we can discern the most drastic

difference between Luther and Paul, between the 16th and
the 1st century.[7]

Stendahl goes on to develop a new understanding of Paul and comments that the

> problem we are trying to isolate could be expressed in
> hermeneutical terms somewhat like this: The Reformers'
> interpretation of Paul rests on an analogism when Pauline
> statements about Faith and Works, Law and Gospel, Jews
> and Gentiles are read in the framework of late medieval
> piety. The Law, the Torah, with its specific requirements of
> circumcision and food restrictions becomes a general prin-
> ciple of "legalism" in religious matters. Where Paul was
> concerned about the possibility for Gentiles to be included
> in the messianic community, his statements are now read
> as answers to the quest for assurance about man's salvation
> out of a common human predicament.[8]

If the essence of Judaism is Torah as constitutive of the covenant
and the formation of a people, then, in the Pauline texts,

> Paul appears to attack the very essence of Israel, and he does
> so from a position of knowledge. Paul the Pharisee, the dis-
> ciple of Rabban Gamaliel, has experienced the best that
> Judaism has to offer and has rejected it completely.... It
> almost seems that Paul is able to proclaim his gospel of
> grace only against the dark foil of Jewish legalism. The
> Judaism that is reflected in his polemic is a joyless, hypo-
> critical, nationalistic means of earning salvation by mechan-
> ically doing the works of the law. The God of the Jews is a
> remote, gloomy tyrant who lays the burden of the law on
> men, and their response is twofold; they either become
> proud and self-righteous hypocrites who are scrupulous
> about food but ignore justice, or they are plunged into guilt
> and anxiety, thinking themselves accursed for breaking a
> single commandment.... Against this kind of background,
> the gospel of freedom from the law is good news indeed,

and only a stiff-necked stubbornness has kept the Jews from welcoming it.[9]

This description of Paul and his theology of justification by faith (as opposed to justification by works) has a long history of acceptance in Christianity, but has been overturned in the last thirty years, as Daniel Harrington frames the issues:

> Paul's attitudes toward Judaism and its Law have been lively topics.... Did Paul convert from Judaism to Christianity, or rather did God call Paul to carry out a special mission in propagating Judaism for Gentiles? Did Paul ever disavow Judaism, or did he remain intensely proud of his Judaism?... Did Paul and other Jewish Christians cease to observe the Law, or did he rather exempt only Gentile Christians from the obligations of Torah?.... The positions articulated in the second half of each of the preceding sentences constitute a scholarly movement toward a "more Jewish" Paul, which has had a strong impact during the past decade [that is, 1977–1987].[10]

The Christian misreading of the meaning of the Torah and the fulfillment of the 613 commandments (the *mitzvot*) according to a reading of Paul based upon Augustine and Luther would have

> every commandment that is obeyed [resulting] in the Jew accumulating a quantity of merit while disobedience results in the accumulation of demerits. At the end, a calculation is made and, depending on which predominates, a positive or negative judgment results.... [The Orthodox Jewish scholar Michael Wyschogrod comments on this description by saying that] such an attitude is not the authentic self-understanding of the Jew. No Jew stands before God and says: "Dear God, judge me according to what I deserve. Please do not give me more than I deserve but also not less. Do me no favors but give me what is coming to me." No Jew I have ever heard of has taken this attitude and it is inconceivable to me that any Jew ever will.[11]

Wyschogrod's testimony concerning the law, along with the books by E. P. Sanders[12] and others, has thoroughly overturned an older understanding of Paul and the Law (Torah).

In light of the changes in Pauline scholarship the last thirty years, a present-day interpretation of Paul includes the following elements:

1. Paul is profoundly Jewish; he is *not* a Christian; he is a Jew who believes that Jesus is the Jewish Messiah because of his personal experience of the risen Lord.
2. Paul is a Jew reaching out to the pagans (Gentiles) with good news, namely, Jesus as Christ (Messiah) has conquered sin and death and because of Jesus' message, deeds, and resurrection a new order of creation has begun.
3. Paul has not rejected his own Jewishness (or Torah, or circumcision, or the Temple); he has only rejected his stance as a Shammaite, rigorous followers of Rabbi Shammai, who were attempting to convert pagans with a particular theological program and praxis.[13] In Paul's new theological view, pagans now became part of Israel through Jesus—through a faith commitment to the words and deeds and person of the risen Lord and not through circumcision and the food laws.
4. The Israel of God (though not in general accepting Jesus as the Messiah) is still God's covenant people; God is responsible for the general nonacceptance of Jesus by the Jewish people. "God has hardened their [the Jews'] hearts" (Rom 11:11–12, 25, 28–29) so that the pagans might be brought into Israel in wholly new ways, according to Paul in Romans 9—11.
5. Paul's distress at the general Jewish nonacceptance of the gospel refers to Paul's particular "good news" (evangelical message and praxis) to the Gentiles and not to Jewish acceptance of Jesus as Lord and Savior. In other words, Paul wishes that his kin would acknowledge the legitimacy and truth of his message to the Gentiles.
6. Israel will acknowledge Jesus as Messiah at the second coming (Parousia)[14] when a sufficient number of (all ?) pagans have become part of Israel.[15]

Any interpretation of Pauline writings that rejects all or part of the above is part of an older interpretation of Paul that set Paul in opposition to his Jewishness and the Law (Torah). This former interpretation is part of the whole history of Christian rejection of the Jews as a covenant people; for it was taught as part of a supersessionist theology that Christians are the new people of God replacing the Israel (Jews) of the Old Covenant.

How did Paul imagine the relationship between his Gentile converts and those born Jews, the people of the covenant of Sinai? Paul's final thoughts on this issue are to be found in Chapters 9—11 of the Letter to the Romans. The Christian community in Rome was a predominantly Gentile community, and in this letter he is attempting to sketch out the relationship between the Gentile followers of Jesus and the Jewish followers of Jesus.[16] Paul begins by saying to them, "They [the Jews] are Israelites; theirs the adoption, the glory, the covenants [note the plural], the giving of the law [the Torah], the worship, and the promises; theirs the patriarchs, and from them, according to the flesh, is the Messiah [the Christ]" (Rom 9:4–5).

Notice that Paul is saying that the covenants are alive—here he is thinking not only of the Mosaic covenant but also the promises made to Abraham that embrace the present Gentile Christians. For the Jews, the Law (Torah), the worship, the promises (including Genesis 12:1–4a and Genesis 15)—that have given us Gentiles hope and the Patriarchs we Gentiles claim by adoption—still exist. The Greek verb used is in the present tense, thus it is not "theirs *was* the covenant," but "theirs *is* (now) the covenant." The Jews are still God's chosen, covenant people. Why? Paul says in Romans 11: 29, "God does not take back the gifts he bestowed or the choice he made." In Romans 11:16–24, Paul uses the imagery of the root and branches. He calls the Gentiles the wild olive shoot grafted on to the good olive tree that is Israel. The root (Israel) and the sap of Israel provide life for the whole olive tree, not the other way around. He admonishes them not to forget that they, the Gentile followers of Jesus, draw their nourishment from the olive tree of Israel, and that what gives life to their community are the roots of this tree, they being but "grafted" on…not being naturally a part of the people Israel. Israel, its sap, its blood, its faith, nourishes us who have been grafted on.[17]

TWO COVENANTS OR ONE COVENANT?

It is clear that Gentile Christians are intimately related to the Christian Jews according to Paul, but how are we to visualize and characterize this relationship? The church has now rejected the supersessionist theology that understood the "New" Covenant of and in Jesus to have replaced the "Old" Covenant of Sinai.[18] Yet is it still possible to speak of multiple, but now related covenants, or is our relationship better characterized by considering there to be but one covenant but one covenant newly defined? If only one covenant, how do Christianity and Judaism retain their individual distinctiveness and integrity?

Before we look at representatives of both groups, we need to consider the recent proposal of Michael A. Signer. He has articulated three "paths" of Jewish covenantal interpretation. The first posits that there is only one covenant, even though God could have established many other foundational covenants. Thus, any other covenants God established are only secondary to the primary covenant of Sinai. Though he does not articulate these other covenants, I assume he is speaking of covenants with Abraham and David. Signer says that the long history between Jews and Christians was a sustained argument as to which group now had the one foundational covenant.

The second "path" is one that is amenable to dialogue and conversation. This "path" was first articulated in the nineteenth century and attempted to "describe the historical situation of the early Church and the 'parting of the ways' between Judaism and Christianity."[19] This view is best characterized by the writings of Franz Rosenzweig, where "Judaism and Christianity have reciprocal roles. Judaism is the center of the star. It provides the 'heat.' Christianity presents the rays of the star reaching outward through space and time" with separate tasks.[20] Signer rejects this "path" too because, according to Rosenzweig, "Jew and Christian both labor at the same task. He cannot dispense with either. He has set enmity between the two for all time, and withal has most intimately bound each to each."[21] Signer rejects this "path" because it "seems odd that the divine plan would provide for a reciprocal relationship between Jews and Christians which is driven by hatred between them."[22]

Signer proposes his own third "path," suggested by the work of Rabbi David Hartman and Paul van Buren, namely, that there is one covenant that is "both revealed and concealed in the language of

Hebrew Scripture…[but that there are] two distinct yet recognizably analogous realizations of the covenant: one in Oral Torah for Jews, and one in the incarnate word for Christians."[23]

In his response, Pawlikowski admits, "[A] single covenantal perspective has clearly dominated the many statements and speeches of Pope John Paul II on the theology of the Church's relationship to the Jewish people."[24] Pawlikowski continues to favor a two-covenant theory, which he believes better "honor(s) [the] classical theological claims about 'newness' in Christ while remaining faithful at the same time to Vatican II's insistence that this 'newness' does not involve the termination of the original covenant with the Jewish people as the Churches have often argued."[25]

Double-Covenant Theories

The most significant proponents of a two-covenant theory are J. Coert Rylaarsdam, James Parkes, and Rosemary Radford Reuther. This group of theologians argues that there are two covenants that are different but complementary. The first, the covenant with Israel, the Sinai covenant, embodies the perspective of history and signifies a socioreligious union called into being by God. It includes a mutual pact of faithfulness and responsibility between God and his people.[26] Such a view of the covenant reflects the belief that in the world of peoples and history special significance has been given to the particularity of Israel, which has been chosen by the LORD. This covenant is future-directed. The events it relates constitute a salvation history filled with "acts of divine rescue." It remains an open history. Such a salvation history cannot easily be blended with the Christ event; hence, it was not as significant for the New Testament writers as was the "second" covenant. The second covenant was a covenant with David, representing the eschatological tradition. The principal characteristics of this covenant were the holiness attached to Mount Zion, and the divine presence as revealed through the dynasty of David. This covenant marked a new beginning and continued to stand in tension with the first covenant to which it was finally accommodated. Rylaarsdam believes that the ongoing tension between these two covenants ultimately produced several sects, one of which became the eschatologically oriented Christian church.

Rylaarsdam emphasizes that the Christians who authored the New Testament were a Jewish sect; they were sectarian because they took a one-sided view of the relation of the two covenants, Sinai's and David's, to one another. They forgot about the paradoxical character of the relationship and thought that the full meaning of human history could be fitted into the perspective of the eschatological.[27] For Rylaarsdam the tension between the two covenants of Sinai and David continues. Whereas Judaism has given priority to the historical Sinai/Torah covenant over the Davidic covenant, Christianity has given priority to the eschatological Davidic covenant over the Sinai covenant. He concludes: "If both Judaism and Christianity always continue to revolve around the same two covenants that are paradoxically related to one another, then their relationship, whatever its tensions, is forever mutually interdependent."[28]

James Parkes has a different type of double-covenant theory that he calls the complementary revelation of "Sinai" and "Calvary." Sinai centers around God's action in and through the Jewish community while Calvary focuses on the understanding and communication with the individual person. Parkes describes these two revelations:

> [The] highest purpose of God which Sinai reveals to men in community, Calvary reveals to man as an end in himself. The difference between the two events…lies in the fact that the first could not be fulfilled by a brief demonstration of a divine community in action; but the second could not be fulfilled except by a life lived under human conditions from birth to death.[29]

What occurred at Sinai was the final development of a long, gradual growth in the human person's understanding of community. In the same manner, the emphasis on the individual that had been developing in Judaism since the period of the Exile attained its full development with Calvary and has been subject to interpretation ever since. For Parkes, "Judaism and Christianity are inextricably linked together as equals." The tension that exists between them is rooted in the "experience of tension in ordinary human life between the human person as social being and as individual, as an ultimate value in himself or herself, as one formed in the likeness of God."[30]

Another probable representative of the double-covenant theology is Rosemary Reuther.[31] In numerous writings and especially in *Faith and Fratricide*, she appears to affirm the validity of the separate individuality of Jewish and Christian peoples and calls, not for a reorientation of traditional Christian theologies, but a radical dismantling of Christian theology—particularly Christology.[32]

Yet another version of a two-covenant theology is given by Joann Spillman, wherein she gives an additional rationale for a two-covenant model by identifying both traditions as valid paths to God in a "theology of recognition."[33] In her view, the differences between Judaism and Christianity—in their histories, in their interpretations of the Old Testament, their practices, and their theologies—are too great to be defined as both sharing one covenant. Rather, what must be practiced is a mutual recognition of the legitimacy of each one's covenant, each one's particular path to God. Her position is critiqued by Eugene Fisher, who proposes a modified model of a single covenant in the images of "one root/two branches," a marriage of "[t]wo very different human beings (but both equally the image of God)" joined in a oneness enhancing "the unique personhood of each" and finally, the image of "interlocking circles."[34] Though he does not elaborate any further these creative suggestions, they are not antithetical to my position, which will be articulated below.

Although all the two-covenant theories attempt to explain both the distinctiveness *and* the interrelatedness of Christianity and Judaism, they fall short of expressing the unity and interconnectedness of the vision of Paul, and the trajectory of common rootedness that the church has been articulating since the Second Vatican Council. Let us turn for support to several proponents of a single-covenant theory: Monika Hellwig, Paul van Buren, A. Roy Eckardt, and Norbert Lohfink, SJ.

Single-Covenant Theories

The Catholic theologian Monika Hellwig believed that Jews and Christians alike are charged with simultaneous and complementary roles within the same covenant of God with his people. With those of the two-covenant school, she shares the opinion that it is inaccurate to say that Jesus fulfilled the Jewish messianic prophecies; however, unfilled or even false messianic expectations are only auxiliary to a neglected or misunderstood notion of "covenant" in the Hebrew scriptures. Hellwig believed that Christians have emphasized the messianic theme in the Hebrew scriptures at the expense of the covenant theme. Jesus' mission is that through him the Gentiles come to worship the one true God. Messiahship is to be understood as a mission for the entire church of God (Christians and Jews) to realize throughout history, not as already completely realized in Jesus. Thus, the Jews witness in a special way to the transcendence and unity of God.

Election is a way of saying that God talks first, so Christians are "elected" by becoming part of the chosen people through Jesus. Jewish election finds its meaning in the messianic meaning that is yet to come. The covenant after Jesus is new only in the sense that now it includes all people.[35] Regarding the institution narratives in the Synoptics (Matt 26:28; Mark 14:24; Luke 22:20) and in Corinthians (1 Cor 11:25), she considers that this is a mystical identification with the blood of the Sinai covenant (see Exod 24:8) in the spirit of the suffering servant (in Isa 42:6) and in the spirit of a renewal in people's hearts (Jer 31:31–34; Ezek 16:59–63).[36] Hellwig suggests that it may be more accurate to assert, in phenomenological terms, that "Jesus is the place of encounter of man with the transcendent God, which Christians have experienced as central in all human existence."[37] Claims of salvation only through Jesus, found in the New Testament, are expressions of kerygmatic urgency produced in, and making sense only from, a background of imminent eschatological expectation. Thus, revelation is not a deposit of propositions about Jesus, but the unformulated speaking of God in the depth of the human heart that finds expression in people's religious traditions.[38] Christians must look then to God's revelation in contemporary Jewish experience to see what God is saying of himself, just as God reveals himself in the experience of the church.

One of the first to develop a single-covenant theology was A. Roy Eckardt. For him, Israel's primary role in the covenant is to face in toward the Jewish people, while Christianity's function in the covenant is to look outward toward the Gentiles. The temptation is that Israel may secularize the kingdom of God, and on the other hand, in going forth into the secular world, Christianity may be tempted to overspiritualize the kingdom of God and negate the goodness of creation.[39]

The Anglican theologian Paul van Buren first proposed a type of single-covenant thesis in 1977 and continued to develop those ideas.[40] He insists that the church has an identity, apart from Judaism, that is a divinely appointed identity. It is not merely one among several Jewish sects. The church is the community of the Gentiles who have been drawn by the God of the Jews to worship him and make his love known among the nations. For those Gentiles, who through the Christ event came for the first time to be drawn into the plan of God, what took place in Jesus could not be understood as merely one episode in the history of salvation. Rather, it "marked a genuinely new beginning, a step out and beyond the circle of God's eternal covenant with his people, the Jews."[41] For van Buren, Jesus is the Christ of the church, but he is not the Jewish Messiah as Christians have traditionally claimed. Through the Jew, Jesus of Nazareth, the nations were finally allowed to experience the Way, though in a manner different from that of the Jews.[42]

The Jesuit biblical scholar Norbert Lohfink, also a proponent of a single-covenant theory for both Jews and Christians, discusses the concept of covenant and analyzes all the biblical texts that speak of the "new" covenant (Heb 8:2, 2 Cor 3, Rom 9—11, and Jer 31) and demonstrates how these texts do not exclude or replace the "old" covenant of Sinai with the Jewish people. He rejects any notion of parallel paths (as all holders of a two-covenant theory argue in favor of) because Paul does not speak this way in Romans 9—11. He concludes that the

> "new covenant" of the book of Jeremiah is the renewal and new institution of the covenant of Sinai. It includes the same torah. The "new covenant" of the New Testament is the eschatological fullness of this "new covenant" which has already begun with the return of the exiles from Babylon; it is in this that contemporaneous Jews also stand who do not believe in Christ. I lean therefore to a *one covenant theory which however embraces Jews and Christians, whatever their differences in the one covenant, and that means Jews and Christians of today* [emphasis added].[43]

Lohfink challenges us to think of two ways but within one Torah—Jews and Christians are not on parallel courses, but on the same course because the Hebrew scriptures' "view is universal throughout, [and] does not permit Israel and the nations each to maintain such reciprocal contact in the future that it outlines [two parallel plans]. God has only one plan of salvation, and at the end He will be 'one.'"[44] Though there is only one covenant in Lohfink's view, he says that from "early Christian times Jews and Christians have been on *two ways* [emphasis added]. Because the two ways run their course within the one covenant which makes God's salvation present in the world, I think that one must speak of a 'twofold way to salvation.'"[45] Lohfink holds that since

> the torah in the 'new covenant' is the same as in the covenant of the exodus from Egypt, it can, so far as it is present in our world in two ways [that is, Jews and Christians], ultimately be only one torah, God's world confronting the world societies structured out of sin, even if that world stemming from God's torah has to be as rich and varied as can possibly be devised.[46]

He adds at the end of his book that what "this might entail concretely must be the subject of a new book, or even of several new books."[47]

For Catholics, the most significant proponent of a single-covenant perspective was Pope John Paul II (1979–2005). In his speeches, his travels and meetings with representatives of the Jewish community, and in his formal documents, he reiterated the intimate and unique bond that exists between Christians and Jews.[48]

In a recent lecture series on "The Catholic Church and the Jewish People from Vatican II to Today," Archbishop Bruno Forte asserted that the theology of the two covenants "inspired the opposition between Judaism and Christianity, pushed to the point where the Church is seen as the New Israel and where the survival of the Chosen People is emptied of all significance."[49] For Forte, "[M]any of the interpretations proposed in the past to understand the relationship between Israel and the Church must be abandoned or left behind…[and we must] move on to the search for an authentic complementarity."[50] He puts this new view in the strongest possible words:

> There is no question of one or of two covenants: the economy of the Covenant is one and consists precisely in the plan of God's love for His people, the plan which Paul calls the mystery kept secret for long ages (cf. Romans 16:25).… Thus between the two people of the economy of the covenant there can be nothing but complementarity.[51]

Forte's model of complementarity has the danger of still meaning that each has things the other does not have, which can potentially lead to a conclusion of the superiority of one over the other. For instance, he speaks of the covenants of Golgotha and of the resurrection as being covenants that do "not negate the earlier covenants, but brings them to fulfillment," implying the superiority of one over the other. Missing still is a clear image of which covenants are complementary: Sinai and Golgotha, Noah and the resurrection. On the other hand, are all of the covenants of the Old Testament (Noah, Abraham, and Sinai) complementary with the New Testament covenants of Golgotha and the resurrection? In addition, in what ways are Golgotha and the resurrection covenants—special bonds between God and the people? Are the people Israel, the church, Gentiles, or all of the above? Although Forte is to be commended for pushing the dialogue forward and challenging us to think in new ways, he does not present enough detail and clarity to justify his theory of complementarity.

In spite of the affirmation of a single-covenant perspective, all the above authors are imprecise with regard to a concrete articulation or image that this new perspective might entail.[52]

CONCLUSION

Although historically Christianity has seen itself, at least since the second century, as the "replacement" people of the "new" covenant as opposed to the "old" covenant of the Jewish people, since the Second Vatican Council we are urged to think of ourselves as bonded together, and the council affirms that the covenant with Israel has never been rejected, superseded, or transcended. The proponents of a two-covenant theory are trying to have it both ways: preserving the "tradition" of two covenants, albeit two covenants now in a positive dynamic relationship with each other, with each having its own validity and permanence. However, Lohfink and others are right to criticize these proponents from the perspective of Paul, the apostle who preeminently reflected upon and struggled with the bonding of Gentiles with the people Israel. Based upon Romans 9—11, two-covenant theories are not acceptable, so others have tried to propose a single-covenant theory that still preserves the identity and distinctiveness of each community while bonding them together.

The following proposal that I would make, in my view, takes the Jewish tradition more seriously, in the light of my more than thirty years of active participation in Catholic/Christian dialogue with the Jewish community, including Orthodox/Traditional, Conservative, Reform, Reconstructionist, and so-called "secular" Jews—mostly in the United States but partly in Israel.

A New Covenant Model

The theological image that I propose[53] comes from an insight in the Gospel of John. It is a christological image that speaks particularly to the present situation of Christian-Jewish relations and, I believe, helps further develop the directions the church has been moving in since the Second Vatican Council. I have a colleague in my seminary who says, "If one is going to die for the gospel, you'd better decide which one you're going to die for!" By this he means that biblical scholars and theologians have known for a very long time that not only is the Jesus of Mark radically different from the Jesus of John— some would even say that they are incompatible Jesuses—but also that we have at least five distinct portraits of Jesus presented by the four evangelists *and* Paul.[54] Therefore, I recognize that the following proposal is not the only possible reimaging of Jesus within the Christian-Jewish relationship, but is one that I believe speaks particularly to today.

Two Modalities—One Covenant

It is clear in the prophet Hosea (4:1–2; 2:21–22) and elsewhere that *hesed* (loving-kindness or covenant love) and *emeth* (covenant fidelity) are the pillars of the covenant between God and his people.[55] In the Gospel of John (1:14), the author says that "the Word became flesh and tabernacled among us, and we beheld the glory of him, glory as of an only begotten from a father, full of grace (*charitos*) and of truth *(aletheias)*."[56] These words, *charis* and *aletheia*, usually translated as "grace and truth" (NAB, NRSV, and others), are the Greek translations[57] of the Hebrew covenant terminology words, *hesed* and *emeth*.[58] Thus, *this word of God (=Jesus) is the flesh and blood incarnation of the covenant. Hesed* (=*charis*, "grace, covenant love") and *emeth* (=*alethia*, "truth, covenant fidelity") are incarnated, that is enfleshed, in the person of Jesus.

This enfleshed covenant presence is further indicated by the phrases just before "grace and truth." The Word was "tabernacled among us" (John 1:14a). This Greek verb *skenoun* ("make a dwelling, pitch a tent") has important associations in Israel's past. In Exodus 25:8–9, Israel is commanded "to make a tent (the Tabernacle — *skene*) so that God can dwell among His people; the Tabernacle became the site of God's localized presence on earth."[59] The Hebrew underlying the Johannine prologue's "dwelling" is the *shekinah*, God's presence, which dwelt in the midst of his people (Exod 13:21–22; 40:34–38). This theology of the *Shekinah* was known in the time of Jesus.[60]

In the next phrase, "we beheld the glory of Him" (John 1:14b), this experience of the Word's "Glory" (*doxa* in Greek; *kabod* in Hebrew) is a visible manifestation of God's "majesty in *acts of power*. While God is invisible, from time to time He manifests Himself to men by a striking action, and this is His *kabod* or glory".[61] Therefore, Jesus is a manifestation, an enfleshment in the human, of God's powerful presence as a physical covenant-reality breaking into history in a new modality.

The Word of God is a powerful, efficacious, and creative word. In the first chapter of Genesis, this Word brings order from chaos, men and women are empowered to people the earth and commanded to be good stewards of it. Out of all creation, after the Flood, God calls Abraham, commands him to go to a new land, blesses and protects him, and promises that he and his descendants will be a blessing to all people (Gen 12:1–4a). Much later, God's Word calls his people out of Egypt and forms them as a special covenant people at Sinai. The first chapter of John's Gospel located this powerful Word of God as existing before creation, and attributes to this "Word" all that has come to be through the power of God. Surely, then, this creative and efficacious Word of God is then incarnated or enfleshed in the person of Jesus, who is the covenant power in our midst. This is the same Word that God spoke at creation, to Abraham, at Sinai, and lastly, and now, in Jesus. In light of this identification of the Word, who is this Jesus for us and what is his mission?

At least since the second century, this Jesus has been the focus of divisiveness and hostility between Christians and Jews. What have we Christians learned from this sordid history? We have learned that disputation, persecution, ghettoizing, pogroms, and the twentieth-century Holocaust/Shoah have not brought about a massive Jewish conversion to Christianity. Unless we take the position of the prayer of the old Good Friday liturgy that Jews are simply a reprobate, callous, and closed-minded people, we must face the fact that perhaps God is still with his Jewish people. Has God not spoken to us about Jesus in these peoples' nineteen centuries of "no" to Christianity? Perhaps to answer fully the question, "Who is Jesus and what is his mission?" we must say that Jesus has in historical fact turned out to be the Christ of the Gentiles and not the Messiah of the Jews.[62] We could describe his earthly mission as either a flawed success (since only a relatively small number of Jews became his followers) or a magnificent failure (since the Gentiles have been brought to the God of Israel because of his failed mission to his own people).[63]

Until very recently we have always couched the question in an either/or mode. Either Jesus is the Messiah of the Jews and our Savior or he is not, and we are vain and foolish to follow him. Thus, the Jewish "no" has been interpreted as a direct challenge, affront, and attack upon the very foundation of Christianity. Yet then we Christians are a people who are forgetting our own roots: We have forgotten that our original historical roots as Gentiles are found in pagan history and in pagan religion. As Paul's teaching to the Gentile Christian community at Rome (Rom 9—11) clearly indicates, we have been brought from a dark religious past to the light of Christ. However, as Gentile followers of Jesus, we are theologically rooted in the good olive tree, the people Israel, and so we are for all times interrelated. *We Jews and Christians are joined together in the one covenant of Sinai, but it is now one covenant with two modalities.* That is, the one covenant of Sinai manifests itself in two different but related modes of activity. We are two communities united in one covenant of Sinai with a common destiny; namely, to bring peace and justice to this world and walk in the Way[64] of our God.

For Jews this mode or "Way" of covenant actualization means life in the covenant of Sinai by walking in the Way of Torah as lived and interpreted by the Talmud and the great rabbis through the centuries— Hillel, Gamaliel, Yohanan ben Zakkai, Akiba, Judah ha-Nasi, Maimonides, the Baal Shem Tov, Abraham Heschel, and others. For Christians, this mode or Way of covenant actualization means that we die to our pagan past[65] and are born into Jesus, the Christ of the Gentiles; we take on Christ ("yet I live, no longer I, but Christ lives in me" [Gal 2:20]), and for us he is "the way[66] and the truth and the life"

(John 14:6). Jesus-the-Jew's universal mission is to bring the Gentiles to the worship and the life of the God of Israel by becoming part of the covenant of Sinai through him.

Again, the one covenant with two modalities is not a new covenant separate, additional, or supersessionist to the covenant at Sinai. In the light of church teaching since the council, and with a new appreciation of and understanding of the apostle Paul, it is clear that the newness of the "new" covenant has to do with the relationship between Jews and Gentiles *as one people* and not (as was formerly taught) the supersession of a new covenant over the old. The covenant continues to be, for the Jews, embodied in Torah, the instruction to the community on how to live, how to walk in the way of Adonai. This word is eternal and is ever forming the community of Israel through the traditions and interpretations through the centuries. This covenant, for the Gentiles, is incarnated in the person of Jesus, and is an individual, personal Word that unites the Gentiles to the covenant of Sinai through Jesus-the-Jew. As Jews are to walk in the way of Torah as their life in the covenant, so Gentiles are to walk in the way of Jesus-the-Jew as their life in the same covenant.

3
The Holy Land

INTRODUCTION

Since the establishment of the modern State of Israel in 1948 and especially since the end of the Second Vatican Council and the 1993 Fundamental Agreement between the Vatican and the State of Israel, the topic of the land has played a critical role in the dialogue between Christians and Jews. The focus on the State of Israel is partly predicated on the importance of the land in our two traditions. In an effort to clarify the role of the land of Israel in a religious perspective, it is necessary to examine the sources of a land tradition in the Hebrew scriptures and the Christian scriptures. This study focuses on this issue from a Roman Catholic perspective, but has implications for the broader Christian community. At the end of this chapter, a proposal is made for a sacramental understanding of the land in the Catholic tradition.

HEBREW SCRIPTURES

Our search for an understanding of the land of Israel must begin with the scriptures.[1] For a Catholic, the Hebrew scriptures are "an indispensable part of Sacred Scripture. Its books are divinely inspired and retain a permanent value," for God's covenant with Israel "has never been revoked."[2] Furthermore, since the Vatican II declaration *Nostra Aetate* in 1965 affirmed that the eternal covenant of God with Israel is unbroken and remains valid, we Catholics view the Jewish people in a new light. Subsequent documents, the 1975 *Guidelines*, the 1985 *Notes*, the 1994 *Catechism of the Catholic Church*, and the recent 2001 document, *The Jewish People and Their Sacred Scriptures in the Christian Bible*, cause us to take to heart, even more intensely,

41

what the American bishops said in 1975—that Christians should learn "by what essential traits the Jews define themselves in the light of their own religious tradition." The *Notes* cites John Paul II, who calls upon catechists and preachers "to assess Judaism carefully and with due awareness of the faith and religious life of the Jewish people as they are professed and practiced still today."

The Vatican *Notes* also speaks of the religious attachment between the "Jewish people and the Land of Israel as one that finds its roots in the Biblical tradition and as an essential aspect of Jewish covenantal fidelity to the one God." If, as the *Notes* claims, this bond is in the biblical tradition, this is the question we need to ask of the Hebrew scriptures: Is there an essential territorial dimension to "Judaism"?[3] That is, is there a special relationship among the God of Israel, the people of Israel, and the land of Israel? And is that relationship primary and essential or is the territorial claim of Judaism accidental and peripheral?

Let us begin to answer these questions by noting that some of the ideas about land in Hebrew scriptures are common to early ancient Near Eastern religions as well as to archaic religious beliefs; other ideas about land are particular to Israel. We will look first at what Israel shared with other Near Eastern religious traditions.

The belief that there were sacred and profane spaces and that the god(s) dwelt in one particular land and place is common to all archaic peoples. That there were certain privileged spots where the gods manifested themselves, be it a hilltop, a stream, a grove of trees, or through a person as an oracle or shaman was also common to the archaic peoples of the ancient Near East. Postbiblical Judaism ultimately came to believe that Israel was the center of the earth, Jerusalem was the center of Israel, Mount Zion the center of Jerusalem, and the holiest place of all was the foundation stone of the earth whereon reposed the Holy of Holies and the Holy Ark. Of course, these assignations of holy places are not the exclusive custom of Israel; other peoples similarly considered places to be holy to them.[4] In the modern age, we have fugitive instances of this tendency, now secularized, as the "sun never setting on the British Empire."[5]

If the concept of the holiness or sacredness of a land and the holiness of a place is not exclusive, then, to Israel, from whence derives the uniqueness of the God of Israel, the identity of its people and its land? One scholar contends that the *"land theme"* is so ubiquitous that it *may have greater claim to be the central motif in the OT than any other, including 'covenant'* [emphasis added]."[6]

The first theme to be distinguished in the Bible after the "prehistory" of Genesis 1 — 11 is that *of the land as a promised land.*[7] Abraham is promised the land five times, beginning with an account in the earliest written tradition, the Yahwist (or J) tradition, dated in writing from the time of the Davidic and Solomonic empire in the tenth century BCE.[8] God says to Abraham in Genesis 12:1–4a:

> "Go forth from the land of your kinsfolk and from your father's house to a land that I will show you. I will make of you a great nation, and I will bless you; I will make your name great, so that you will be a blessing. I will bless those who bless you and curse those who curse you. All the communities of the earth shall find blessing in you." Abram went as the LORD directed him.

The second promise, also from the J tradition, is given after his return from a sojourn in Egypt and his separation from Lot (Gen 13:14–17). In a later passage, Genesis 15, probably a redaction of the J tradition and the Elohist tradition (a tradition from Northern Israel put into writing sometime after J), recounts a covenant that is made between God and Abraham:

> When the sun had set and it was dark, there appeared a smoking brazier and a flaming torch, which passed between those pieces. It was on that occasion that the LORD made a covenant with Abram, saying: "To your descendants I give this land, from the Wadi of Egypt to the Great River [the Euphrates], the land of the Kenites, the Kenizzites, the Kadmonites, the Hittites, the Perizzites, the Rephaim, the Amorites, the Canaanites, the Gigashites, and the Jebusites. (Gen 15:17–21)

The same covenant relationship is reconfirmed in the E tradition in the story of the "sacrifice of Isaac" (Gen 22:1–18).[9] What is essential in these passages is "the recognition that that promise [of the land of Israel] was so reinterpreted from age to age that it became a living power in the life of the people of Israel." It operated "as a formative, dynamic, seminal force in the history of Israel."[10]

The content of the promise to Abraham (Gen 12) consists of progeny, blessing, and a land. A later redactor may have joined the theologies embedded in Genesis 12 and 15 to connect the Abraham and David traditions; many have argued that in King David the Abrahamic covenant found its fulfillment in the creation of the Davidic empire and the secure establishment of Israel as a people on a land.[11]

The next stage of development occurred when the Deuteronomic tradition joined together the promise of the land made to the patriarchs with the tradition of the Law given at Sinai. The commandments (Hebrew: *mitzvot*) are regulatory, that is, they provide for how one lives on the land. They are also conditional, that is, if Israel the people disobeys the commandments she can be expelled from the land (see Deuteronomy 28—29). The redemption of Israel begun in the Exodus experience finds its completion in the possession of the land, that is, God's mighty acts wrought in Egypt have as their conclusion the entry into and settlement on the land. As von Rad comments, "[I]n this work [Deuteronomy] the land is undeniably the most important factor in the state of redemption to which Israel has been brought, and on this basis the nation is to expect an additional gift from Yahweh—'rest from all enemies round about.'"[12] Many times Deuteronomy stresses that Israel did nothing to deserve this land; it was only God's desire to give her the land and because of his faithfulness to his promises that Israel possesses it. Therefore,

one must not fail to recognize the theological justification given for Israel's possession of a land inhabited by others—and thus also for her dispossession of the former inhabitants. Their wickedness and God's gracious gift of the land in fulfillment of his promises form a rationale for Israel's possession of it. At the same time and over against this, however, is the Deuteronomic self-criticism of Israel's life and obedience and the assertion that Possession of the land is not automatic or eternal.... Israel cannot justify her *original* possession of the land on the basis of her behavior; she must, however, *justify or preserve her continuing and future possession on the basis of her behavior both in*

*terms of the worship of God and a proper use of the pos-
session which is her salvation gift* [emphasis added].[13]

In Deuteronomy there are found two strong traditions: (1) that of
the figure of Abraham, who is the model of a wandering people, leaving home and land to go to a place promised by God; this is a
"nomadic" model,[14] and (2) the image of Israel as a *sedentary* people,
enjoying the gifts of God and living a life of particular service in this
land. These two traditions, nomadic and sedentary, overlap, with the
consequent result in Deuteronomy of the requirement that Israel continue to justify her continued existence in the land by doing good
deeds—especially those of a proper religious worship and the building of a community of justice including both the Israelite and the resident alien (*ger*) in their midst.[15]

In the Priestly tradition, put into final written form during the
Exile in Babylon between 587 and 539 BCE,[16] the promise to
Abraham in Genesis 17 takes on a different cast. In the covenant of
circumcision, God says:

> "Between you and me I will establish my covenant, and I
> will multiply you exceedingly." When Abram prostrated
> himself, God continued to speak to him: "My covenant
> with you is this: you are to become the father of a host of
> nations. No longer shall you be called Abram; your name
> shall be Abraham, for I am making you the father of a host
> of nations. I will render you exceedingly fertile; I will make
> nations of you; kings shall stem from you. I will maintain
> my covenant with you and your descendants after you. I
> will give to you and to your descendants after you the land
> in which you are now staying, the whole land of Canaan,
> as a permanent possession; and I will be their God.... Thus
> my covenant [of circumcision] shall be in your flesh as an
> everlasting pact." (Gen 17:2–8, 13)

God's words to Abraham in this Priestly tradition are *an unconditional statement*. The Abrahamic covenant of Genesis 17 means that
Israel's election and its possession of the land can never become conditional upon obedience to the Law—it cannot be annulled by human

disobedience.[17] These covenant promises of land and blessings are repeated with each of the succeeding patriarchs.

In contrast with the last two patriarchs, there is no question of personal merit or reward. The covenant with Isaac is explicitly rooted in both the promise to and the merit of his father (Gen 26:3–5 [J]). Isaac in turn conveys "the blessing of Abraham," that he "possess the land which God gave to Abraham" (Gen 28:4), to his own son. And, in the subsequent covenant-making encounters between Jacob and God, the first two patriarchs again serve as the point of reference for transmission of the land promise.[18]

Thus the tradition of the land as promised and given to Israel is attested to in the traditions embedded in the Torah in all the major periods of Israel's life from the time of David and Solomon (tenth century BCE) through the period of Exile in Babylon (586–539 BCE). Whether one can trace it back prior to David depends on the position one takes on the historical reliability and age of the patriarchal narratives. The most ancient promise, of Genesis 12:1–4a, can be reasonably associated with a (semi)nomadic life style: Promises of land, progeny, and protection (blessings and curses) are essential for this type of existence. That land promise put into writing during the time of David, associated with earlier promises to Israel's (presumed) ancestors, indicates, at minimum, their belief in their God's ownership of the earth and all the lands thereof, and his beneficence in giving Israel this gift.[19] But it is clear that God's *unconditional gift of the land* does *not* carry with it the *unconditional right to live on the land*, because both Deuteronomy and numerous prophets make Israel's continued residence on the land dependent upon certain ethical requirements.[20]

The first distinctive characteristic of the concept of Israel's land in the Hebrew scriptures is that it is a *Promised Land*; the second is that it is *cultic*, that is, the land is God's own possession, and religious obligations flow from this fact. As Leviticus 25:23 says: "The land shall not be sold in perpetuity, for the land is mine; and you are but aliens [*ger*] who have become my tenants." The Hebrew scriptures also tell us that the offering of firstfruits to God was because he was the true owner of the land; that the land should keep a Sabbath-year rest once every seven years; and that the land was holy because it was separated out ("chosen") and consecrated to the LORD.

One of the reasons given in scripture for the displacement of the "native" inhabitants in the land (Canaanites, Amorites, Jebusites, et al.)

is "rooted in the moral quality of the occupants' life in the Land rather than in the patriarch's merit."²¹ But what applied to these prior inhabitants applies to Israel's life in the same land. Because of the wickedness of the "natives," the LORD drove out the former inhabitants and gave this land to Israel (Deut 1:8). Yet Jeremiah says, during the time of King Josiah of Judah (ca. 627 BCE), "[W]hen I brought you [Israel] into the garden land to eat its goodly fruits, you entered and defiled my land, you made my heritage loathsome" (Jer 2:7). The LORD further says that he "will at once repay them [Israel] double for their crime and their sin of profaning my land with their detestable corpses of idols, and filling my heritage with their abominations" (Jer 16:18). However, those who take the land away from Israel by conquest fare no better in the prophet's denunciations!

> [The LORD] speaks jealously against Edom and other nations "who gave *my* land to themselves as a possession" (Ezek 36:5). Joel 1:6 speaks of "a nation that has come up against *my* land." Enemies will attack the land in vain. Thus we read concerning Assyria in Is 14:25: "I will break the Assyrian in *my* land, and upon my mountains trample him under foot." Joel 2:18 says: "[the LORD] became jealous for *his* land, and had pity on his people." And Joel 4:2 (3:2) predicts that the nations will be judged in the valley of Jehoshaphat "because they have divided up *my* land." It is said by God, "I will bring you [Gog, a symbol of Israel's enemies²²] against *my* land, that the nations may know me" (Ezek 38:16).²³

The primary thrust of the preexilic prophets was that the people would be punished with exile for the sins of covenant-infidelity in the kingdom of Israel and the kingdom of Judah. However, although punishment and exile were deserved by Israel for her sins, it was also unthinkable to the prophets that Israel should be permanently deprived of her land. The exilic addition to the end of the Book of Amos promises a return:

> I will bring about the restoration of my people Israel; they shall rebuild and inhabit their ruined cities. Plant vineyards and drink the wine, set out gardens and eat the fruits. I will

plant them upon their own ground; never again shall they be plucked from the land I have given them, say I, the LORD, your God. (Amos 9:14–15)[24]

The most eloquent prophet of a return to the Land of Israel is Ezekiel, who prophesied during the Exile in Babylon. His vision of the dry bones coming back to life bespeaks Israel's return to her land. The LORD says:

> I will deliver them from all their sins of apostasy, and cleanse them so that they may be my people and I may be their God.... They shall live on the land which I gave to my servant Jacob, the land where their fathers lived; they shall live on it forever, they, and their children, and their children's children, with my servant David their prince forever. I will make with them a covenant of peace; it shall be an everlasting covenant with them.... My dwelling shall be with them: I will be their God, and they shall be my people. (Ezek 37:23, 25–27)

After the return from Exile, Israel never enjoyed the glorious reign of peace, prosperity, and ingathering of all exiles that the prophets had proclaimed. Israel's history continued to be one of domination by foreign powers—Persian, Greek, and Roman. Yet even in exile, the entity of the land continued to play a central role in Judaism.

W. D. Davies concludes his study of the territorial dimension of Judaism by noting that "just as Christians recognize 'the scandal of particularity' in the Incarnation, in Christ, so for many religious Jews...there is a scandal of territorial particularity in Judaism. The Land is so embedded in the heart of Judaism, the Torah, that—so its sources, worship, theology, and often its history attest—it is finally inseparable from it."[25]

CHRISTIAN SCRIPTURES

At this point, it is clear that the land of Israel was a basic component of Jewish belief and religious practice as found in the Hebrew scriptures. Walter Brueggemann argues, "Land is a central, if not *the central theme* of biblical faith."[26] As a Catholic Christian, I am certainly called upon to acknowledge this bond between the people Israel and Eretz Yisra'el and their continuing attachment to the land through postbiblical history up to the present. The question that still remains for us Christians is: Does Christian scripture sever this bond in light of the Jesus experience or does this bond endure, and secondly, does the land have any special significance for us as Christians?

Most Christians believe that we have passed beyond the claims of and need for the particularity of and commitment to any particular land—our commitment is to the person Jesus, and *not* to a land. Without yet attempting to affirm or deny this frequently held belief, let us examine the references in the Christian scriptures, the New Testament, regarding the land.

The earliest existing writings from Jesus' first followers are the letters of Paul dating from 44 to 58 CE.[27] These letters are particularly interesting because Paul is a Jew born in Tarsus, the Hellenistic capital of the province of Cilicia (in modern-day Turkey). He describes himself as a Pharisee (Phil 3:5) before he became a follower of Jesus. He was probably a follower of Rabbi Shammai (d. 30 CE), one of the most rigorous interpreters of the Torah in his day.[28]

Nowhere in Paul's writings is the idea of the land of Israel *explicitly* mentioned. This is not surprising, since one of Paul's primary concerns was with the bonding together of his Gentile converts with the Jewish followers of Jesus. However, Romans 9—11 gives an eloquent defense of the continuing validity of God's covenant with Israel and its continuing election. He tells the Gentile Christian community in Rome that they are wild olive shoots grafted onto the cultivated tree that is Israel. It is the roots that support the branches and not the other way around (Rom 11:11–24).

Thus, it is Israel that supports the Gentile community grafted onto the olive tree and not the reverse. In an earlier passage, Paul says that his own people "are Israelites; theirs is the adoption, the glory, the *covenants* [emphasis added], the giving of the law, the worship, and the *promises* [emphasis added]; theirs the patriarchs, and from them, according to the flesh, is the Messiah" (Rom 9:4–5). Foremost among the "promises" are the land promises made to Abraham in Genesis as well as the prophetic messianic expectations, including the rule of the Messiah, the return of political self-rule over the land of Israel, and a great age of peace for all humankind—and including the acknowledgment of the importance of God's rule and his presence on Mount Zion in the Temple.

Paul also places great stress upon Abraham as the paradigm for our faith in Romans 3—4 and Galatians 3—4; his primary thrust is to assure his pagan converts that it is by faith in Jesus the Jew, as Christ [Messiah, anointed one], that they become members of the covenant community and children of Abraham, and not by circumcision and food laws. As a first-century Jew, Paul approaches the biblical text in the Torah in a linear historic mode; namely, he posits that since the Law was given on Sinai many centuries after the time of Abraham and since Abraham's faith made him righteous in God's eyes (Gen 15:6),[29] Paul's pagan converts become members of the covenant community of Israel through faith, and not by circumcision.[30] Because Abraham's faith affirmation is the key for Paul to our relationship with God in Christ and because constituent to this faith affirmation are the promises of progeny, land, and protection, the importance of the land of Israel remains part of the Abrahamic faith and promise. Brueggemann could not state it more strongly when he says:

> Abraham imagery apart from the land promise is an empty form. No matter how spiritualized, transcendentalized, or existentialized, it has its primary focus undeniably on land. That is what is promised, not to the competent deserving or to the dutifully obedient, but freely given (as in the beginning) to one who had no claim....[31]

On other occasions, Paul was at pains to demonstrate that no division existed between the Christian-Jewish community at Jerusalem and his Diaspora non-Jewish Christian communities. Paul exhorts the Gentile community at Corinth to set aside monies, and, when Paul arrives, he will send emissaries with the collection to the Jerusalem community (1 Cor 16:1–4; 2 Cor 8–9). This action was probably, first of all, based upon an understanding that Paul would preach to the non-Jews while Peter, James, and John would minister to their fellow Jews in Jerusalem (Gal 2:6–10) and, secondly, was based upon Paul's contention that his Gentile converts were in complete communion with the Christian-Jewish community in Jerusalem. We also know that the Jewish Jerusalem followers of Jesus continued their distinctive Jewish practices, including daily praying in the Temple (Acts 2—3).

Although Paul did not require pagans to become first Jews through commonly accepted Second Temple conversion practices and only after that to accept Jesus as Messiah,[32] he was at pains to ensure that there was a common covenant bond between Jesus' Jewish believers and his pagan converts. The content of this religious identity is made explicit in Romans 9:4–5, and Gentile converts, by virtue of their bonding with Israel, are heirs of this same content. Included in this identity as people of the covenant is a religious (and political) bond to the land of Israel for all Christians—both Gentile and Jewish believers.

After Paul's death[33] Christian perspective toward the land of Israel changes radically with the four gospels. Mark's Gospel's final composition was ca. 70 CE and probably written in Rome for the persecuted Christians there.[34] It has as its focus the coming of the kingdom of God. It was Jewish expectation that God's lordship would be definitively manifested at the end of history with a universal acknowledgment of his rule by all peoples and nations. In order not to inflame the Roman authorities, the author was careful not to emphasize the political and military functions of the expected Jewish Messiah. In fact, he goes out of his way to make clear that Jesus conceals his messiahship during his earthly life.[35] Although in this Gospel, Galilee becomes the place of revelation and redemption while Jerusalem is the place of Jesus' rejection, there are no grounds given to elevate Galilee to a land of central importance to Christians.

The Gospel of Matthew was written in the late 80s CE by a Jew who accepted Jesus as Messiah. This person was probably a leader in the local community—perhaps in Caesarea, the capital of Roman government of the province of Judea.[36] This Gospel represents a predominantly Christian-Jewish perspective;[37] thus, we would expect to find great theological importance given to the concept of the land of Israel. However, two events intervened that negated this possible development. First, in the year 70, after four years of Jewish revolt against Roman rule, the Roman general Titus and his tenth legion destroyed the city of Jerusalem and the Temple. We know that at that time the Christian-Jews fled from the city and refused to defend it against the Romans. Second, after this catastrophe, the Pharisaic leaders gathered at Javneh to develop what has become Rabbinic Judaism—a religious way of life that now functioned without the Temple, priesthood, and sacrifices. They met as a rabbinic academy from about 75 to 135 CE, in this period becoming less amenable to the theology and community of the Jewish/Gentile messianic sect of Jesus' followers.[38] It was in this milieu that Matthew attempted to assert the Christian-Jewish community's Jewish roots and to demonstrate its continuity with the Torah, the prophets, and the tradition. Both because of Roman rule and new directions the Pharisees were beginning to take at Javneh, the land becomes a moot question for Matthew's Gospel.

The Gentile author of Luke-Acts addressed a primarily Gentile audience when he wrote from Antioch in Syria between 85 and 90 CE. The main theme in his work is the relationship of Christianity to Judaism—especially its growth from a small Jewish sect to reaching "the ends of the earth" in the Book of Acts. By the time of Luke's writing, Gentiles greatly outnumbered Jews in the church. This fact underscores the reason why there is little interest in the theme of the land of Israel: The Gentiles had no roots in Jewish tradition and religious practice and thus no attachment to the land. Luke does not explicitly separate the Christian message from the land or consciously negate it, but the end result is the same: its absence from his Gospel. Luke concentrates on the Word of God coming from Jerusalem and from the land of Israel to the Gentile world focused in Rome, and from there to the "ends of the earth." Jerusalem and the land of Israel are only important because they are the place of origin for Jesus and God's Word; they have no abiding significance for Christians.

Of the Christian scriptures, the Gospel of John is probably the most radical in its severing of the importance of the land from Christian belief. Written in the late 90s CE, this Gospel presents special problems to interpreters because of its apparent hostility to Jews, their practices, their Temple, and Jerusalem. The prologue (chapter 1) of John establishes Jesus as the incarnate Word (the Logos) of God. This Logos is no longer attached to a land, as was the Torah, but to a Person who came to his own land, and was not received. The abandonment of any special relationship with the land is seemingly completed in the Gospel of John.

INITIAL CONCLUSIONS

It is clear from this brief survey that in the Hebrew scriptures the importance of the idea of the land plays a central role, but that in the

Christian scriptures the role the land plays is at best ambiguous. Why? Because at a very early date Gentiles, for whom interest and commitment to the land had no previous history, became a majority in this Jewish messianic movement. With the fall of Jerusalem in 70 CE, Christian-Jewish communities declined in the land of Israel, and with the diminishing of these believers there was no voice for the enduring bond with the land of Israel.[39] Also, although early Christian-Jews proclaimed the advent of the messianic age and the future return of Jesus as Lord, before this came to pass a new reality appeared on the scene. Before the new Israel on Mount Zion and the earthly and cosmic rule of Jesus in his return took place, there "emerged a community, in response to Jesus, the Messiah, which dispensed with the Oral Law as unnecessary to salvation. Outside the land, outside the Law there was a Messianic activity."[40] Although Christian-Jews tried to reconcile this activity with traditional expectations (a struggle reflected in Paul's letters and Matthew's Gospel), Rabbinic/Pharisaic Judaism ultimately rejected this new movement. Early Christians, probably by the time of Luke, if not earlier, and certainly by the time of John, were moved by the question: "What shall we do now that the End is delayed? How are we to understand our Faith in the light of the emergence of these Gentile Christians, who are without the Law and outside the land but yet share in the redemption?"[41]

Was the ultimate result the breaking of the linkage between covenant, peoplehood, and the land of Israel[42] for the Gentile Christian movement? Or rather, did the land take on a different kind of importance for this Gentile Christian movement?

LAND AS "HOLY LAND"

Introduction

The focus of this next section is to consider the meaning and significance that the land of Israel has had for Christians; it is not our concern to consider the meaning that the land has had and continues to have in the Jewish tradition.[43]

Surprising, our story does not end at the time of the Bar Kochba revolt (132–35 CE) with the separation into "church" and "synagogue," and the dismissal of any importance of the land of Israel in Christianity. Even though the link with the land of Israel/covenant/

peoplehood appeared to be sundered, a Christian connection with the land continued unbroken. From the beginning, there were permanent Christian communities established in the land, and very soon this land became a place of Christian pilgrimage.

If it is true, as Father Edward Flannery contends, that Christians are totally ignorant of the history of anti-Semitism,[44] then it is even more powerfully true to say that Christians are also totally ignorant of the history of Christian presence in the land of Israel—even in this present century!

"Holy Land" as Place of Pilgrimage

The first known pilgrim to the land of Israel for whom we have documentary evidence is a bishop from western Asia Minor, Melito of Sardis, who in the second century made a journey to this land "to the 'place where these things had been proclaimed and accomplished.' His purpose in going there was to obtain 'precise information' about the books of the 'Old Testament.' He wanted to know the number as well as the order of the books that Christians shared with the Jews."[45]

Even prior to the beginning of the Christianization of the empire at the time of the emperor Constantine and the building of churches in the Holy Land at sacred Christian sites under his orders, pilgrims were journeying to the Holy Land. In the third century, "pilgrims had begun to visit Palestine 'for prayer' and 'investigation of the holy places.'"[46]

Both Origen (185–254) and Jerome (340–420) took up residence there to study the scriptures, compile manuscripts of biblical texts, write commentaries and live out their lives there. The first historian of Christian history, Eusebius (260–339), bishop of Caesarea, also wrote "a book on biblical place names (*Onomasticon*), several other biblical studies, a commentary on the book of Psalms (fragmentary), and a complete, verse-by-verse exposition of the book of Isaiah."[47] With the discovery of the tomb of Christ in Jerusalem, "located not in the heavens but in Judea,"[48] Eusebius was the first to sense a "profound shift in devotion that was taking place in his day and to lay the foundations for a Christian idea of the holy land."[49]

While this work of scholarship and study was going on, Christian pilgrims were undertaking the difficult journey to the land of Jesus' birth, life, death, and resurrection. As it was clear to them that "Christ's sojourn on earth, it seems, had sanctified not only the specific places where he lived and died, but the very soil of the land itself."[50] Consequently, we have a substantial record of journeys made by pilgrims from the fourth to the eleventh century.

Some of these writings are first-person accounts and others are secondhand reports of pilgrim journeys. What is clear is that in the first thousand years of Christianity, irrespective of how the land was understood from the scriptures, there was a continuing importance given to journeying to the land as a pilgrim. Moreover, this has continued to the present day.

Although, unlike Judaism and Islam,[51] Christianity does not mandate its adherents to make a pilgrimage to any place, yet Christian pilgrims have come to the Holy Land from the early centuries to the present day.

Modern-day Pilgrimages

In viewing contemporary Catholic pilgrimages to the Holy Land, Catholic groups come to the Holy Land throughout the year, and while many come as individuals or in families the larger proportion come in groups active as organizations—oftentimes as members of a particular parish community. In a study of modern pilgrimages, Glenn Bowman notes that

> [i]n large part Catholic pilgrimage is inspirational;…[that is, people] come to the Holy Land to be renewed in their faith so that they can subsequently reengage their ordinary lives with renewed energy and a renewed sense of purpose. The idea that pilgrimage serves as a revitalization of spiritual energies drained by involvement in the labors of the secular world makes Catholic pilgrimage much more individuated than that of the Orthodox; instead of a cosmological celebration of the community of mankind in Christ, Catholics engage, as individuals or in groups bound by a shared purpose, in a process of being repossessed by the power that gives meaning to their personal lives and labors.[52]

Bowman goes on to note that Catholic groups are generally given great amounts of secular and historical information about the holy places, both inside and outside them, by knowledgeable Catholic and

Israeli guides who instruct the pilgrims and speak of the significance of what, by tradition, is believed to have happened on that site. For Catholics the most significant act is to celebrate the Eucharist at the holy sites. These liturgies of the Eucharist differ in essence and structure not at all from Eucharists celebrated in their own worldwide home communities, however, save for perhaps special commemorations or readings associated with the site; but it is in the eucharistic celebrations on these holy spots that God is felt especially and intensely present in ways that do not occur in the same way when this same Eucharist is celebrated in one's home churches. The power of these celebrations would seem to imply a sacramentality connected with the sites and thus inextricably to the land itself also, making more intense the reality of God's presence.

Leaving aside the incredibly rich diversity of Christian communities in the Holy Land, not because they are not important nor have much to teach us, but because of space constraints, let us briefly consider the Holy Land in light of a theology of presence. How might we reimage the meaning of the "Holy Land" in light of the history of Christian presence in the land and the experience of pilgrimages to this land?

THE HOLY LAND: A THEOLOGY OF PRESENCE

Sacramental Theology

Catholics have often been called "sacramentalists," which means that we are a church based on sacrament and word.[53] "'The Church' is the People that God gathers in from the whole world. She exists in local communities and is made real as a liturgical, above all a Eucharistic, assembly. She draws her life from the word and the Body of Christ and so herself becomes Christ's Body."[54] What is the meaning of Christ's presence here, and how does this take place in the church?

The early Greek and Latin literature spoke of *mysterion* and *sacramentum*, from which we get our modern term, *sacrament*. Originally, *mysterion* "meant something secret, something hidden, and something not fully manifest. This sense of *mysterion* is retained in both…Testaments. In the Book of Daniel, *mysterion*[55] refers simultaneously to the plan of God for the end times and to some obscure revelation of this plan. In Paul *mysterion* refers to the divine plan to save all…in Christ, a plan determined by God from the beginning and kept secret, but now revealed through the Spirit, through the prophets, through the apostles."[56]

The third-century Alexandrians, Clement and Origen, first began to adapt the mystery language to ritual practices of Christians; and by the fourth and fifth centuries, this language usage was fully established. The Latin translation of the Greek word *mysterion* was *sacramentum*, which referred to sacred realities proclaimed and realized in symbols in general and particularly in sacramental symbols.[57] This development continued through Augustine (fourth century) until it was more precisely defined in the twelfth century by Hugh of St. Victor, who said that a sacrament was a sign which signifies something, and also efficaciously confers it. That is, because "by a visible reality seen externally, another invisible, interior reality is signified."[58] It was Thomas Aquinas, in the thirteenth century, who gave the definition and explanation of sacrament that continues in the church until the present day.[59]

Following the Second Vatican Council's decree *Dei Verbum*, describing "the sacramental character of revelation" and implicitly also the "description of the sacramental character of the whole economy of salvation,"[60] many modern theologians have attempted to expound the fuller implications and meaning of the direction of the council. We can now say that in

> contemporary Catholic theology the use of the word sacrament has been extended. It is applied to Christ, who is described as the sacrament of God [Schillebeeckx, *Christ the Sacrament*]. It is applied also to the Church, which is described as "a kind of sacrament" [*Constitution on the Church*], "the sacrament of unity" [*Constitution on the Sacred Liturgy*], "the universal sacrament of salvation" [*Constitution on the Church in the Modern World*]. The application of [this] word to Christ and to the Church and to the individual Christian is an analogical use of the word. Christ, the Church, the Christian and many elements of the Christian life are called sacraments, legitimately, insofar as they are in some way akin to but still quite different from the ritual sacraments, signs and instruments of the grace of God mediated to men and women. The growing extension

of the analogical use of the word sacrament marks a *renewed emphasis on the traditional Catholic theme that the grace of God is mediated to men and women in created reality* [emphasis added].... God always speaks and communicates himself, the Catholic tradition holds, in created "deeds and words."[61]

Each of the traditional seven sacraments has been reexamined in light of the new understandings and insights of modern theology, biblical studies, and other modern disciplines. More recently, some sacramental theologians have begun to look at sacraments "based less on the history and theology of the rites than on the actual experiences of women and men at prayer."[62] This approach, used in the early church and practiced most extensively in the fourth century, is called *mystagogy*.[63] This practice is "a form of instruction that attempted to plumb the depths of the rites that had been experienced for their spiritual import. First the experience, then the teaching...."[64] While this approach is found in the great teachers of the fourth century, it is ultimately grounded in scripture. St. Paul is using the approach we have called mystagogic when he challenges those who died to sin in baptism to longer live in sin (Rom 6:1–4) and the Gentile Christian community in Corinth to properly live out their eucharistic experience in the way they treat the poor in their community (1 Cor 11:17–33).

In this approach, "the experience of participants is also always in the forefront."[65] The primary focus of mystagogy is the community's sacramental life—especially baptism, confirmation, and Eucharist, but the whole sacramental life of the community is appropriate for mystagogical reflection.[66] "Personal experience is [an] indispensable focus of mystagogy. Thus, imagination and memory are critical to the mystagogical process."[67]

Applying this mystagogical process to a reexamination of the Eucharist includes an attempt to understand the sense of real presence in terms more meaningful to, and resonant with, our present-day experience of personal communication. These views in no way deny the reality of Jesus' presence in Eucharist as risen Lord, but are a modern attempt to explicate the meaning of Christ's real presence in contemporary idioms.

In this purview, Schillebeeckx posits "that the real eucharistic presence cannot be isolated from the real presence of Christ in the whole liturgical mystery and in the souls of the faithful.... [Thus] the eucharistic presence in the consecrated bread and wine is ordered to the *ever more intimate presence of Christ* [emphasis added] in the assembled community and in each member of the church."[68]

These new ways of reflecting on sacraments, especially that of the Eucharist, led Pope Paul VI to issue his Encyclical, *Mysterium Fidei*, in which he says that he wishes "to review at greater length the...doctrine which was briefly set forth in the constitution *De Sacra Liturgia*,"[69] of the ways in which Christ is present in his church. Those ways are, in order:

1. The presence of Christ first of all in the church at prayer ["where two or three are gathered in my name"]
2. In the church performing works of mercy
3. In general, with us and in us on our pilgrimage through life
4. As the church preaches or proclaims the word of God
5. In the governance of the people of God through pastoral care
6. "In a manner still more sublime" as the church offers the Sacrifice of the Mass
7. As the church "administers" the sacraments
8. "There is yet another manner in which Christ is present in His Church, a manner which surpasses all the others; it is His presence in the Sacrament of the Eucharist."

Then Paul VI adds a very important note on eucharistic presence vis-à-vis other forms of presence: "this presence [in the Eucharist] is called 'real'—by which *it is not intended to exclude all other types of presence as if they could not be 'real' too* [emphasis added], but because it is presence in the fullest sense."

A Reimaging of the Holy Land as Sacrament of Encounter

If indeed there are multiple senses of Christ's presence as the *Constitution on the Sacred Liturgy* and Paul VI teach, let us reflect upon what this might mean regarding a new Christian imaging and understanding of the "Holy Land."

At the level of personal communication, there are various degrees of presence. For example, when we think of someone dear to us and bring him or her to mind there is a sense in which they are present to us. There is a yet-more-intense sense of presence when we receive a letter or e-mail from them, and an even more intense sense of presence when we speak to them over the phone. The most intense experience is, of course, a person-to-person meeting with someone. If, as we have demonstrated, a sacrament is the mediation and encounter of a Christian with God (in fact, Schillebeeckx speaks of Christ as *the* "sacrament of our encounter with God"), then perhaps the different kinds of encounter with Christ, as well as the degrees of intensity of these encounters as described above, have a parallel with a pilgrim's experience in the Holy Land. When one brings to mind the land where the great events of our redemption took place—whether by reading scripture or meditating—there is a sense of the presence of these events and an experience of Christ's presence being brought about by the land. Seeing pictures of and reading books about the land can also increase the sense of Christ's presence being mediated through the land. The most intense sense of presence, of course, is making a pilgrimage to the Holy Land, visiting and praying at the sites where Jesus lived and walked and the early church took root. (It has been said that tourists pass through the land, but the land passes through the pilgrim.)[70]

From this description of our experience of reading, reflecting, viewing pictures, and finally personally visiting the Holy Land, we can experience the essential role that the land plays in making Christ present to us. In a reimaging of our relationship to the Holy Land, we can say: *As Christ is the sacrament of our encounter with God, the Holy Land is a sacrament of our encounter with Christ.* As surely as Christ is mediated in multiple ways and present in multiple ways as taught by the Second Vatican Council, Paul VI, and various theologians, so he is most assuredly present and mediated in the land we call holy. We can call this mediation of Christ in the Holy Land, a sacramental encounter; thus, *the Holy Land, itself, becomes for us a sacramental experience.*

This sacramental experience neither invalidates nor supersedes the Jewish experience and covenantal connection to the land of Israel, but adds a new dimension of experience and meaning specific to Catholic Christians, who, since the Second Vatican Council, are called upon to understand, appreciate, and affirm the reality of the Jewish experience in the twenty-first century—in addition, I would argue, especially the Jewish experience of their connection to the land of Israel.

4
Between Land and State: Palestinian Perspectives

Having acknowledged the importance of and the validity of the Jewish attachment to the land of Israel along with having presented a Christian affirmation of it as the Holy Land in a sacramental context, and before a discussion of the State of Israel can ensue, it is necessary to present a Palestinian perspective, both Christian and Muslim, on the land and on Jerusalem.

Palestinian Christians claim attachment to the land and to Jerusalem on several grounds. First, many still hold the traditional view held over the centuries that Christianity has superseded Judaism and that Christians are the new "people of God"—heir to all the promises made to Israel, now to the exclusion of the Jewish people. In this light, all the land promises to the patriarchs in the Torah as well as those to David and throughout the Hebrew scriptures are the exclusive prerogative of Christianity. In the Roman Catholic tradition this is called supersessionism and in the Protestant tradition, replacement theology. Characterizing two Arab-Christian scholars,[1] Haddad says:

> The Jewish people can no longer think of themselves as God's Chosen People since Christians are the New Israel. Therefore, the Arab-Israeli conflict will be solved when all of the Jewish people accept Christ.[2]

After the Second Vatican Council and subsequent documents indicating the ongoing validity of the Jewish covenant and the promises therein, some, but not all, Arab Christians and their leaders changed their views. However, most notably, Eastern Orthodoxy has been reluctant to change its supersessionist view.[3] Father

61

George Makhlour of St. George's Greek Orthodox Church in Ramallah has said:

> The church has inherited the promises of Israel. The church is actually the new Israel. What Abraham was promised, Christians now possess because they are Abraham's true spiritual children just as the New Testament teaches.[4]

Merkley concludes that in this extreme point of view it can be said that

> *the land itself belongs to the Christians.* This is not a manner of speaking or a metaphor. The land *literally belongs* to the People of God, the Christians. And the Christians on the land are *Palestinians.*[5]

Catholic-Christian Arabs generally hold a more moderate view, prescinding from the argument of who "owns" the land, namely, that both Arabs and Jews have a right to the land and both must learn to share this patrimony.[6]

The second claim that Palestinian Christians make is that the Arabs were the earliest Christians, along with the Jewish followers of Jesus. They claim longevity of residence in the land since the first century[7] and assert that this claim has priority over that of the majority of Jews in the land who arrived much later. That arrival, beginning in the nineteenth century, but with the bulk of Jewish immigration taking place after World War II, the Holocaust, and the establishment of the present-day State of Israel in May 1948, accounts for almost all of the present Jewish population.[8] As evidence of Palestinian-Arab longevity in the land they cite the Pentecost event in the Acts of the Apostles 2:2–13, where many different peoples and races are listed, including "Arabs" who all "hear them speaking in our own tongues of the mighty acts of God" (Acts 2:11).[9]

The third claim to the land made by Palestinian Christians is that the Israelis in the war of 1948 drove them off the land. In Arabic, this is called the *Nakba*, which means the "catastrophe." In the past, Israelis claimed that either the Palestinians all voluntarily fled their homes because of the approaching Israeli army or because Arab radio stations told them to flee so that the Arab armies could destroy this new State and that in a short time they would be able to return to their homes. On the other hand, Arab apologists for the Palestinians claimed that the Palestinian exodus was a planned expulsion. Although there is some truth to each of these two claims,[10] it is now clear from the recent book by the Israeli historian Benny Morris that the situation is much more complex. In an analysis of 377 abandoned Arab villages in Israel, Morris gives six reasons for the Palestinian-Arab exodus:

1. Abandonment on Arab orders
2. The influence of a nearby town's fall
3. Expulsion by Jewish forces
4. Fear of being caught up in fighting
5. Actual (or expected) military assault on a settlement
6. Whispering campaigns—psychological warfare conducted by the Haganah/IDF[11]

Meron Benvenisti, the deputy mayor of Jerusalem from 1971 to 1978, "who often accompanied his father, a distinguished geographer, explains how the Arab landscape, both physical and human, was transformed into an Israeli, Jewish state in his book," *Sacred Landscape: The Buried History of the Holy Land since 1948.*[12] While Palestinians no doubt know much of this account, it is a painful read to discover how Arabic names of over nine thousand natural features, villages, and ruins were given new Hebrew names—thus obliterating their Arabic past.

Of the three dominant claims to the land by Palestinians, the latter certainly carries the most weight, and justice would seem to, at minimum, require compensation for the land taken by Israelis.

In addition to the claims to the land, Palestinian Christians believe and experience the land as holy.[13] If the land is holy, then Jerusalem bears a special holiness for Palestinian Christians because of Jesus' association with Jerusalem. It was in the Temple that Jesus was presented after his birth and where he was lost when the Holy Family returned to Nazareth. John's Gospel tells of his journeys to Jerusalem to celebrate the feasts of Passover, Pentecost, Tabernacles, and Hanukkah, and it was in Jerusalem that his passion, death, resurrection, and ascension took place.[14] While Bethlehem bears a special holiness as Jesus' birthplace and the Galilee as the place of his ministry, it is Jerusalem[15] that is the holiest place to Christians—focused particularly on the Church of the Holy Sepulcher.[16]

Palestinian Muslims also have claims to the land and its holiness. Islam's paramount claim is that Abraham was the first Muslim.[17] In the Qur'an, Abraham is spoken of as a Muslim because he was the first monotheist. In addition, unlike the Bible where Abraham is identified as the ancestor of a chosen people with a special status including a covenant established with him and the guarantee of the Promised Land, the Qur'an "claims to set the biblical record straight by presenting Abraham as a more universal ancestor who is not just the proto-Israelite but the ideal person of faith whom all should emulate."[18] However, the first Arab inhabitants of the land preceded even Abraham. It is claimed that Arabs came to this land

> from the Arabian peninsula during the successive waves of immigration thousands of years ago, and that they called it the Land of Canaan (i.e. the Lowland) as an Arabic way of describing the land according to its geographical features.... This land continued to be prosperous with its Canaanite Arabs in both war and peace times, regardless of misfortunes or successive invasions.... During this history, the land was invaded by intruders like the Hebrew tribes, which did not settle in it except for a short while, whereas the native inhabitants of the land stuck to it, which truly emphasized and confirmed the historical Arabic identity of this land over more than six thousand years.[19]

Based both upon length of settlement in the land and their stories in the Qur'an (that find their duplicates in the Bible, although often with variant details and interpretations), Muslims claim this land, which is a holy possession to them.

> The Holy Land, from the point of view of religion and legitimacy, *is an Islamic territory* (emphasis added). It is characterized by a holy status which distinguishes it from the rest of the Islamic territories.... Hence, it is imperative for Muslims, regardless of where they live, to *defend it and maintain it as an Islamic property* (emphasis added).[20]

In the biblical story of the sacrifice of Isaac, the Qur'an tells the story with Ishmael as the intended victim rather than Isaac (Gen

22:1–19).[21] The consequences of this Islamization of this tradition are significant. In the biblical tradition, Isaac is the bearer of the covenant (Gen 17:19–21; 18:14), whereas in the Qur'an "neither son is the sole heir of the promise…nor Allah does not prefer one over the other."[22] Thus, the Qur'an has reinterpreted both Abraham and Isaac out of the promises of the covenant and the land.

Although Muhammad was born in the year 570 CE and died in 632 CE, and thus the formal date of the beginning of Islam as an organized religious community dates to this time period, Muslims claim their tradition actually dates from the time of Abraham. It is difficult to adjudicate this claim since many Jews base their claims of covenant and possession of the land on the religious truth of the Hebrew scriptures and, on the other hand, many Muslims base their claims on the religious truth of the Qur'an and its revelation through Muhammad of the will of Allah (God) that gives them prior claims to the land—claims that are in conflict with Jewish claims.[23]

The second principal claim of Palestinian Muslims to the Holy Land is also religious, namely, that since the conquest by Islam of the land in the seventh century and the fact of the hegemony of Islam on the land until the twentieth century, the land may never be given away to the infidel, that is, the non-Muslim.[24]

> According to Islamic law, once an area becomes a part of the Islamic world, it must never withdraw or lose Islamic political hegemony. Therefore, the very existence of a Jewish State within what used to be the Islamic world is a serious problem to many Muslims.[25]

This doctrine is called *dar al-islam*, "which literally means 'the house or abode of Islam,'"[26] and it was first proposed when Islam was in its early expansionist period in the seventh and eighth centuries CE. This doctrine is connected with the term *dar al-harb*, "which literally means 'the house or abode of war.'"[27] The term

> denotes the territories bordering the *dar al-Islam* whose leaders are called up, under threat of invasion, to convert to the Muslim religion. Jurists trace the concept of *dar al-harb* back to the time of the Prophet and cite the messages sent by Islam's founder to the emperors of Persia,

Abyssinia, and Byzantium, and to other leaders, summoning them to choose between conversion and war.[28]

These two doctrines are highly controverted today by Islamic scholars; many question the applicability of these concepts in today's world.[29]

A third claim to the land by Palestinian Muslims is identical to a claim made by Palestinian Christians, namely, that they were expelled from the land during the war of 1948.[30] Since the 1967 war and the establishment of many settlements on the West Bank, Palestinian Christians and Muslims claim that much of their land has been illegally confiscated and they have not given up title to this land. It is on this land, 22 percent of the original mandate land, that Palestinians hope to establish their own independent State.[31]

The religious attachment to Jerusalem is very strong among Muslims. Jerusalem ranks as the third-holiest city in Islam after Mecca and Medina. About a year before the Hijra[32] the Qur'an relates an account of Muhammad's night journey to the Dome of the Rock in Jerusalem, where the mosque now stands, his being taken up to the heavens from there, then his returning to earth and returning to Mecca.[33]

According to al-Hasan al-Basri, one who was in the relationship of a son to him, the angel Gabriel came to the prophet while sleeping at a place close to al-Kaaba. Gabriel stirred the prophet with his foot three times before the Prophet sat up anticipating a serious event. Gabriel took him by the arm to the door, whereupon the prophet saw a white animal, half mule and half donkey, with wings on its side. The apostle and Gabriel then rode the animal until they reached the shrine at Jerusalem. The Apostle then ascended from rock to heaven, where he found Moses and Jesus in the company of other Prophets. The apostle of Allah led these in prayers. When he returned during the same evening and told other Qurayshis of his journey, they thought this had been an absurd claim since the journey to Syria by caravan takes a month and another month to return. When his listeners remained incredulous, the apostle was asked by Abu Bakr to describe Jerusalem, and he did, in great detail. This dispelled doubts from the followers' minds. According to A'isha, the Apostle's wife, the body of the Messenger of God was not missed during the nocturnal journey. The climb to heaven, she added, occurred with his spirit. Another tradition claimed that it was a vision that occurred in Muhammad's sleep. However, most traditions by the Companions of the Prophet assert differently [that this was a real physical, material journey].... One of the traditions added, Muhammad stopped to pray at Bethlehem where Jesus, the Messiah, the son of Mary, was born. Several traditions asserted that while in Jerusalem, Muhammad's fabled winged horse, known as al-Buraq was tethered against the Temple Wall....

Even before Muhammad made his Hijra (emigration) to Medina in 622, he followed the Jewish custom of turning towards Jerusalem at the time of prayer.[34]

Because of this association, the Umayyad caliph Abd al-Malik began construction of a shrine over the exposed bedrock face on the Temple Mount in Jerusalem in 688 CE and completed it in 691. The El Aksa Mosque[35] was built by the caliph al-Walid (709–715 CE). Though twice destroyed by earthquakes and restored in 780 CE, its present structure was again rebuilt after an earthquake in 1033.[36] After the 1948 war, Jordan annexed the Old City of Jerusalem, including the entire area of the Temple Mount, as part of "the West Bank," a large area initially designated for an Arab state, and no Jews were allowed to pray at the Western Wall.[37] Since the 1967 war, the Temple Mount[38] (called the Haram esh-Sharif,[39] the Noble Sanctuary, by Muslims) has been under the exclusive control of the Muslim Waqf.[40] In addition to these sites holy to Islam, the site of the cave of Machpelah[41]—believed to be the burial site of Abraham, Isaac, and Jacob[42]—is "encased" by an impressive structure. It is a place of pilgrimage and prayer for Muslims. The outer wall around the cave dates to Herod the Great (37–4 BCE), while the existing structure dates from the time of the Crusader king Baldwin II (1118–1131 CE).[43] Yet it remains that the most important city for Muslims is Jerusalem:

As for Jerusalem's position in Muslim worship, the preference of living, praying and even visiting Jerusalem upon other cities in the Islamic regions has been emphasized by many sources. The Prophet (PBUH)[44] said, 'He who goes to Jerusalem for nothing but praying and prays the five prayers, i.e. morning, midday, afternoon, sunset and evening, will be as free from his sins as the day his mother gave him birth.'[45]

CONCLUSION

Palestinian-Christian and Palestinian-Muslim perspectives on the State of Israel are diverse. Most Palestinian Christians and Muslims within the borders of the 1948 State of Israel hold Israeli passports, vote in Israeli elections and are de jure citizens of the State with the equal rights of all citizens, including universal health care, social services, and other benefits given to all citizens in the state.[46] The only exception is that they are not required to render any military service, compulsory for all other Israelis. Druze are an exception to this Arab exemption as they are accepted into military service and many serve. Although equal in legal standing, de facto, Israeli-Christian Arabs and Israeli-Muslim Arabs are discriminated against in employment, government benefits to their towns and villages, and in many other subtle ways.[47]

In conclusion, the Israeli-Arab population (both Christian and Muslim) within the State of Israel has a connection to the land that is both historic and religious. This connection neither invalidates nor diminishes the Jewish attachment to the land, but it is all too often overlooked and/or denied. American Catholic Christians need to understand Palestinian Christians in Israel as well as the role that Palestinian Muslims have played in the land historically and continue to do. Since the Second Vatican Council with its new understanding of our relationship to the Jewish people, we have a serious obligation to understand our bond with the Jewish people, land, and state. While doing this, we must not diminish nor negate the bond we have with Christians in this land, nor fail to understand and respect the Muslim presence in this same land. We have a responsibility to work for a just solution for all the parties — three religions sharing one land in a two-state solution — with justice, security, and shalom for all.

The following chapter will consider what theological valuation a Catholic Christian might place upon the State of Israel. Such a proposal in no way negates the rights and history of the Palestinians as discussed in this chapter — in fact it lays greater responsibility upon all parties to effect a just solution to what has been called the "Palestinian Problem."

5
The State of Israel

INTRODUCTION

Every morning, the religious Jew prays in the Amidah:[1]

Sound the great Shofar proclaiming our freedom. Raise the banner to assemble our exiles, and gather us together from the four corners of the earth. Blessed are you, O God, who will gather the dispersed of Your people Israel.... Return in mercy to Jerusalem, your city, and dwell therein as you have promised. Rebuild it in our own day as an enduring habitation, and speedily set up therein the throne of David. Blessed are you, O Lord, who rebuilds Jerusalem.[2]

After every meal, Jews also pray for the rebuilding of Zion and the ingathering of the exiles:

We thank thee, O Lord our God, because thou didst give as a heritage unto our fathers a desirable, good and ample land.... And rebuild Jerusalem the holy city speedily in our days. Blessed art thou, O Lord, who in thy compassion rebuildest Jerusalem. Amen.... May the All-merciful break the yoke from off our neck, and lead us upright to our land.[3]

Dan Cohn-Sherbok says that "throughout history Jews have longed to return to the Holy Land they inhabited in ancient times, and this quest has animated messianic aspirations through the centuries as well as the creation of a Zionist movement in the nineteenth century," which finally culminated in the reestablishment of the State of Israel "on May 14, 1948 [when] Prime Minister David Ben Gurion read out the Scroll of Independence in the Tel Aviv Museum."[4]

How did the Catholic Church respond to this aspiration of Jews in the nineteenth century? The first Zionist Congress was held in Basel, Switzerland, in 1897. At issue was a discussion of the possible return of Jews to Palestine as a national homeland.[5] On January 25, 1904, in a private meeting, Pius X replied to Herzl's plea for a sympathetic understanding of the Zionist cause:

> We are unable to favour the movement. We cannot prevent the Jews from going to Jerusalem, but we could never sanction it. The ground of Jerusalem…has been sanctified by the life of Christ. As head of the Church, I cannot answer you otherwise. *The Jews have not recognized our Lord, therefore we cannot recognize the Jewish people* [emphasis added].[6]

The church's view was no better when the State of Israel was proclaimed in 1948:

> Immediately following the establishment of the State of Israel, the unofficial organ of the Vatican, *Osservatore Romano*, wrote: "Modern Zionism is not the authentic heir of biblical Israel, but constitutes a lay State.… This is why the Holy Land and its sacred places belong to Christianity, the Veritable Israel."[7]

Forty-five years after that article was written, on December 29, 1993, the Holy See (that is, the Vatican) and the State of Israel established diplomatic relations.[8] The following year in an interview in *Parade* magazine with Tad Szulc, Pope John Paul II said:

> It must be understood that Jews, who for two thousand years were dispersed among the nations of the world, had decided to return to the land of their ancestors. *This is their right* [emphasis added].
> And this right is recognized even by those who look upon the nation of Israel with an unsympathetic eye. This right was also recognized from the outset by the Holy See,[9] and the act of establishing diplomatic relations with Israel is simply an international affirmation of this relationship.[10]

It seemed extraordinary that this event of diplomatic recognition occurred. To this query from Szulc, the Pope answered:

> Because you ask how the present rapprochement has developed between the Holy See and Israel, I shall answer citing the words of the Second Vatican Council. In the *Nostra Aetate* declaration, the Council states: "The Church ever keeps in mind the words of the apostle Paul about his kinsmen 'who have adopted as sons, and the glory and the Covenant and the legislation and the worship and the promise; who have the fathers, and from whom is Christ, according to the flesh'" [Rom 9:4–5].[11]
>
> If we stand by the declaration of the Council, we must conclude that the Church's attitude toward Israel results from *the same mystery of the Church that the Council undertook to plumb anew* [emphasis added].[12]

As the saying goes, "How did we get from here to there?" given the initial reactions of the church in the nineteenth century, and exactly what does the church now teach about its relationship with the State of Israel? Are there any indications of what a Catholic's relationship should or could be toward the Jewish State?

DEVELOPMENT OF CATHOLIC CHURCH TEACHING ON THE STATE OF ISRAEL

On October 28, 1948, Pius XII issued the encyclical *In Multiplicibus Curis*, in which he sympathized with the "thousands of refugees, homeless and driven, [who] wander from their fatherland in search of shelter and food."[13] The pope notes that before the conflict began he spoke to "a delegation of Arab dignitaries…condemning any recourse to violence." He several times reiterates the need for settling matters with justice and peace; however, not once does he refer to the Jewish population or the State of Israel. He calls it only Palestine, a country that does not exist, not even alluding to or hinting at Jewish suffering or the invasion of the Arab armies after the State of Israel was declared following the Jewish acceptance of the November 29, 1947, United Nations vote for partition into two states,[14] Jewish and Arab, along with the subsequent rejection of the UN partition by all the Arab parties. Though Pius XII said that "when war was declared, without abandoning the attitude of impartiality...which places Us above the conflicts which agitate human society," his actions belie quite the contrary! He ends this document by advocating the internationalization of Jerusalem and all of the holy places "scattered throughout Palestine" in order through international guarantees to assure free access to these places and also guarantee "the freedom of worship and the respect of customs and religious traditions." He clearly has no confidence that the newly declared State of Israel will insure this.

Although the language of the encyclical is rather restrained, the article of commentary following it in *Civiltà Cattolica* is not:

> A detailed description is given of the fate of the Arab refugees; they had fled from the pursuing Jewish gangs, wandering along the roads from Haifa and Jerusalem and having nothing to eat except olive leaves. Nothing must be expected from American justice (it is said) as Truman needed the Jewish vote. No one should wonder at Jewish military successes since the Soviets sent them all the arms. Russia would like to see a communist state established in Palestine and there were at least three hundred Russian "observers" in the country. Their hopes were nearly fulfilled, for the first Israeli elections had resulted in a socialist government.[15]

Sister Charlotte Klein thoroughly documents the hostile and rejectionist views of the Vatican toward the rise of modern Zionism with Herzl, Zionist immigrations to the land and the State of Israel. She says that it is not until 1964 that any positive change takes place, which she attributes to Vatican II, Cardinal Bea, many American bishops and Pope John XXIII.[16]

Anthony Kenny, in a masterfully comprehensive book, *Catholics, Jews and the State of Israel*,[17] traces the official Catholic teaching on the State of Israel from the time of the Second Vatican Council until the early 1990s.[18] Prior to the first official Vatican mention of the State of Israel in the *Notes* (1985), Pope John Paul II made a strong positive reference to the state in his encyclical *Redemptionis Anno* ("Year of Redemption") of April 20, 1984. He dealt mostly with the topic of Jerusalem—its holiness and importance for Christians,

Jews, and Muslims. Regarding Jerusalem, the Holy See supported a plan to internationalize Jerusalem and its suburbs as a separate entity, prior to the United Nations vote of November 29, 1947.

> This demand was based on the religious and pragmatic interests of the church in the Holy City, and on the presence of Christian communities and holy places in the city. The demand was modified in 1967 with plans for an internationally guaranteed statute, a vague formula not further defined.[19]

Pope John Paul II reiterated this call, since 1967, by urging for Jerusalem "a special statute internationally guaranteed so that no party could jeopardize it,"[20] that is, jeopardize the interests and aspirations of the diverse communities and their holy places in Jerusalem. The pope believed that Jerusalem is the most important question and the key to the final settlement of the crisis in the Middle East. He continues: "It is natural in this context to recall that in the area two peoples, the Israelis and the Palestinians, have been opposed to each other for decades in an antagonism that appears insoluble."[21]

The Middle East is always full of surprises. Who would have thought that in less than ten years after that "gloomy" observation of the insolubility of the problem, the Oslo accords would be signed with the Palestinians and soon afterwards the Vatican would establish diplomatic relations with Israel, and Israel would sign a peace treaty with Jordan!

Nevertheless, back in 1984, the pope still invoked peace and reconciliation:

> For the Jewish people who live in the State of Israel and who preserve in that land such precious testimonies to their history and their faith, we must ask for the desired security and the due tranquility that is the prerogative of every nation and condition of life and of progress for every society.[22]

After explicitly speaking of the State of Israel, for the first time in a papal document, and acknowledging their right to live in security and tranquility, he speaks of the needs of the Palestinian people:

> The Palestinian people, who find their historical roots in that land and who, for decades, have been dispersed, have

the natural right in justice to find once more a homeland
and to be able to live in peace and tranquility with the other
peoples of the area.[23]

In this document, the pope very carefully speaks to the needs of
each group: for the Jews the need for security since their state has
been besieged from the beginning by hostile forces, and for the
Palestinians, who are also acknowledged as having roots in this land,
that they live in peace with the other peoples, that is, the Jews. That
both need tranquility is clear!

From 1984 until the Gulf War of January 1991, followed in the
fall by the Madrid Conference, which brought Israelis and
Palestinians together face-to-face for the first time at an official level,
the church continued to slowly develop its understanding of the State
of Israel and the concomitant need for diplomatic recognition.[24]
Suddenly, on September 13, 1993, as a result of secret talks (called
unofficially the "Oslo Agreement") the Israeli-Palestinian Declaration
of Principles was signed on the lawn of the White House with the public handshake between the then prime minister of Israel, Yitzhak
Rabin, and the chairman of the Palestine Liberation Organization
(P.L.O.), Yasser Arafat — bringing together two implacable enemies in
a pledge of friendship and cooperation for the establishment of a permanent peace in the Middle East!

The time was at hand for a dramatic move by the church.
Anthony Kenny's book, *Catholics, Jews and the State of Israel*, concludes with an eloquent plea for the Vatican recognition of the State of
Israel; however, by the end of 1993 (the year of publication of the
book), this event occurred. What influence this book may have had
will probably never be known, but its documentation is a valuable
resource. He concludes his study, speaking to Catholics:

> It is clearly apparent that the immense change of heart and
> attitudes developed and demonstrated by the Catholic
> Church since the Second Vatican Council is lost to Jews
> while the Catholic Magisterium remains prudently silent
> about the State of Israel.... While silence and prudence are
> wisdom for the Catholic Church, they are folly for the dia-
> logue with the Jews, since so many Jews interpret them as
> being malevolent in character and intention. Such silence

evokes from the corporate Jewish memory the most serious doubts about the Catholic Church.[25]

Just as the Vatican Council's document on the Jews, *Nostra
Aetate*, was a turning point in the history of the church, I believe that
the diplomatic recognition of Israel is another important turning point
in the relationship, not only of the official Catholic Church but also of
the Catholic people and the Jewish people as a community of faith.
Therefore, let us now examine the "Fundamental Agreement" in some
detail and reflect on its explicit and implicit consequences.

THE FUNDAMENTAL AGREEMENT BETWEEN
THE HOLY SEE AND THE STATE OF ISRAEL

On July 29, 1992, a meeting was held between then Foreign
Ministry director-general Yosef Hadass and Vatican undersecretary for
foreign affairs Msgr. Claudio Maria Celli. The talks, the announcement said, were aimed at establishing relations between Israel and the
Vatican.

The announcement was followed by a protest from some
Christian leaders, including Latin Patriarch Michel Sabbah, the first
Palestinian Arab to be appointed to that position. On the Jewish side,
there were protests from the Haredi, or ultra-Orthodox, community.[26]

These talks caught most people by surprise. This first meeting in
July set up a Bilateral Permanent Working Commission with groups
of "experts" from each side quietly working without publicity. The
commission held its next plenary session on November 19, 1992; and,
a year later on December 29, 1993, in a joint communiqué issued by
the commission from the Vatican Apostolic Palace came the
announcement of the approval of the draft of the "Fundamental
Agreement between the Holy See and the State of Israel." The formal
signing by the parties was to take place the next day in Jerusalem.[27]

A momentous event transpired with the signing by Dr. Yossi
Beilin, deputy foreign minister of Israel, and Msgr. Claudio M. Celli,
Vatican undersecretary for relations with the states. Both signatories
noted its overwhelming significance as Dr. Yossi Beilin said:

> In a formal sense, the Agreement today is an agreement
> between us, a small state, and an even smaller one. However,

its impact reaches beyond those geographic boundaries, and touches the hearts of millions of Jews and more than a billion Christians throughout the world....[28]

Msgr. Celli also affirmed

...as Mr. Shimon Peres, Foreign Minister of the State of Israel, pointed out a few days ago, the signing of the agreement, while certainly marking an important historic event, must also be acknowledged to have a *fundamental religious and spiritual significance* [emphasis added]—not only for the Holy See and the State of Israel, but for millions of people throughout the world.... [T]he dialogue and respectful cooperation between Catholics and Jews will now be given new impetus and energy, both in Israel and throughout the world. The Preamble of the accord explicitly mentions this religious dimension.[29]

The Preamble says:

The Holy See and the State of Israel,
   Mindful of the singular character and universal significance of the Holy Land; Aware of the unique nature of the relationship between the Catholic Church and the Jewish people, and of the historic process of reconciliation and growth in mutual understanding and friendship between Catholics and Jews....[30]

Though, at face value, this Agreement is between two states, they are not like any other states in the world. Each one, while it possesses, more or less, the institutions and structures of a nation state,[31] has meaning far transcending its apparent "reality." The preamble speaks of the specialness of the Holy Land wherein is found the State of Israel and the "unique nature of the relationship between the Catholic Church and the Jewish people"; thus an identification is made at the very beginning of a reality beyond the states of Vatican and Israel. Also linked to this diplomatic recognition is "the historic process of reconciliation and growth in mutual understanding and friendship between Catholics and Jews." The universality of this action is immediately apparent, for neither do all Catholics live in

Vatican City State nor all Jews live in the State of Israel, but this action deeply affects these peoples and the action between these peoples effects a change upon these legal entities of the Vatican and the State of Israel.

The Agreement goes on to discuss issues of theological import as well as more mundane affairs. Article 2 commits both parties to combat "all forms of anti-Semitism and all kinds of racism and of religious intolerance" as well as positively promoting understanding, tolerance, and "respect for human life and dignity" (par. 1). The next paragraph is a reiteration of the Holy See's condemnation of all manifestations of anti-Semitism "directed against the Jewish people and individual Jews anywhere, at any time and by anyone" and it "deplores attacks on Jews and desecration of Jewish synagogues and cemeteries, acts which offend the memory of the victims of the Holocaust…" (par. 2). The extraordinary nature of the Agreement is absolutely clear: Recognition of Israel marks another step in the reconciliation between Catholics everywhere and the whole Jewish people, who, by implication, finds identification with the State of Israel. If there were no identification of the whole Jewish people with the State of Israel, there would be no need for the Vatican to have made such sweeping statements thus far in the Agreement. It is clear that the church has taken seriously what it said in the *Guidelines* of 1975 and the *Notes* of 1985 that Christians should learn "by what essential traits the Jews define themselves in the light of their own religious tradition" and what the American Catholic bishops said in their 1975 statement on the bond that the Jewish people feel with the land of Israel.[32]

Most of the Agreement now touches upon the "mundane" issues one would expect in a concordat between a nation state and the Holy See. Article 3 acknowledges the right of the Catholic Church to operate various types of religious institutions and the commitment to negotiate giving canon law the "full effect in Israeli law." Article 4 insures the continuance of the "status quo" of the Christian holy places,[33] continuing respect for Catholic places/institutions and freedom of worship. Article 5 acknowledges a *mutual* interest in promoting pilgrimages and *both* express the hope that these pilgrimages "will provide an occasion for better understanding between the pilgrims and the people and religions in Israel." A pilgrimage is not seen as simply a personal private activity, but one that has communal and

interfaith relations dimensions! The church has the right to establish
and maintain schools (Article 6) and maintain communications media
(Article 8). Both "recognize a common interest in promoting and
encouraging cultural exchanges" worldwide between Catholic institutions and Israeli institutions (Article 7) as well as the right of the
church to carry out "charitable functions through its health care and
social welfare institutions" (Article 9). Property rights and all that
entails are the topic of a rather extended Article 10. Article 11 commits both to commit to promote "peaceful resolution of conflicts
among States and nations" (par. 1), and then paragraph 2 apparently
removes the church from being a "player" in the final status talks on
the borders with the nascent Palestinian State and the settlement of the
claims and issues surrounding Jerusalem:

> The Holy see, while maintaining in every case the right to
> exercise its moral and spiritual teaching-office, deems it
> opportune to recall that, owing to its own character, it is
> solemnly committed to remaining a stranger to *all merely
> temporal conflicts, which principle applies specifically to
> disputed territories and unsettled borders* [emphasis
> added].[34]

In spite of the apparent removal of the church from these issues,
it could claim, and probably will, that issues surrounding Jerusalem
are not "merely temporal conflicts" since they involve holy places,
and so on. In the event of a dispute involving this overall Agreement,
Article 12 commits the parties to continued negotiating, and while
there are two copies, in the English and Hebrew languages, with "both
texts being equally authentic," in the case of divergency, "the English
text shall prevail" (Article 15).

On September 29, 1994, the first ambassador of the State of
Israel to the Holy See, Mr. Shmuel Hadas,[35] presented his credentials
personally to the Holy Father. In his address he spoke of a "Jewish-
Catholic rapprochement" and the fact that this agreement "was more
than a diplomatic initiative; it was a step of historical significance. A
unique act, for its protagonists are unique."[36] He continues by stating:

> The establishment of diplomatic relations between the
> Holy See and the State of Israel is not the point of arrival,

but on the contrary, a starting point, a new and constructive dimension in which to bring together in dialogue the Catholic Church and the Jewish People.[37]

He continues by speaking of the contributions of the pope in his "declarations and gestures of fellowship" toward the Jewish people and extends an invitation "on behalf of all Israelis, Jews, Christians and Muslims" to "make a pilgrimage to the Holy Land."

On his part, John Paul II acknowledges the special nature of the relationship between the State of Israel and the Holy See and the historic significance of this ceremony and says that "all this will help intensify the dialogue between the Catholic Church and the Jewish people of Israel and of the *whole world*" [emphasis added].[38]

In the "Report of the Commission for Religious Relations with the Jews," headed at that time by Cardinal Edward I. Cassidy, it noted that "the Fundamental Agreement includes areas in which both parties commit themselves to mutual cooperation, areas which go beyond the questions regarding Church-State relations."[39] In addition, Rabbi Ronald Kronish, the director of the Interreligious Co-ordinating Council in Israel (ICCI),[40] says that this Agreement "has changed the relationship between the Church and the Jewish people in a major way. This was not just a diplomatic agreement. It was a recognition of the centrality of the State of Israel to the Jewish People everywhere in the world."[41]

On February 10–11, 1997, the ICCI along with four other bodies sponsored a symposium on "The Future of Jewish-Catholic Relations in the World and in Israel/The Holy Land."[42] This "conference was designed to help cement the positive effects of the new diplomatic relations between the Holy See and the State of Israel…and to keep the issue of Catholic-Jewish relations in the public during the ensuing period of transition."[43]

In discussing the impact of the Fundamental Agreement, Cardinal Cassidy, president of the Vatican Commission for Religious Relations with the Jews, said we have entered a new stage in Catholic-Jewish relations and that three issues must now occupy our attention. First, since there is much of the work of the last thirty years that remains generally unknown, communication of this work and of the church's teaching since Vatican II is a priority; second, there is a need for a healing of memories; and third, he stressed the importance of formation (in seminaries and rabbinical schools), information, and education. He concluded by saying that the church will not, indeed cannot, go back on the changes since Vatican II, but we must enflesh them in our local communities.[44]

In speaking of visions for the future, both Rabbi Mark Winer, the newly elected president of the National Council of Synagogues (USA)[45] and Bishop Alexander Brunett, the chairman of the National Conference of Catholic Bishops Committee on Ecumenical and Interreligious Affairs, emphasized the uniqueness of the Fundamental Agreement and the fact that its significance extended beyond a "mere" recognition of two states to profound religious significance between the State of Israel/Jewish people and the Vatican/worldwide Catholic community.

In discussion with Archbishop Andrea di Montezemolo, the papal nuncio (ambassador) to Israel and member of the negotiating team of the Fundamental Agreement, he emphasized that there were three points to keep in mind: (1) that peace between Israel and her neighboring states is a goal of the Agreement, (2) that it fosters and confirms reconciliation between Jews and Christians, and (3) that there is diplomatic recognition between two *entities*, not states in the "usual" sense — both are very different, Vatican City State and the State of Israel, and there is not a parity between them. He also emphasized that the consequent global and religious interpretation of the significance of this Agreement was not in the mind of the framers of this document, but is a development since the signing of the Agreement. He also indicated that he approves of this consequent interpretation and development.[46]

There has been a clear movement, it seems to me, at the official and quasi-official levels of the church to begin to see a religious/ theological significance in the State of Israel beyond what one would expect in the Vatican's relationship with "ordinary" nation states. How this might eventually evolve remains yet to be seen; it remains part of the future agenda of Catholic-Jewish relations of which this book is attempting to make a contribution.

CHRISTIAN THEOLOGICAL APPROACHES
TO THE STATE OF ISRAEL

General Overview

Can we make some generalizations about basic Christian theological attitudes toward the State of Israel?

The Reverend Petra Heldt, the executive secretary of the Ecumenical Theological Research Fraternity in Israel,[47] has been studying basic Christian attitudes toward the State of Israel for many years. She divides them into four major groups:[48]

1. *Israel of No Importance.* This position is held by mainly the non-Chalcedonian Churches of the East—the Syrian Orthodox Church, the Coptic and Ethiopian Churches and the Armenian Church.[49] Although they have independent histories and residence in the Holy Land from the earliest centuries, they share certain common characteristics. For them, "life is devoted to holiness, devotion and tranquility."[50] Over the centuries they have been indifferent to who rules the Holy Land, be it Muslim invaders, Crusaders, Turks, or British. Though they are theologically indifferent, they all want to survive as communities so they try to have good relations with the State of Israel.

2. *Israel of Paramount Importance.* Some 90 million evangelical, charismatic, and fundamentalist Christians all over the world hold this view according to Petra Heldt. The International Christian Embassy Jerusalem claims to represent this constituency.[51] For these Christians, the Jews of Israel are an instrument of God's will and the reestablishment of the State of Israel is the realization of biblical prophecy. They are very vocal and active in their support of Israel, which usually includes an uncritical affirmation of whatever the state does.

3. *The Middle Ground of Developing Appreciation.* This includes a large group of churches with perhaps the most progressive being the Roman Catholic Church, especially in the last twenty years and in light of the establishment of diplomatic relations with Israel in late 1993. Among Protestant churches, the Netherlands Reformed Church has made the greatest strides, including having a minister officially representing the church in Israel to pursue Jewish-Christian dialogue in Israel.[52] Many

mainline American Protestant churches would be "more or less" in this grouping. The common denominator in this group would be the ascription of a positive theological significance to the return of the Jewish people to the land of Israel. How this is spelled out in detail would diverge widely.

4. *Resistance to Positive Evolution.* According to Reverend Petra Heldt, the World Council of Churches, with more than three hundred member churches in more than one hundred countries (of which the Roman Catholic Church has only observer status), and the Middle East Council of Churches (MECC), including all the Christian churches in the Middle East (Catholics as well since 1989), have resisted and challenged the positive developments indicated above. Yet even here, there are exceptions:

a. The policy statement of the MECC says that "the MECC has sought to *build bridges of mutual understanding and respect* [emphasized in original] between Christians and people of other faiths, particularly Muslims and Jews."[53] One of their program units under the General Secretariat is the "Interreligious Dialogue for Justice and Peace" described as having the aim "to facilitate understanding between people especially of the three Abrahamic faiths."[54]

b. The Latin Patriarch, led by His Beatitude Michel Sabbah, the first Arab Catholic patriarch, has done much to improve relations with the State of Israel and the Jewish people.

A Catholic Theology of the State of Israel

This brings us to the final question: Is it possible to construct a *Catholic* theology of the State of Israel that is consistent with the teaching and direction of our relationship with the Jewish people that the church has been moving in since Vatican II? I believe that it is. We have seen above the different Christian approaches to the state as sketched out by Petra Heldt and the different attempts of Christians to articulate a positive Catholic theology of the State of Israel. None of these has received wide acceptance in the church, although some are clearly more well received than others. In general, there has been some reluctance to do so, as noted by Rev. John Pawlikowski, who said in *PACE* that a clear consensus has not yet emerged:

David Tracy has argued that events such as the Holocaust and the State of Israel force us to return to a theological outlook in which concrete historical events are decisive. Msgr. John Oesterreicher, Charlotte Klein, Bruce William OP, and Kurt Hruby have argued that in one way or another the re-birth of Israel must be understood as a sign of God's continuing concern for the Jewish people as well as a divine plan for Israel. Klein and Williams have been the strongest voices within theological circles for a specifically *redemptive dimension* [emphasis in original] to the State of Israel from the Catholic perspective.... Dr. Eugene Fisher who directs the U.S. Bishops' Office for Catholic-Jewish Relations has not gone quite as far as the others, but does regard Israel (especially when seen in connection with the Holocaust) as a sign of hope not only for Christians and Jews, but also for all of humanity, victims of oppression in particular. However, clearly the reflections of the theologians are still at an embryonic stage.[55]

Pawlikowski goes on to list his three principal beliefs, which he indicates he has not yet adequately interrelated:

First, I would certainly wish to maintain some significant differences between Christianity and Judaism regarding the present meaning of the land tradition. It is my firm belief that one result of the Christian theology of the Incarnation is an equalization of all land in terms of sacredness. Jerusalem is from the standpoint of theological principle no holier than Geneva, Rome, the favellas of Rio, or the inner city of Chicago.[56]

Second, I clearly acknowledge the centrality of the land to the overall sense of a divine covenant among the Jewish people; and third, since I acknowledge from a theological perspective an inherent bonding between the Church and the Jewish people, I recognize that the Jewish sense of land as part of the covenant makes some claims on my faith as well.[57]

Not everyone would be willing to go as far as the late Father Edward Flannery, who said that "any Christian who assisted the

Jewish return to Israel or who supports and aids Israel today can be considered a Christian Zionist."[58] Flannery often urged that a "theological significance on the latest return of Jews to Israel"[59] be given, and that "Israel today constitutes an important sign of the times for the Christian as well as for the Jewish theologian."[60] However, he never sketched out an actual theology of the state.

One of the tensions felt in Catholicism, and in Christianity in general, has been the dialectic between realized and unrealized eschatology. The apostle Paul was driven by the conviction, born of his experience, that the resurrection of Jesus ushered in the "new creation" (2 Cor 5:17 and Gal 6:14–15), that the power of sin and death was conquered (Rom 6:1–14), and most importantly, Jesus would soon return as risen Lord to bring all things to their final completion (1 Thess 4:13–18 and Rom 13:11–12). There is an apocalyptic urgency to the mission of the church since Jesus may come at any moment. Our task is to be always ready[61] as Paul never seems to tire of saying.

When the end-time completion was delayed, although Paul expected it during his lifetime (1 Thess 4:13—5:3),[62] the Christian community tried to come to terms with this delay, particularly in Luke-Acts where Christ's return is put off for a long time.[63] The community was also sensitive to Jewish charges of unrealized eschatology and the lack of messianic fulfillment in the daily experience of sin, death, suffering, evil, war, injustice—experiences that the prophets said would come to an end in the messianic age.[64] Thus, part of the battle between Jews and Christians becomes an interpretive disagreement concerning eschatological/end-time theology. The Christians stressed the positive experiences in peoples' lives that the risen Lord had made—thus a beginning of this new age. Yet there was still a consciousness that a complete fulfillment was in the future. On the other hand, Jews tended to stress the uncompleted nature of the Christian claim of the messianic age—how can one claim it has begun, is indeed really instituted, when the world still seems to be such an imperfect place? Both groups have, to some extent, "painted themselves into a corner" and need to find a way out. Perhaps we are victims of our own undoing because of the way we framed our messianic understanding.

TRADITIONAL JEWISH MESSIANIC UNDERSTANDING

Throughout much of Jewish history, there have been two under-standings of the messianic age: a prophetic eschatology and an apocalyptic eschatology.

Those in a prophetic mode say that our task here is to build a world of justice and peace. God has told us how we should live in community, how we should treat others, and how we are given the task of being a "light to the Gentiles" (Isa 42:6; 60:1–3; 49:6). Therefore, when *the world is a fit place for the Messiah, God will send the Messiah*. Clearly, our task is proactive; we must work in the human community to change the world around us. When our task has been completed, God will send the Messiah to us.[65]

Those in an apocalyptic mode say that we are living in an out-of-control world, that everything is just getting worse and worse. And what we have to do is "draw our wagons in a circle" and protect ourselves from the outside. A fortress mentality says we need to preserve the purity and integrity of our own community and await God's coming. In other words, *when the world is such a hopelessly wicked and evil place, God will intervene and send the Messiah, who will set things straight*.[66]

Both communities have fought over the application of the prophetic and the apocalyptic interpretation. Both communities need a way out of this impasse that over the centuries has produced enmity and persecutions. Perhaps we both need to make much more modest claims for our religious insights. In chapter 2, I argued for a new understanding of our covenant relationship between Christians and Jews in one covenant. That is, that we are one covenant people in the covenant of Sinai with two different modalities. For Jews, they are commanded to walk in the way of the Torah as interpreted by the Pharisees since the destruction of the Temple in 70 CE. For Christians, we are commanded to walk in the way of the Torah as interpreted for us by Jesus-the-Jew and articulated to us Gentiles through the revelation received by the apostle Paul. The normative writings for the Jewish community are the *Mishnah* and *Gamara* (= the Talmud) and its long tradition of interpretation; the normative writings for the Christian community are the Christian scriptures (the New Testament) and its long history of interpretation with implications of how we should live the Christian life. Each of these writings is an interpretation of the earlier received texts that Jews call TANAKH,[67] with an emphasis on the Torah, and the Christians call the "Old Testament."

Might we not also understand the State of Israel in this same context of two different *modes* of understanding the one and same covenant? To begin this journey of understanding, we Catholics are instructed to listen to how Jews articulate their experience and understand themselves.[68] Yet, there is no universally accepted Jewish understanding of Zionism and the State of Israel—there are many understandings; although all Jews, save for a very small number, find a significant and essential meaning in the existence of the State of Israel, as the American bishops noted in 1975:

> [A]n overwhelming majority of Jews see themselves
> bound in one way or another to the land of Israel. Most
> Jews see this tie to the land as essential to their Jewishness.
> Whatever difficulties Christians may experience in sharing
> this view they should strive to understand this link
> between land and people that Jews have expressed in their
> writing and worship throughout two millennia....[69]

Although there are many current interpretations, the one that most harmonizes with a new understanding of covenant relationship in this book is that of Rabbi David Hartman.[70] In his books, *The Living Covenant* (1985) and *Conflicting Visions* (1990), he sets forth his thesis about covenant and the State of Israel.[71]

According to Hartman, there are three stages of covenantal fidelity and life for the Jewish people. The first occurs at Sinai and encompasses the biblical period. God's divine love makes room for the other: human beings in a created universe. God's identity is defined in a relational matrix: God longs to be loved and mediated within the context of human freedom. God says, "I have set before you life and death, the blessing and the curse. Choose life..." (Deut 30:19).

The second phase of this covenantal life is the rabbinic tradition, that period beginning after the destruction of the Temple in 70 CE, which inaugurates a new period of Jewish existence. Now human beings have to be responsible for discerning and interpreting God's word. As Rabbi Hartman says, "[I]n the Bible you hear God's voice and in the Talmud you hear Rabbi so and so says…this means that the biblical God is prepared to live with risks."[72] The Torah, which descends from heaven, is now on earth and subject to "earthly" interpretation.[73]

The third phase of the covenant is Zionism. Hartman acknowledges that "Zionism began over a century ago as a revolt against the conception of the Jewish people as a community of prayer and learning that had resolved to restrict the covenant of political action in history until the days of the Messiah."[74]

Although the initial "reaction of the traditional religious circles to early Zionism was intensely hostile,"[75] most all traditional religious groups have come to either actively support the state, as does the National Religious Party, or tacitly work with the state and benefit from its financial support as do all the Haredi institutions.[76] Hartman summarizes his position, which is shaped by his experience in the State of Israel:

> Secular Zionism created the conditions under which individuals committed to a covenantal perception of Judaism are capable of restoring to Jewish life a national existence not grounded in the need for supernatural grace. The Zionist revolution thus opened up new domains of life to the rabbinic spirit of human initiative by liberating the community from the dominant mood of helpless dependency upon the Lord of history. The drama of the State of Israel is not a messianic unfolding of the final stages in Jewish religious eschatology, but a process that began at Sinai in which Israel was prepared to build its religious life on God's self-limiting love in human history. The lack of God's visible, triumphant victory in history was met in the rabbinic tradition with a new enlivened sense of covenantal intellectual responsibility.… One can summarize the different stages of the covenant under the following three headings. The [1] Bible liberated the will of the community to act with responsibility. The [2] Talmud liberated the intellect to define the contents of Torah. [3] Zionism liberated the will of the nation to become politically responsible and to promote the Ingathering of the Exiles without

the need for miraculous grace as the condition for reestablishing Israel as a covenantal nation in history.[77]

Hartman understands the covenant of Sinai to have accepted
Israel with all its human limitations and foibles:

> Weak and fragile human beings are given the command-
> ments. So when I put on my *tefillin*[78] in the morning, it is
> not human grandeur which is confirmed, but human vul-
> nerability, my weakness in which I can nonetheless love
> God and sense God's acceptance. I am a "commanded
> one" within the context of human limitations. *The covenant,
> therefore, signifies for me the re-establishment of the dig-
> nity of the concrete. It is the celebration of human finitude*
> [emphasis added]. It is the ability to love in spite of human
> limitations, to build meaning in the face of death, to affirm
> today without the certainty of tomorrow.[79]

This is an understanding of covenant and the State of Israel that
is a "secular" model that expands the Jewish existence in a human
context while never ceasing to acknowledge the transcendent. In this
state, you articulate an historical course of action. "Therefore the
Jews have returned to be present to Christians and Muslims in this
land. Our role is not to be forerunners to some eschatological finale
but to be alive in our own tradition. If this has implications for
Christianity and Islam that is fine," says Hartman. "I'm trying to re-
shift our theologies of history away from redemptive messianic dra-
mas into another mode, *a different spiritual metaphor* [emphasis
added], coming out of the biblical tradition." [80]

By these comments, Hartman does not mean that God's grace and
guidance are not involved in this action of the Jewish people that
involves a reconstituting a Jewish State of Israel. He is rather alluding
to the long tradition in Judaism (and in Christianity) of the distinction
between prophetic eschatology and apocalyptic eschatology and the
expectation of the events when the Messiah comes. The prophetic end-
time tradition (*eschaton*) teaches that when you build a world of justice
and peace, God will send the Messiah. Thus, our task is to be agents of
change in the world to prepare the world to be a fit place for the
Messiah. On the other hand, apocalyptic end-time tradition teaches that

only when the world is such an evil and wicked place that only God can change this situation will God send the Messiah. In this apocalyptic end-time view, our task is an internal one to build up our own community and not worry about the outside world, which is hopelessly wicked and irreformable. How do these views relate to reestablishing a State of Israel? The more consistent and traditional Jewish (and Christian) expectation is that only when the apocalyptic end-time comes and God sends the Messiah will the State of Israel be reestablished. This will include the ingathering of all the Jewish exiles from the four corners of the earth and the rebuilding of the Temple. Orthodox Jews, in the past centuries and in the early years of the Zionist movement, considered it a sin and a going against God to return to the land of Israel and reestablish a state there. That was to be the task of the Messiah at the end-time. Hartman says that Zionism said that we are not going to wait for this eschatological end-time but build the kingdom now with the reestablishment of a state. Many Jews said that we are not going to wait for a miraculous intervention of God to bring this about, but take our destiny into our own hands. This movement began in the late nineteenth century with the Austrian writer and journalist, founder of political Zionism, Theodor Herzl (1869–1904).

Having said this, Hartman, nevertheless believes that although Zionism began as a secular movement we can now say that the State of Israel is the manifestation of the living covenant tradition of the Jewish people and has a religious and spiritual dimension to it as well as the human dimension of a nation among other nations.[81] Hartman believes that God is active in this process, but not as a miracle-working deity.

What does this new interpretation mean for Christians? In light of Rabbi Hartman's understanding of the state and my thesis of covenantal modality, it means that for us Christians *the State of Israel and Zionism is a new modality of covenantal fidelity of the Jewish people in the twenty-first century.* Since we and the Jews are brothers and sisters in the one covenant, we ought to acknowledge the validity and reality of the profoundly religious meaning of the State of Israel as an institution of covenantal life. Just as for us Catholics, there is a profoundly religious meaning and identity to our membership in the Roman Catholic Church as a living institution forged by a long history, influenced by culture and secular political institutions over the many long centuries of its existence. It is an institution that has been sinful, imperfect, and in need of reform, yet it is a vehicle of God's love and relationship with the community of believers. Can we Catholics say less about the State of Israel? And are there Jews who may acknowledge the importance of the state in the world of Judaism yet do not want to make *aliya*, to immigrate, to take up permanent residence and citizenship in this state? Of course! Are there Jews living as citizens of the State of Israel who want changes, even radical changes in the state? Of course! Do even Jews who reject the State of Israel acknowledge that it has an important impact upon world Jewish life? Of course! Now to each of the above statements change *Israel* to *the Roman Catholic Church*. Are there those who acknowledge the importance in Christianity of the Roman Catholic Church, but who do not want to belong, who can live the Christian life without being Roman Catholics? Of course! Are there faithful Roman Catholics who want change in their church, who fight for change because they are members of the community, because it is their church? Of course! Are there Christians who reject the Catholic Church totally, but who acknowledge its great influence in the history of Christianity in the past and in the present? Of course!

As the Catholic Church is related to worldwide Christianity, so, in many ways, is the State of Israel related to worldwide Jewry. This new view of comparative understanding is made possible by the dramatic change in our understanding of the Roman Catholic Church flowing from the Second Vatican Council, in particular *Lumen Gentium*, the Dogmatic Constitution on the Church.

The bishops of the Vatican Council speak in this document of Christ, who "established and ever sustains here on earth His holy Church, the community of faith, hope and charity."[82] The document on the Church continues: "This is the sole Church of Christ which in the Creed we profess to be one, holy, catholic and apostolic...*[t]his Church, constituted and organized as a society in the present world, subsists in the Catholic Church, which is governed by the successor of Peter and by the bishops in communion with him* [emphasis added]."[83] In the thought of Vatican II, we now describe the church as the pilgrim people of God in movement through history, sharing in Christ's three-fold mission as Prophet, Priest, and King. The Body of Christ "subsists in" the Catholic Church, which is to say that it is present in its fullness there, but not exclusively. The verb *subsists in* was explicitly chosen to replace the copulative verb *is* in a previous draft.[84]

In responding to some critics who denied that this was the meaning of *subsists in*, Cardinal Johannes Willebrands, president of the
Vatican Secretariat for Promoting Christian Unity, said "that the
church [emphasis added] of Christ is not limited to the visible structure of the Catholic Church."[85] He goes on to articulate that "*subsistit
in*…is meant to indicate that the church, which in the Creed we profess to be one, holy, catholic and apostolic, is found in this world—
constituted and organized as a society [emphasis added]—in the
Catholic Church, though indeed it [that is, the church of God] goes
beyond the visible limits of the latter."[86]

This new understanding of the Roman Catholic Church suggests
that we can make some profound new parallels with the State of Israel
that will reimage the identity and the relationship of the State of Israel
with us as Roman Catholics.

To reiterate: In light of Vatican II, as the Catholic Church is
related to worldwide Christianity, so, in many ways, is the State of
Israel related to worldwide Jewry. The Jewish State is a structure that
provides a new rich possibility for a Jewish way of life for the Jewish
people; the Roman Catholic Church also provides a rich and full possibility for a Christian way of life for Christians. Neither one is the
only way; but both are "institutional structures" within which a
fidelity to God can be lived out in concrete ways.

There is a somewhat ironic reversal of movement in the change
in self-identity as institutions between the two religious communities.
Roman Catholics are coming to see that their "God-instituted church"
is a very human church—yet God's action in and through this institution is not negated. Jews, on the other hand, are making the move
from what began as an almost solely "secular" movement, Zionism,
to a more spiritual interpretation such as Rabbi Hartman's. Yet
Hartman's covenantal interpretation does not negate the human, secular, and political in the State of Israel. The issue for both the Roman
Catholic Church and the State of Israel is the balance between the
divine and the human in the lives of Christians and Jews.

This new image of the State of Israel makes it an institutional
analogue to the Roman Catholic Church, *mutatis mutandis* (that is,
with respective differences having been considered) as the Catholic
Church is related to all of Christendom, so the State of Israel is related
to all of the Jewish people. This does not make the State of Israel or
the Jewish people a church. The U.S. bishops' 1975 "Statement on

Catholic-Jewish Relations" taught that it must be acknowledged that the Jewish people "do not consider themselves as a church, a sect, or a denomination, as is the case among Christian communities, but rather as a peoplehood that is not solely racial, ethnic or religious, but *in a sense a composite of all these* [emphasis added]."[87] Nevertheless, the relationship of *all* the Christian people to the Roman Catholic Church as an instrument and manifestation of covenant fidelity to God and the relationship of *all* the Jewish people to the State of Israel as an instrument and manifestation of covenant fidelity to God has a surprising and life-giving parity!

In sum, the proposal that the State of Israel and the Roman Catholic Church are both covenantal institutional structures within which a fidelity to God can be lived out in concrete ways has some consequences.

How might these images be incorporated into our spirituality? First of all, it means that our spirituality, our way of being a Catholic Christian, is intimately bound up with the Jewish people and covenantal theology as manifested in the State of Israel. This means that they should be in our frequent prayers and thoughts extending into our liturgical actions, such as the prayers of the faithful, which should regularly include prayers for the well-being of the Jewish people, for Jews in the State of Israel, and for peace in the Middle East. It ought also to include our personal and parish interaction with the Jewish community and in particular with area synagogues. The celebration of important shared holidays ought to be joint celebrations, and in particular we ought to collaborate on Yom HaShoah (Holocaust Remembrance) services. Our pilgrimages to the "Holy Land" must include more than Christian holy sites; they must include Jewish holy places and interaction with the rich Jewish communities in the State of Israel.

If we take seriously the mandates of the Second Vatican Council and the subsequent development of our relationship with the Jewish people and the State of Israel, including a new mutual understanding articulated above, we must begin to live differently as Catholics by re-imaging our prayer life, our relationships with the Jewish community, and our views of the State of Israel. As we begin this new millennium, let us also look forward to a new era in Catholic-Jewish relations so that the errors and sins of the previous millennium will not be repeated but will bring the dawn of new life for us all—Catholics and Jews together.

6
Issues, Reflections, and Conclusions

The points that I have demonstrated in the preceding chapters may be summarized in six propositions:

1. Since the Second Vatican Council there has developed a whole new understanding of the relationship of the Catholic Church to the Jewish people.

2. This understanding acknowledges the ongoing validity of the covenant of Sinai between God and the Jewish people, and the legitimacy of the rabbinic tradition that has developed since the destruction of the Temple in the year 70 CE.

3. Christianity is related to the Jewish people in covenant with God at a deep and abiding level.

4. A corrected and reinvigorated understanding of the theology of Paul, the Jewish Apostle to the Gentiles, opens the possibility of understanding ourselves as members of that same covenant with the Jewish people. With the insight from John 1:14 that Jesus is the incarnation of the *Hesed* (covenant love) and *Emeth* (covenant fidelity) of Yahweh we can understand our traditions in a new light, that while Jews walk in the way (the *Halakhah*) of the Torah, and its developed and developing rabbinic tradition, we Christians walk in the way (the *Halakhah*) of Jesus-the-Jew, and our bond with him binds us to the Jewish people. Thus, Christians and Jews are brothers and sisters in the same Sinai covenant, but one covenant with two modalities.

5. As an outgrowth of this new understanding of Jewish and Catholic covenantal theology, we can reimage our relationship to the Holy Land in terms of a post-Vatican II expansion of our understanding of Catholic sacramental theology, that as Christ

is the sacrament of encounter with God, the Holy Land is a sacrament of our encounter with Christ.

6. The modern State of Israel can be viewed as the twenty-first-century Jewish embodiment of the living covenant as the church is the Christian covenantal embodiment of our faith life, our walking in the way of Jesus. As the Catholic Church is both a human and divine society, the State of Israel is both a human and divine society by virtue of the living covenant tradition of the Jewish people. **Both are institutions that are instruments and manifestations of God's covenant with his people**.

CONSEQUENCES

What are some of the consequences of, and challenges to, these reimages, of one covenant with two modalities, of the Holy Land as a sacrament of our encounter with Christ, and of the Roman Catholic Church and the modern State of Israel as instruments and manifestations of God's covenant with us?

One Covenant—Two Modalities

Jews have had great difficulty moving beyond the traditional view that Christians are simply a manifestation of the fidelity of Gentiles to the covenant of Noah. What are the terms of this Noahide covenant? Since the Middle Ages, general Jewish interpretation has followed Maimonides, who says that everyone who accepts the seven Noahide commandments and observes them carefully is one of the righteous of the nations of the world and has a share in the world to come. While Maimonides has given the classic codification and interpretation to the seven minimal moral duties enjoined by the Bible on all,[1] we know that they, in general, can be dated to at least the period of the Hasmoneans (152–37 BCE).[2] How were these "righteous" of the nations to be defined? We know that in the first century of the common era (contemporary with Jesus and Paul), in addition to the proselytes there were many in the ancient world who were attracted to Judaism as a kind of religious philosophy and attached themselves to synagogues, keeping many of the customs (commandments) without in any sense being Jews: the so-called "God-fearers."[3] It is these

"God-fearers" that are the precursors for the later description of "righteous Gentiles."

While this view describing Christians as "righteous Gentiles" may be comforting and nonthreatening to Jews—especially given the long history of anti-Semitism and the persecution of the Jewish people—it is not ultimately acceptable to Catholic Christians. Since the Second Vatican Council and the tremendous changes in Christian theology and practice regarding Jews, Christians have found it demeaning and trivializing to be placed in the same religious category as all non-Jewish and non-Christian religions, since the claims of Christianity are based upon the acceptance of the validity and truth of Hebrew scripture itself. Indeed, in the past, Christianity has traditionally understood itself as the fulfillment of, or completion of, the biblical revelation to the Jewish people. This makes it a religion unlike all other non-Jewish religions. In light of the declarations of Vatican II, Catholic Christians have seen themselves as intimately connected to the Jewish people, so to say that we are merely those Gentiles who are faithful to the so-called Noahide covenant and thus are "righteous Gentiles" is woefully inadequate. On their side, Jews have not been able to find a way to affirm Christianity without delegitimizing their own religious tradition.[4] Thus it has been an either/or theological affirmation on each side of the religious divide.

The German Jewish philosopher Franz Rosenzweig (1886–1929) tried to ameliorate this description of Christians in his book, *The Star of Redemption*.[5] It has been erroneously attributed to him that he proposed a two-covenant theory of Judaism and Christianity, wherein Judaism was God's covenant for the Jews, and Christianity was the covenant for all others.[6] Yet Rosenzweig's conception is nuanced and complex. The image of the star for Rosenzweig best described the relationship between Judaism and Christianity. The inner fire and heat of the star is Judaism, which "for now looks within, to the maintenance of its own life,"[7] while the bright rays of light from the star are Christianity, which "goes out, converting the nations, conquering paganism and preparing (unwittingly) for the messianic age."[8] This view is neither a two-covenant theology nor a one-covenant theology since Rosenzweig does not use this terminology, but a single, metaphoric image that tries to connect the two traditions intimately, but gives each different missions. In my view, this ultimately makes of Christianity a "Judaism for Gentiles," since the fire and heat of the star radiate either inward (Judaism) or outward (Christianity); this image accounts neither for the differences in the traditions nor acknowledges the inherent and distinct identity of each. Nevertheless, it is an improvement on the Jewish view of Christians as the righteous Gentiles of the Noahide covenant.

However, the Jewish scholar Michael Kogan recognized the fallaciousness of identifying Christians as "Noahides":

> To appeal to the Noahide Laws in dealing with Christianity today is evidence that the Jews who do so continue to ignore Christianity as a distinct movement. No Christian can recognize herself or himself in this limited list of minimal requirements for civilized life.... Christians must be addressed as Christians, not simply as gentiles.[9]

Kogan is the first Jewish scholar to call for a one-covenant identification of Jews and Christians:

> It seems to me that the multiple-covenant model is not suited to explicating the special relationship existing between Judaism and Christianity. A single-covenant model is to be preferred, because it reflects more faithfully the events through which the covenant between God and Israel was broken open by Christianity to include the nations of the world.[10]

Thus, the covenant has been opened to the nations so that "Christianity is not a worldly threat to Judaism but a Jewish outreach into the world.... Through our 'great brother,' they [the pagans] have come to know Israel's God.... Christianity came not for us but for the nations. Our covenant with God is eternal and self-sustaining."[11] Although Kogan can be interpreted as saying that Christianity is a developmental function of Judaism ("a Jewish outreach into the world"), he concludes his article by positing that "there are not two truths here, but one: *the God of Israel's redemptive plan differently mediated for different peoples* [emphasis added]."[12] His view is compatible with my description of one covenant with two modalities, although he doesn't explain how this could be possible from a Jewish point of view except to say that "[i]n Christianity we see a partial fulfillment of this summons"[13] that was given to Abraham to be a blessing to all the nations in Genesis 12:1–4a.

The most significant steps forward to recognition of, and acknowledgment of, shared theology and vision are found in the Jewish document *Dabru Emet*, published in September 2000 and signed by 169 Jewish professors, rabbis, and community leaders mostly from the United States, but including some from Canada, England, and Israel.[14] *Dabru Emet* does not deal explicitly with the controversial question of Judaism and Christianity as being in a two-covenant or one-covenant relationship, although it does speak of covenant in relation to the promise of the land to the Jews. Regarding the "new relationship between Jews and Christians" they say that "[w]e respect Christianity as a faith that originated within Judaism and that still has significant contacts with it. *We do not see it as an extension of Judaism* [emphasis added]." This, too, like Kogan's, is an attempt to interrelate the two faiths, while retaining their distinctiveness. It fails in not making an attempt to spell out how this can be possible.

It is not only Jews who may object to a new imaging, but some Christians also may consider this proposal as simply a "Judaism for Gentiles." Nothing could be further from the truth: The issue is covenant peoplehood, that is, how does one become a member of the covenant community? As has been indicated, the way in which one becomes a member is different for each of the two peoples, and for each the modality of existence in this covenant is also different—yet they are related and partly shared.

We have come to call the faith tradition that developed among the Jewish people after the destruction of the Temple "rabbinic Judaism" (or Pharisaic Judaism). It became the *Halakhah*, the "way," the praxis of living as a member of the covenant community of Israel according to a lifestyle proposed by the Pharisees.[15] Both Judaism and Christianity are in fact children of this Second Temple Jewish life, which revolved around the sacrificial system in the Jerusalem Temple. The subsequent relationship between Judaism and Christianity is not a mother/daughter or father/son relationship, but rather a sibling relationship that has been one of rivalry since the second century CE. It is neither accurate nor fair to call this proposal "Judaism for Gentiles," Christianity being no more a "type" of rabbinic Judaism than is rabbinic Judaism a "type" of "inferior" Christianity.

To clarify further our origins in Second Temple Jewish life, Christians need to do a rigorous historical description of the phenomena of the kerygma of the early community of Jesus' followers, and the dramatic change that occurred after 70 CE: I believe that one can mutually affirm each other and yet maintain and affirm the distinctive differences. To recapitulate some of what was said in chapter 2, the historical Jesus came to call his own people to *teshuvah* in preparation for the in-breaking of the kingdom. It was an internal Jewish renewal movement. After his death on the cross in the year 30 CE, his closest followers (among others) experienced him as risen and alive. They began to proclaim to their Jewish kinfolk this "good news." Many Jews became followers of Jesus and proclaimed him as the Messiah. Sometime in 31/32 CE, Saul of Tarsus had a profound religious experience and began proclaiming "good news" to the Gentiles and inviting them to become part of the people Israel through this Jesus. There were then multiple missions and missionaries reaching out to the Gentiles and much turmoil within the movement over this move to incorporate Gentiles into Israel in new ways. The controversy is reflected in Paul's letters. The Temple and cultic worship still formed the central focus for all these Jewish, "Christian"-Jewish, and probably also the Gentile "Christian" groups until the year 70 CE.

After the destruction of Jerusalem and the Temple, a dramatic shift begins to take place. What were once multiple ways of living "Jewishly" (Sadducees, Pharisees, Essenes, and followers of Jesus) now began to coalesce into two major groups: one living a Jewish life following the teaching of the Pharisees (notably in two major camps, that of Hillel and that of Shammai) and those following Jesus. This competition can be discerned throughout Matthew's Gospel. The way of living a Jewish life is beginning to divide according to two major interpretations, and one became "Judaism," the other became "Christianity." Though this occurred over many decades, after 70 CE the two groups became more and more antagonistic and competitive toward each other. Examining the reality of what happened and recognizing that both modes of Jewish life were rooted in Second Temple religious life (not in "Judaism," which was "born" after 70 CE), we can say that each is a mode of covenant fidelity and the interpretation of the one covenant of Sinai.

Taking John 1:14 as a model for a Christology, we can say that Jesus is the enfleshment/incarnation of the covenant of Sinai in that the fullness of God's *Hesed/Charis/Grace* and *Emeth/Aletheia/Truth* is found in Jesus. Thus, the God of Israel has self-revealed the covenant of Sinai in new ways in this Jesus. In fact, this message and movement of Jesus' followers became almost exclusively Gentile within a hundred years of Jesus' death and resurrection.

The covenant of God is, for the Jews, embodied in Torah, the instruction to the community on how to live, how to walk in the way of Adonai. This word is eternal and is ever forming the community of Israel through the traditions and interpretations through the centuries. The covenant word is, for the Gentiles, incarnated in the person of Jesus and is an individual personal Word that unites the Gentiles to the covenant of Sinai through Jesus-the-Jew. Just as Jews are to walk in the way of Torah as their life in the covenant, so also Gentiles are to walk in the way of Jesus-the-Jew as their life in this same covenant.

In accepting this, we both can affirm and acknowledge our separate ways without positing the superiority (or inferiority) of one or the other. This manifestation of God's covenant in each people is God's doing. Our common task is that identified by *Dabru Emet*:

> Jews and Christians, each in their own way, recognize the unredeemed state of the world as reflected in the persistence of persecution, poverty, and human degradation and misery. Although justice and peace are finally God's, our joint efforts, together with those of other faith communities, will help bring the kingdom of God for which we hope and long. Separately and together, we must work to bring justice and peace to our world.[16]

Holy Land as Sacramental Encounter with Christ

If, as I have proposed, *as Christ is the sacrament of our encounter with God, the Holy Land is a sacrament of our encounter with Christ*, what are some examples/manifestations of this type of experience? In a letter anticipating a pilgrimage to the Holy Land, Pope John Paul II said that he has

> a strong desire to go personally to pray in the most important places that, from the Old to the New Testament, have seen God's interventions, which culminate in the mysteries of the incarnation and of the passion, death and resurrec-

tion of Christ. These places [are] already indelibly etched in [my] memory from the time when in 1965 [I] had the opportunity to visit the Holy Land. It was an unforgettable experience.[17]

Clearly the simple memory of past experiences being recalled to mind and bringing a sense of the presence of Christ's actions were not sufficient for the pope. He wanted to rekindle the most intense sense of presence *in* this land that he had once experienced—might we say a sacramental sense of presence? Although noting that "God is equally present in every corner of the world,"[18] the pope goes on to note

that this universal presence of God in the world does not take away from the fact that, just as time can be marked by *kairoi*, by special moments of grace, space too may by analogy bear the stamp of particular saving actions of God...[all religions] not only have sacred times but also *sacred spaces, where the encounter with the divine may be experienced more intensely* [emphasis added] than it would normally be in the vastness of the cosmos.[19]

Thus, in March 2000, John Paul II made an historic pilgrimage to the Holy Land, visiting Egypt, Jordan, the Palestinian Territories, and the State of Israel.[20] In his Angelus Message in Jerusalem on March 26, 2000, John Paul said,

These have been days of intense emotion, a time when our soul has been stirred not only by the memory of what God has done but *by his very presence, walking with us once again in the land of Christ's birth, death, and resurrection* [emphasis added].[21]

The pope has clearly sensed that the Holy Land itself has brought about a special intensity and a particular encounter with Christ. In his earlier visit to Bethlehem, in Manger Square, the pope quoted the Venerable Bede: "Still today, and every day until the end of the ages, the Lord will be continually conceived in Nazareth and born in Bethlehem. Because it is always Christmas in Bethlehem, every day is Christmas in the hearts of Christians...."[22] Jesus Christ is made intensely and especially present in the Holy Land, specifically in Bethlehem, a holy place in a Holy Land.

At each of the places the Holy Father visited: the Upper Room, Nazareth, the Mount of the Beatitudes, the Church of the Holy Sepulcher in Jerusalem, and other places, he speaks of Christ's presence in a special way at eucharistic celebrations and in elocutions to the crowds. It is clear that the pope experienced the same power of Christ's presence, a sacramental presence, in this Holy Land that other Catholic pilgrims have experienced (see above, pp. 54-60).

An apparently dissonant voice against special sacred places is raised by the Russian Orthodox theologian Alexander Schmemann, who says about place and the Land of Israel:

> Christians had no concern for any sacred geography, no temples, no cult that could be recognized as such by the generations fed with the solemnities of the mystery cults. There was no specific religious interest in the places where Jesus had lived. There were no pilgrimages. The old religion [paganism] had its thousand sacred places and temples: for the Christians all this was past and gone. There was no need for temples built of stone: Christ's Body, the Church itself, the new people gathered in Him, was the only real temple. "Destroy this temple, and in three days I will raise it up."… (John 2:19).
>
> The Church itself was the new and heavenly Jerusalem: the Church *in* Jerusalem was by contrast unimportant. The fact that Christ *comes* and is *present* was far more significant than the places where He had been. The historical reality of Christ was of course the undisputed ground of the early Christians' faith.…"[23]

Schmemann is speaking primarily about the contrast between the pagan religions and the early church and the fact that pagans accused Christians of being atheists because of their lack of a sacred geography, that is, sacred places and temples. Yet it is clear that Orthodox praxis places great importance upon celebrating the salvific events of Christ's life during Holy Week in the Church of the Holy Sepulcher in Jerusalem. In another work, Schmemann himself notes that since the fourth century the "cult of holy places" did not so much "arouse historical interest so much as it was in the fact that it expressed the sense and need of the sacred as something materialized, localized and introduced into the very fabric of natural life...."[24] Although it is clear that Orthodox Christians may not give the same theological description to the Holy Land and its sacred sites as we might, their experience there is not too dissimilar from Western Christians.

There are other pilgrims who have had similar experiences in the Holy Land: The Franciscan biblical scholar Father Stephen Doyle has guided more than one hundred pilgrimages to the Holy Land. In a book he has written specifically for pilgrims he says:

> There are major differences between going to the Holy Land as a pilgrim, and going there as a tourist, or even as a student of history of archaeology. One joins a pilgrimage from faith and for faith. This is not the same as a deepening of theological insight, or becoming more knowledgeable about the facts and beliefs of Christianity.[25]

It is clear that Father Doyle is speaking of a religious experience, an encounter with Christ in this land. For each site in his book, he gives the appropriate biblical verses (in his own translation), meditations, prayers, and hymn suggestions—forty-two hymn texts are included in an appendix. He comments that "for Christian pilgrims, Jesus is their companion to the places made holy by his life, and he is also the goal of the pilgrimage."[26] In a pilgrim's prayer at the beginning of the book, he urges us to pray:

> Lord Jesus, your feet made this land holy.
> You came as a pilgrim to this City of Peace.
> As we follow your steps
> Open our eyes that we may see.
> May we see you not only in the stones,
> but in your people and each other....[27]

The Jewish author Bruce Feiler, in three very engaging and lively books, has written the most popular series about a journey to holy sites. In his first book, *Walking the Bible*,[28] he says that he got an idea to write about the Bible but that

[n]o sooner had I made this realization than I discovered how daunting it seemed. For starters, the idea of reading the Bible from cover to cover seemed undoable. The text was too long; its structure too convoluted; its language too remote. I went to the bookstore seeking help, but found instead fifty different translations, with assorted concordances, interpretations, and daily inspirations. Other options seemed equally unappealing. Though there are shelves of books on every aspect of the Bible—from spelling to sex—none seemed to offer what I craved.[29]

He soon realized that he would have to

enter the Bible as if it were any other world and seek to become a part of it. Once inside, I would walk in its footsteps, live in its canyons, meet its characters, and ask its questions in an effort to understand why its stories had become so timeless and, despite years of neglect, once again so vitally important to me.[30]

This is no curmudgeonly book like the one Mark Twain wrote in the nineteenth century about his journeys through the Middle East and the Holy Land in which he brings his sharp wit to bear but leaves us with scant impression that he had any kind of a religious experience in going to these holy places.[31] Feiler travels his way through the five books of Moses, seeking to connect with the religious experience of the Jewish people through his journeys to holy sites. For Feiler's second journey, to seek out Abraham, he says:

If my previous experience in the region involved a journey through place—three continents, five continents, five countries, four war zones—this would be a journey through place *and* time—three religions, four millennia, one never-ending war. I would read, travel, seek out scholars, talk to religious leaders, visit his natural domain, even go home to mine....[32]

Does Feiler connect with Abraham in a sacred place? Well, yes and no. He says:

I found him—not in the books, in the religious leaders, in
the caves. Not in any particular place at all. I found him
everywhere, in a sense.... Abraham *is* like water.... He's a
vast, underground aquifer that stretches from Mesopotamia
to the Nile, from Jerusalem to Mecca, from Kandahar to
Kansas City. He's an ever-present, ever-flowing stream
that represents the basic desire all people have to form a
union with God. He's a physical manifestation of the fundamental yearning to be descended from a sacred source.[33]

It seems that, for Feiler, Abraham becomes a metaphor for the
religious longing in all of us. Nevertheless, Feiler comes into contact
with this longing through his engagement with places and people in
the lands of Abraham. Thus place does matter and becomes the cata-
lyst for a religious experience.

The end of Bruce Feiler's book, *Where God Was Born*,[34] took
him on a great odyssey through the Middle East, in which his engagement with holy sites and many people brought him into living contact
with the biblical story. He says that "[a]t the end of my travels, I came
to view my relationship with religion as I do my relationship with
God, I can no longer be a passive recipient. I must be an active partner."[35] This journey of engagement with the land and the people has
clearly brought him into a living relationship with the God of Israel.
In the end

the act of touching these places, walking these roads, and
asking these questions had added another column to my
being. And the only possible explanation I could find for
that feeling was that a spirit existed in many of the places I
visited, and a spirit existed in me, and the two had some-
how met in the course of my travels. It's as if the *godliness
of the land* [emphasis added] and the godliness of my
being had fused.[36]

This was experience of the land for a Jewish believer like Feiler;
for a Christian we would say that the Christ who abides in us[37] con-
nects with the sacramental presence of Christ in the Holy Land, which
intensifies the Christ present in us in new, more intimate, and height-

ened ways. Feiler comes to the conclusion after his ten-thousand mile journey that he

> returned to the essential triad at the heart of the Bible: the people, the land, and God. I had gone to the land, I had encountered a spirit, and in so doing I had become more human. That equation drew me back to one of the defining moments of the Pentateuch, Jacob's wrestling with the messenger of God in the valley of Jabbok [Gen 32:23–33].... Humans experience God, the text seems to be saying...by walking with him [in the land].... After all my travels, I had reached the destination that the Five Books, at least, may have intended all along. I had reached the promised Land—Israel—the place where one strives with God.[38]

In this way, the Jewish believer Bruce Feiler came into contact with the God of the covenant, the God who guided Israel's history, who came alive from the pages of the biblical text in the journey into the land that he had taken.

For the Roman Catholic author Thomas Cahill, whose popular series, "The Hinges of History," includes *How the Irish Saved Civilization*[39] and *The Gifts of the Jews*,[40] identifies an important historical figure in his 1999 book:

> Two thousand years ago a man was born into a family of carpenters in occupied Palestine. He was a small-town Jew, born in a bad time for Jews. Their land was no longer their own, and they had been made to bow before a succession of conquerors who had diluted their proud culture and, as many would have said, infected it. His name, as everyone knows, was Jesus of Nazareth—or, as the Jews of his own day called him, Yeshua. As everyone knows, he preached a message of mercy, love, and peace and was crucified for his trouble. This unlikely character has long been accounted the central figure of Western civilization.[41]

Cahill writes about Jesus as an "armchair traveler." There is no indication he ever left his study or research library to connect actually with the land, its living history, or its people. His perspective is solely from historical documents—Greek, Roman, Jewish, and Christian—aided by a broad spectrum of scholarly interpretations. While well written and interesting, it lacks the realism of someone who has walked the land, engaged with the people, and encountered the sacred.

On the other hand, a sympathetic view of the Holy Land as a sacrament of our encounter with Christ comes from Elias Chacour, a Palestinian Melkite priest from the Galilee who works tirelessly for reconciliation in the conflict between Palestinians and Jews.[42] While pilgrims to the Holy Land encounter Christ in the land, we also need to hear Father Chacour's voice, who says, at the end of his book:

> We Palestinians and Jews live in what the world calls the Holy Land, but what makes the land holy? Is it the stones or trees? Is it the churches? The shrines? The paths on which the patriarchs and our Lord Jesus Christ walked? Or is the land sanctified by what we *do* to make God present?[43]

The native Christian populations in the Holy Land are often called the "living stones," that is, they manifest Christ's presence in the living Christian communities in the land that we call holy.[44] The different, but not contradictory, expressions of what constitutes holiness arise from the difference between being rooted and living on the land and being a pilgrim on the land. All Christians must manifest their identity with Christ by how they live—and this includes not only the Palestinian Christian communities in Israel, but also wherever Christians live. The issue at hand is how the land functions for Christian pilgrims to the land, especially in the context of the eucharistic celebration. For Palestinian Christians, the land manifests a sacramental identity of encounter with Christ—a presence that abides with the resident Palestinian Christian populations in Israel. Also for them, more is called for, that is, as Chacour says, "to make God present" to Israelis, Palestinians, and all others in their actions. This is a fuller development of the initial encounter with Christ in the land. As a Palestinian Christian, Chacour himself reflects during a BBC interview about his destroyed home village of Biram:[45] "I saw the people in my Melkite community in Ibillin.[46] But most of all, I saw Jesus, striding toward me over the Galilee hills, smiling holding out his hand to me."[47] A more eloquent statement of Christ's presence in the land could not be found.

The State of Israel and the Catholic Church as Covenantal Institutions

It has become axiomatic for liberal Christians, both Catholic and Protestant, to seethe with anger at the State of Israel and wax eloquent in defense and support of the Palestinians, berating the Israelis for the injustices they have perpetrated upon the native Palestinian population. Equally adamant is the voice of conservative Christians — Catholic, Protestant, and Evangelical — in support of Israel — usually including whatever the current prime minister is doing and to grant virtually no hearing to the Palestinians, whom they broadly connect to the suicide bombers and other terrorists.

It seems time for both groups to take a step back and reflect on the consequences of institutionally equating the Roman Catholic Church with the modern State of Israel. To repeat briefly the points made in the previous chapter:

1. The State of Israel vis-à-vis Zionism is a new modality of covenantal fidelity of the Jewish people in the twenty-first century.
2. Since the Vatican Council teaching in *Lumen Gentium*, the Dogmatic Constitution on the Church, we can say that the Catholic Church is an institutional embodiment of the church of Christ as it exists in society today.
3. Both the State of Israel and the Catholic Church are institutional structures within which a fidelity to God can be lived out in concrete ways.
4. The issue for both the Roman Catholic Church and the State of Israel is the balance between the divine and the human in the lives of Christians and Jews.

God calls Jews and Christians to covenantal fidelity and invites them to express it in the real world of institutions and organizations. Each is a response to God. There is a sense in which each is "divinely instituted" but also a sense in which each is fully human. The sin of the human does not obliterate the divine, nor does the divine aspect liberate the human from criticism and sin.

Each institution, Catholic Church and State of Israel, is called upon to live out its covenantal identity in the world—each does so partly successfully and partly unsuccessfully. The church of sexual abuse scandals and the Israel of unjust treatment of Palestinians must each repent of its sins, resolve to do better in the future, and work toward different future relationships. Each may need structural transformations to fulfill this task, each may need to look to new leadership models.

Do Jews and specifically the State of Israel have a religious right to the land? Clearly, God gives the land of Canaan to the Jewish people, it is part of God's covenant bond with the Jewish people, and the Roman Catholic Church recognizes that God's covenant with the Jewish people still endures. Thus, they have a religious right to the land. But what of their political and juridical right to the land? No one doubted or questioned the Ottoman Empire's right to rule over its empire with the land of Israel being under its control and authority from 1517 to 1918. After the Ottoman Empire lost World War I to the Allies, by the traditional rules of war the victors appropriated the spoils of war that created some new national states, and placed temporary rule over other areas under the authorship of the League of Nations, the precursor to the United Nations. France had jurisdiction over what became Syria and Lebanon as its mandate, and Great Britain had jurisdiction over what became Jordan and Israel (part of which will eventually become Palestine) as its mandate. The "Byzantine" intrigues began almost the day after Britain assumed authority with the ultimate consequence of the vote of the United Nations on November 29, 1947, to partition this land into two states—a Jewish and an Arab Palestinian State.

The Jews accepted the vote of this international body, the successor body to the League of Nations, but the Arab governments of the surrounding areas and those living within Mandate Palestine did not, and war ensued after the May 14, 1948, declaration of the reestablishment of the State of Israel. Wars were subsequently fought in 1955, 1967, and 1973. After the 1991 Gulf War, the State of Israel and the PLO signed the Oslo Agreement in 1993. Presently, Israelis and Palestinians are pursuing an "on-again, off-again" road to the creation of a Palestinian State alongside of a Jewish State with secure and safe boundaries. Both peoples are struggling to learn to live together and share space on this land with the presence of three great monotheistic religious traditions—Jewish, Christian, and Muslim.

This brings us back to a description of the Roman Catholic Church and the State of Israel. This description, as two covenantal institutions, should help Catholics to value more their church and the State of Israel, but not silence prophetic voices of reform and renewal in either institution, knowing that there is a foundation of faith, love, and support for both. We are always a people both holy and sinful and our institutions reflect this identity, too.[48]

Notes

1. PRESENT CATHOLIC CHURCH TEACHING
ON JEWS AND JUDAISM

1. Anti-Judaism is a theological description that includes opposition to Judaism or Jewish opinion as it expresses positions contrary to Christian belief or practice. The theological polemics of the first century of believing Christians against the Jews were superseded by violent, anti-Jewish teachings in the second century. The term *anti-Semitism*, coined in the nineteenth century, has come to mean hateful stereotyping of the Jewish people simply because they are Jewish. See the helpful discussion by a Jewish and Christian scholar on "Antisemitism" in *A Dictionary of the Jewish-Christian Dialogue*, expanded edition, edited by Leon Klenicki and Geoffrey Wigoder (Mahwah, NJ: Paulist Press, 1995), 9–15.

2. This history has been divided into six periods, beginning with the first period of Jesus' ministry to the beginning of the sixth period with the liberation of the Nazi death camps in 1945. See Eugene J. Fisher, "Epilogue," in *Interwoven Destinies: Jews and Christians Through the Ages*, edited by Eugene J. Fisher (Mahwah, NJ: Paulist Press, 1993), 143–46.

3. Edward Flannery, *The Anguish of the Jews*, revised and updated (New York: Paulist Press, 1985), 1–2. Also see the excellent works by an Anglican priest/theologian, William Nicholls, *Christian Antisemitism: A History of Hate* (Northvale, NJ: Jason Aronson, 1993) and by a British rabbi, Dan Cohn-Sherbok, *The Crucified Jew: Twenty Centuries of Christian Anti-Semitism* (San Francisco: Harper Collins, 1992).

4. Claire Huchet Bishop, introduction to Jules Isaac, *The Teaching of Contempt: The Christian Roots of Anti-Semitism* (New York: Holt, Rinehart and Winston, 1964), 10.

5. See the illuminating and tortuous history of this declaration and especially *Nostra Aetate* in *Declaration on the Relation of the Church to Non-Christian Religions of Vatican Council II*, commentary by Rene Laurentin and Joseph Neuner, SJ (Glen Rock, NJ: Paulist Press, 1966), 17–77. For a more thorough history of the development of *Nostra Aetate* see Alberto Melloni's unedited transcript of a lecture delivered at the Pontifical Gregorian University in Rome on November 9, 2004, as part of a series "The

Catholic Church and the Jewish People from Vatican II to Today," by Alberto Melloni, "*Nostra Aetate* and the Discovery of the Sacrament of Otherness" at www.bc.edu/research/cjl/meta-elements/texts/center/conferences/Bea_Centre_C–J_Relations_04–05/melloni.htm.

6. There has been significant improvement from the late 1950s into the early 1990s. The principal studies in Catholic textbooks have been done by Sister Rose Thering, OP (1960), Dr. Eugene J. Fisher (1976), and Dr. Philip A. Cunningham (1992). Cunningham's doctoral research has been published as *Education for Shalom: Religions Textbooks and the Enhancement of the Catholic and Jewish Relationship* (Collegeville, MN: Liturgical Press, 1995). For an analysis of the changes, see the review article by Eugene J. Fisher, "Update on Catholic Education on Jews and Judaism," *SIDIC* 27, no. 3 (1994): 24–30.

7. This term has been used historically to characterize the Jewish "crime" of killing God, namely, Jesus as the God-man and Second Person of the Trinity.

8. The teaching of contempt as summarized by Padraic O'Hare, "The Reform of Christian Religious Education: The End of 'The Teaching of Contempt,'" *Interfaith Focus*. 1, no. 2 (1994): 1–2.

9. Ibid., 2.

10. Pope John Paul II, "The Roots of Anti-Judaism," *Origins* 27 (November 13, 1997): 365.

11. "Anti-Semitism," in *HarperCollins Dictionary of Religion*, edited by Jonathan Z. Smith (San Francisco: HarperCollins, 1995), 53. Also see the excellent brief article, "Antisemitism," in *A Dictionary of the Jewish-Christian Dialogue*, expanded edition, edited by Leon Klenicki and Geoffrey Wigoder (Mahwah, NJ: Paulist Press, 1995): "Jewish View" by David Blumenthal (9–12) and "Christian View" by Michael McGarry (12–14).

12. Sidney G. Hall III, *Christian Anti-Semitism and Paul's Theology* (Minneapolis: Fortress Press, 1993), x. Hall cites his description of conversion, expulsion, and annihilation from Raul Hilberg, *The Destruction of the European Jews* (Chicago: Quadrangle Books, 1961), 3–4.

13. Padraic O'Hare, "The Reform of Christian Religious Education," 2.

14. Mary C. Boys, "A More Faithful Portrait of Judaism: An Imperative for Christian Educators" in David P. Efroymson, Eugene J. Fisher, and Leon Klenicki, eds., *Within Context: Essays on Jews and Judaism in the New Testament* (Mahwah, NJ: Paulist Press, 1993), 5.

15. This is particularly well documented in the collection of papal statements, *Spiritual Pilgrimage: Texts on Jews and Judaism*, 1979–1995 (by Pope John Paul II),with commentary and introduction by Eugene J. Fisher and Leon Klenicki, eds., (New York: Crossroad Publishing Company, 1995).

16. Full text can be found at www.bc.edu/research/cjl/meta-elements/texts/cjrelations.

17. Ibid.

18. After the promulgation of *Nostra Aetate* in 1966, the *Vatican Office for Catholic-Jewish Relations* was established and Cardinal Bea entrusted it to the care of Rev. Adriaan Cornelius Rijk (+1979). After the death of Cardinal Bea in 1968, Cardinal Johannes Willebrands became President of the Secretariat for Chrisitan Unity and the Office for relations with the Jews which was linked with it. Archbishop (now Cardinal) Edward I. Cassidy succeeded him in 1990 until 2001 when Cardinal Walter Kasper became the current President. Pier Francesco Fumagalli, "The Church and the Jewish People—Twenty-Five years after the Second Vatican Council (1963–1965)," *SIDIC* 25, no. 2 (1992): 19. See the collection of major addresses and essays of Cardinal Willebrands, *Church and Jewish People: New Considerations* (Mahwah, NJ: Paulist Press, 1992) for an appreciation of his contributions during his tenure.

19. For a fascinating first-person account of the development of this document from the time of the meeting of Jules Isaac until it was passed by the council fathers and the challenges for the future of the dialogue, see Thomas F. Stransky, CSP, "Holy Diplomacy: Making the Impossible Possible," in *Unanswered Questions: Theological Views of Jewish-Catholic Relations*, edited by Roger Brooks (Notre Dame: University of Notre Dame Press, 1988), 51–69. Thomas Stransky has also written a briefer account, "The Genesis of Nostra Aetate," *America* 193, no. 12 (October 24, 2005): 8–12; this whole issue of *America* is devoted to reflecting on *Nostra Aetate* after forty years.

20. See *In Our Time: The Flowering of Jewish-Catholic Dialogue*, edited by Eugene J. Fisher and Leon Klenicki (Mahwah, NJ: Paulist Press, 1990), 36. This book contains a collection of documents including *Nostra Aetate*, the *Guidelines*, the *Notes*, and other documentation and annotated bibliography from 1975 to 1989 in Christian-Jewish dialogue issues.

21. See the detailed chart by Eugene Fisher, "The Development of a Tradition," *SIDIC* 19, no. 2 (1986): 20–23.

22. Commission for Religious Relations with the Jews, "We Remember: A Reflection on the 'Shoah'" (March 16, 1998) in *Origins* 27 (March 26, 1998): 669, 671–75.

23. See reactions to this document: Cardinal Keeler/Eugene Fisher, "Implications of the Document on the 'Shoah,'" *Origins* 27 (March 26, 1998): 675 ; Cardinal O'Connor, "A Step Forward in an Ongoing Dialogue," *Origins* 27 (March 26, 1998): 676; and Communique on the Vatican document on the "Shoah" by the International Catholic-Jewish Liaison Committee meeting at the Vatican, *Origins* 27 (April 9, 1998): 701, 703–4.

Over a year later, Eugene Fisher comments on Jewish criticism of the document and the intent and direction the Vatican points Catholics toward: see Eugene J. Fisher, "Catholics and Jews Confront the Holocaust and Each Other," *America* 181 (September 11, 1999): 9–14. John Pawlikowski has made a cogent critique of "We Remember" in the areas of (1) the flaws of drawing the distinction between the sinfulness of the "sons and daughters" of the church vis-à-vis the holiness of the church itself, (2) the lack of "inherent connection between Nazi ideology and classical Christian antisemitism," and (3) the problematic depiction of Pius XII in the document; original article by John T. Pawlikowski, OSM, in *Kirche und Israel* (2000) with an English version, "We Remember: A Constructive Critique," on the Web site: www.nclci.org/Articles/art-remember.htm.

24. *Declaration of the U.S. Conference of Catholic Bishops*, November 20, 1975. Complete document can be found in *Stepping Stones to Further Jewish-Christian Relations: An Unabridged Collection of Christian Documents*, edited by Helga Croner (Mahwah, NJ: Paulist Press, 1977), 29–34.

25. Both in the *Declaration of the U.S. Conference of Catholic Bishops* (cited above) and in the *Notes* there is a caution, "The existence of the State of Israel and its political options should be envisaged not in a perspective which is in itself religious, but in their reference to the common principles of international law" (Notes # 25). This does not mean that there is no religious/theological meaning to the State of Israel, but the Vatican and U.S. Bishops are cautioning against a certain type of theological interpretation, namely, the fundamentalist interpretation that would seek to determine current geographical boundaries of the modern state by citing certain biblical passages. Eugene Fisher has argued that the authors of the *Declaration* and the *Notes* had in mind the views espoused by Rev. Jerry Falwell (on the Christian "Right") and the late Rabbi Meir Kahane (on the Jewish Fundamentalist "Right"). See Anthony Kenny, *Catholics, Jews and the State of Israel* (Mahwah, NJ: Paulist Press, 1993), 49–51.

26. In modern biblical studies, the development of the historical-critical method (beginning in the late nineteenth century) has come to characterize these periods as the *Sitz im Leben Jesu* [setting in the life of Jesus], *Sitz im Kirche* [setting in the church] and *Sitz im Evangelium* [setting in the evangelist/gospel]. This development in New Testament studies began with Martin Debelius in 1920 and continued through the development of form criticism, redaction criticism, and tradition criticism. First given church approval in the encyclical *Divino Afflante Spiritu* by Pius XII in 1943 and reaffirmed in the 1964 Vatican document, *Instruction on the Historical Truth of the Gospels*. Guidelines and positions in these documents have become the commonly

accepted approach of Catholic biblical scholars as well as mainline Protestants and Reform, Conservative, and Reconstructionist Jewish scholars.

27. Marcion, a deacon in the church of Rome, posited that there were two "Gods," namely, the God of the Old Testament, who was a God of law, justice, and punishment, and the God of Jesus (and the New Testament), who was a God of love, mercy, and forgiveness. Therefore, he rejected the Old Testament entirely because of the nature of the God (as opposed to the God of Jesus) and edited the Christian writings to include only a version of Luke and some of Paul's letters. The Synoptics were too "Jewish" for him — among other reasons. The church of Rome excommunicated him in 140 CE and expelled him from the city. Nevertheless, his caricature of the Hebrew scriptures and Judaism often continues to this day!

28. Fisher, *In Our Time*, 42.

29. The NAB footnote best explains this passage in context: "[T]he Torah speaks only about a rock from which water issued, but rabbinic legend amplified this into a spring that followed the Israelites throughout their migration. Paul uses this legend as a literary type: he makes the rock itself accompany the Israelites, and he gives it a spiritual sense. *The rock was the Christ*: in the Old Testament, Yahweh is the Rock of his people (cf Dt 32, Moses' song to Yahweh the Rock). Paul now applies this image to the Christ, the source of the living water, the true rock that accompanied Israel, guiding their experiences in the desert." Paul has made a pastoral application/interpretation to solve a pressing problem in Corinth; this instance does not justify elevating this example into a universal principle of interpretation (typology) of the Old Testament.

30. Fisher, *In Our Time*, 42–43.

31. *Catechism of the Catholic Church*, English translation for the United States of America, copyright 1994, United States Catholic Conference (New York: Doubleday, 1995). See the excellent analyses of this catechism in its ecclesial context, its authority, its treatment of the issues of interreligious dialogue, justice and peace, and many other topics in the collection of essays: *Introducing the Catechism of the Catholic Church: Traditional Themes and Contemporary Issues*, edited by Bernard L. Marthaler (Mahwah, NJ: Paulist Press, 1994).

32. Mary C. Boys traces the history of the development of the *Catechism* in "How Shall We Christians Understand Jews and Judaism? Questions about the New Catechism," *Theology Today* 53 (1995): 165–67.

33. The *Catechism* is now in its second edition (*Catechism of the Catholic Church* [Vatican: Libreria Editrice Vaticana, 2000]) based upon *Catechism of the Catholic Church: Modifications from the Editio Typica* (Vatican: Liberia Editrice Vaticana, 1998), USCC publication no. 5–166.

None of these revisions effects changes in the first edition's presentation of Jews and Judaism.

34. An example of this is the *Catechism*'s use of typology in its interpretation of biblical texts that would seem to render other interpretations current in the Jewish community at best irrelevant and at worst in error. Both Peter Phan ("Preaching Jews and Judaism") and Mary C. Boys ("How shall We Christians Understand") are highly critical of this presentation, along with the prophet-fulfillment themes, its supersessionist Christology, and its discussion of the "Old Law."

35. See this remarkable critique: Rabbi Jack Bemporad, "The Universal *Cathechism*'s (sic) Teaching on the Jews and Judaism in the Context of the Documents Stemming From Vatican II and the Statements of Pope John Paul II," in *The Catholic Catechism on Jews and Judaism*, Institute Paper (South Orange, NJ: Institute of Judaeo-Christian Studies, Seton Hall University, 1996), 15–32. This presentation was the second Monsignor John M. Oesterreicher Memorial Lecture given at Seton Hall University on October 39, 1994.

36. Eugene J. Fisher, "Reflections on the Catechism of the Catholic Church, *SIDIC* 27, no. 2 (1994): 2; additional article on this topic by Fisher, "Reflections on the Catechism of the Catholic Church" in *Interfaith Focus*, vol. 1, no. 2 (1994): 10–21, in a special issue entitled "Catechism of the Catholic Church: Catholic and Jewish Readings."

37. Ibid.

38. These eight catechetical principles are taken from the brief list given by Eugene J. Fisher in "The Catechism and 'Our Elder Brothers in the Faith,'" *Explorations* 10, no. 2 (1996): 5.

39. This is yet one more ringing condemnation of the ancient heresy of Marcionism to which the church has so often fallen prey over the centuries in both official teaching and popular religious sentiment.

40. *Interfaith Focus*, 2.

41. "Today's visit is meant to make a decisive contribution to the consolidation of the good relations between our two communities, in imitation of the example of so many men and women who have worked and who are still working today, on both sides, to overcome old prejudices and to secure ever wider and fuller recognition of that 'bond' and that 'common spiritual patrimony' that exists between Jews and Christians" (*Spiritual Pilgrimage: Texts on Jews and Judaism, 1979–1995 by Pope John Paul II*, edited by Eugene J. Fisher and Leon Klenicki [New York: Crossroad, 1995], 62).Later he adds "that the Church of Christ discovers her 'bond' with Judaism by 'searching into her own mystery' [cf. *Nostra Aetate*]. The Jewish religion is not 'extrinsic' to us, but in a certain way is 'intrinsic' to our own religion. With Judaism, therefore, we have a relationship which we do not have with

any other religion. You are our dearly beloved brothers and, in a certain way, it could be said that you are our elder brothers" (*Spiritual Pilgrimage*, 63). The pope reemphasized this teaching ten years later in an address on June 23, 1996, in Berlin. This time he added that "*further intensification of this relationship continues to be a major interest of the Church* [emphasis added]." His complete address can be found in *SIDIC* 29, nos. 2–3 (1996): 54–56.

42. "Let us pray for the Jewish people, the first to hear the word of God, that they may continue to grow in the love of his name and in faithfulness to his covenant" (*Roman Missal*, ed. 1983).

43. *Interfaith Focus*, 2.

44. Bemporad, "The Universal *Cathechism*'s Teaching," 31.

45. See the excellent summary of thirteen studies on this text by Joan E. Cook, SC, "The New PBC Document: Continuity, Discontinuity, and Progression Revisited," delivered at the Catholic Biblical Association meeting in San Francisco on August 5, 2003, and available from http://www.bc. edu/research/cjl/meta-elements/texts/cjrelations/resources/articles/ cook.htm. References are to this fourteen page article posted on the Web site of the Center for Christian-Jewish Learning at Boston College, directed by Dr. Philip A. Cunningham. The center's Web site can be found at: http://www.bc. edu/cjlearning. This site is clearly the best source for documentation and articles relative to Christian-Jewish relations.

46. See previous footnote.

47. Cook, "The New PBC Document," 2.

48. Ibid.

49. See Cook, 2–14, where she summarizes comments from diverse authors.

50. Paragraph 21.

51. Ibid.

52. Ibid.

53. Ibid.

54. Ibid.

55. Paragraph 22 as corrected on Boston College Web site (see n. 40) by Charles H. Miller, "Translation Errors in the Pontifical Biblical Commission's 'The Jewish People and Their Sacred Scriptures in the Christian Bible'" *Biblical Theology Bulletin* [*BTB*] 36 (2005): 34–39.

56. Paragraph 22.

57. Paragraph 65 as corrected by C. H. Miller.

58. The English translation of the French original reads "the" key, whereas the French original posits that Jesus as the Davidic Messiah is *a* key, that is, one legitimate way to read and interpret the scriptures, but not the only way. See Miller, "Translation Errors," 38, referring to original page 162 in the official English translation.

59. See Cook, 11–12.

60. See Cook, 13, and above, note 26.

61. Paragraph 87.

62. Ibid.

63. Amy-Jill Levine, "Roland Murphy, the Pontifical Biblical Commission, Jews, and the Bible," *BTB* 33 (2003): 104–13; see her earlier critique, "The Jewish People and Their Sacred Scriptures in the Christian Bible: A Jewish Reading of the Document," *The Bible Today* [*TBT*] 32 (2003): 167–72. Only a few of her comments will be highlighted; the reader is encouraged to read the complete articles.

64. Levine, "Roland Murphy," 105.

65. Ibid., 107.

66. Ibid., 109.

67. Ibid., 106.

68. Ibid., 113.

2. THE JEWISH PEOPLE

1. Fisher and Klenicki, *Spiritual Pilgrimage*, 4.

2. Ibid., 14–15.

3. The great importance of this statement is that it is *not* in the presence of any Jews or any Jewish committee or community. Some in the church (especially those opposed and unaccepting of the sweeping changes in church teaching regarding the Jews) have criticized the pope's statements on Jewish relations, accusing him of "playing to his audience," that is, saying positive, encouraging things to Jewish audiences to be merely tolerant and polite. This address to a solely Christian audience, including many non-Catholic Christians, serves notice that profound changes in church teaching have taken place and there is to be no retreat from these new directions.

4. Fisher and Klenicki, *Spiritual Pilgrimage*, 18–19.

5. Daniel J. Harrington, "A New Paradigm For Paul," *America* 157 (1987): 290–93; "Paul the Jew," *The Catholic World* (March/April 1992): 68–73; and "Paul and Judaism: 5 Puzzles," *Bible Review* 9, no. 2 (April 1993): 19–25, 52. See also the book by Sidney G. Hall III, *Christian Anti-Semitism and Paul's Theology* (Minneapolis: Fortress Press, 1993), which traces the development of Paul's theology through Augustine and the Reformation and develops a new view based upon Pauline research and publications in the 1970s and 1980s. The most thorough analysis and presentation of the traditional view of Paul, new views of Paul, and their application and interpretation of Galatians and Romans is to be found in John G. Gager, *Reinventing Paul* (New York: Oxford University Press, 2000).

6. Found in Krister Stendahl, *Paul Among Jews and Gentiles* (Philadelphia: Fortress Press, 1976), 78–96.

7. Ibid., 79.

8. Ibid., 85–86.

9. Lloyd Gaston, "Paul and the Torah," in *Antisemitism and the Foundations of Christianity*, ed. Alan T. Davies (New York: Paulist Press, 1979), 49.

10. Harrington, "A New Paradigm," 293.

11. Michael Wyschogrod, "The Torah as Law in Judaism," *SIDIC* 19, no. 3 (1986): 10.

12. E. P. Sanders, *Paul, the Law and the Jewish People* (Philadelphia: Fortress Press, 1983). His earlier work, *Paul and Palestinian Judaism* (Philadelphia: Fortress, 1977), thoroughly demolishes the "old" Pauline theological interpretation of justification by faith (Luther) versus a works-righteousness interpretation of the Torah.

13. In the Second Temple period, Jews required four things from their Gentile converts for a complete conversion to the Jewish community: (1) acceptance of the one God of Israel, including the revelation of the Torah, which meant observance of all 613 commandments (*mitzvot*), including the food laws; (2) circumcision (as the sign of the covenant) and mandated in Genesis 17; (3) immersion in a *mikvah* (ritual bath of water)—required even of men in a conversion ceremony though usually used by women, and (4) the offering of a sacrifice in the Temple. Details, documentation, and discussion are found in the excellent work by Lawrence H. Schiffman, *Who Was a Jew? Rabbinic and Halakhic Perspectives on the Jewish-Christian Schism* (Hoboken, NJ: KTAV Publishing, 1985). Paul self- identifies himself as a zealous Jew and acknowledges he persecuted and tried to destroy the communities of the followers of Jesus (Gal 1:13–15). If, as Raymond Brown proposes, there was a circumcision-free evangelical missionary program before Paul, that would explain his persecution of this group. As a follower of the strict Rabbi Shammai (as opposed to more "liberal/pastoral" Rabbi Hillel), he would be outraged that "Christian"-Jews would try to make converts and indeed claim they were now part of Israel without requiring circumcision. See below, note 17 for discussion of Brown's theory.

14. It is a debatable question whether Paul means (as traditionally interpreted) that Jews will accept Jesus as their Messiah at the Parousia or whether Paul has in mind that they will acknowledge Paul's gospel to the Gentiles as a valid message from God and Jesus as the Messiah for the Gentiles, but not necessarily Messiah for the Jews. Church teaching since the council acknowledges this latter possibility (see above pp. 17–19); Paul's Letter to the Romans admits of both possible interpretations.

15. An excellent popular explanation of the foundation of this new interpretation and the scholarship upon which it is based can be found in Philip A. Cunningham, *Jewish Apostle to the Gentiles: Paul as He Saw Himself* (Mystic, CT: Twenty-Third Publications, 1986).

16. Paul did not evangelize this community, and its Christian origins are somewhat obscure. From the years 49–55 the emperor Claudius banned all Jews from Rome, and during this time the probably mostly Christian-Jewish community became a completely Gentile Christian community. When the Jews were allowed to return to Rome after the death of Claudius, the Christian-Jews found themselves vastly outnumbered, and considerable tensions arose—presumably the Gentiles were "lording it over" the Jews, and in 58 Paul writes to "straighten out" the attitudes of the Gentiles toward the Jews and simultaneously introduce himself to the community, which he has for so long been eager to visit. See the excellent introductions and commentaries to this letter that read Paul in light of the revolution that has taken place in Pauline scholarship: John Ziesler, *Paul's Letter to the Romans* (Philadelphia: Trinity Press International, 1989), and James D.G. Dunn, *Romans*, 2 vols. (Dallas: Word Books, 1988). For a popular summary of this letter by Krister Stendahl, see his short monograph, *Final Account: Paul's Letter to the Romans* (Minneapolis: Fortress Press, 1995), and Daniel Harrington, SJ, *Romans: The Good News According to Paul* (Hyde Park: New City Press, 1998).

17. The plurality of Christian-Jewish/Gentile missions is far more complex than most interpreters imagine. See Raymond E. Brown, "Not Jewish Christianity and Gentile Christianity, but Types of Jewish/Gentile Christianity," *Catholic Biblical Quarterly* 45 (1983): 74–79. His theory can be explained briefly as follows: There are *four groups of Christian Jews with their Gentile converts*, from the most strict and demanding in their requirements to join this community of followers of Jesus, to the most "lax" in their requirements. **Type 1** required full observance of the Mosaic Law, including circumcision; originated in Jerusalem and found success in Galatia, Philippi, and perhaps elsewhere (see Galatians, especially chapter 2, Philippians 3, and Acts 15, especially verses 1 and 24). This group were opponents of Paul. **Type 2** did *not* require circumcision, but did require some Jewish purity laws and the food laws (see Acts 15:20; Galatians 2:12 on marriage; 1 Corinthians 5:1=Acts 15:20, 29); it originated also in Jerusalem with James (the brother of the Lord as the leader of the community) and Peter as the leader of the Twelve along with John as the "pillars" of the community (Gal 2:9). It was dominant in Antioch (thus Saul/Paul's earlier opposition to the "Way," since they did not require circumcision), Rome, Pontus, Cappadocia, and sections of the Province of Asia (see Galatians 2:7 versus Acts 15:7), the Cephas party in Corinth (see 1 Corinthians 1:12; 9:5); also 1 Peter to Gentile Christians in

northern Asia Minor. Note that Peter acquiesced in the food laws and they were enforced at Antioch (Acts 15:23). This type of "evangelical missionary program" was a middle ground between type 1 and type 3. **Type 3** did *not* require circumcision nor the food laws, but probably did require other purity laws, especially regarding marriage (1 Corinthians 5:1=Acts 15:20, 29). It originated with Paul and his companions who departed from Antioch. After 49 CE, Barnabas and John Mark aligned themselves with Type 2 and broke with Paul. There was *no* break with the cultic practices of Judaism (feasts, Temple, and so on) *nor* were *Christian Jews* to abandon the *Torah* and *circumcision*. **Type 4** did *not* require circumcision, food laws, or any abiding significance to the Jerusalem Temple. These Christians spoke only Greek and were thoroughly acculturated to the Greco-Roman world. They probably originated in Jerusalem and spread to Samaria with Philip (Acts 8:4–6) and to the Gentiles (Acts 11:19–20) in Phoenicia, Cyprus, and Antioch. This type developed into a more radicalized type of Christianity found in John's Gospel and the Book of Hebrews, where "Judaism" is treated almost as another religion.

18. Incredibly, there are still books still being written with a single covenant supersessionist theology—books that completely ignore modern Pauline studies and the last forty years of Christian-Jewish dialogue. Although not written by a Catholic, the book by David E. Holwerda (*Jesus & Israel: One Covenant or Two*? [Grand Rapids, MI: Eerdmans, 1995]) sums up the status of Second Temple "Judaism": "Because of its failure to comprehend, Israel loses what it had and continues to manifest the judgement that Isaiah pronounced on his own unbelieving generation (Matt 13:14)." And "the position of privilege in Israel now belongs to the disciples" (p. 55); the church is Israel and carries out Israel's mission to the world.

19. Michael A. Signer, "One Covenant or Two: Can We sing a New Song," in *Reinterpreting Revelation and Tradition: Jews and Christians in Conversation*, ed. John T. Pawlikowski, OSM, and Hayim Goren Perelmuter (Franklin [WI]: Sheed & Ward, 2000), 16

20. Ibid.

21. Ibid. Signer quotes from Rosenzweig, *Star of Redemption*, trans. William Hallo (New York: Holt, Rinehart, Winston, 1971), 415–16.

22. Signer, "One Covenant," 17–18.

23. Ibid., 19. This is not far from the idea I first proposed in a 1982 article (see below, note 53); although Signer doesn't develop the grounds for this possibility nor its implications.

24. Ibid., 28.

25. Ibid., 27. Pawlikowski has often reaffirmed his position as accepting only a two-covenant theory because it "more faithfully represents the reality of the Christian-Jewish relationship both historically and theologi-

cally," and a single-covenant theory "fails to safeguard the unique contribution of the revelation in Christ" as well as safeguarding "the distinctive experiences of the two communities since separation" (John T. Pawlikowski, "Single or Double Covenant? Contemporary Perspectives" in *Peace in Deed. Essays in Honor of Harry James Cargas*, ed. Zev Garber and Richard Libowitz [Atlanta: Scholars Press, 1998], 147–62).

26. J. Coert Rylaarsdam, "Jewish-Christian Relationship: The Two Covenants and the Dilemmas of Christology," *Journal of Ecumenical Studies* 9 (1972): 249–70.

27. John Pawlikowski builds upon this analysis in "The Historicizing of the Eschatological; The Spiritualizing of the Eschatological: Some Reflections," in Alan T. Davies, ed., *Antisemitism and the Foundations of Christianity* (New York: Paulist Press, 1979), 151–66.

28. Rylaarsdam, "Jewish-Christian Relationship," 267–68.

29. James Parkes, *Judaism and Christianity* (Chicago: University of Chicago Press, 1948), 30.

30. John T. Pawlikowski, *What Are They Saying About Christian-Jewish Relations?* (New York: Paulist Press, 1980), 45.

31. It is difficult to judge how she might accept two covenants, since she spends much time refuting the old supersessionist view of the superiority of the New Covenant (in Jesus) over the Old Covenant (of Sinai). See Rosemary Radford Ruether, *Faith and Fratricide: the Theological Roots of Anti-Semitism* (New York: Seabury Press, 1974), 251–57.

32. Ibid. Pawlikowski, *What Are They Saying*, 48–49, also places E. P. Sanders in the group of those proposing a two-covenant theory to explain the relationship between Christianity and Judaism.

33. Joann Spillman, "The Image of Covenant in Christian Understandings of Judaism," *Journal of Ecumenical Studies* 35 (1998): 63–84.

34. Eugene J. Fisher, "A Word for Continuity: A Response to Joann Spillman," *Journal of Ecumenical Studies* 35 (1998): 85–87.

35. Monika Hellwig, "Christian Theology and the Covenant of Israel," *Journal of Ecumenical Studies* 7 (1970): 37–51.

36. Ibid., 48.

37. Ibid., 50. She acknowledges her dependence here upon Edward Schillebeeckx's vision of Jesus as the sacrament of our encounter with God.

38. Ibid., 51. These ideas are developed further in her essay, "From the Jesus Story to the Christ of Dogma," in Davies, *Antisemitism*, 118–36.

39. A. Roy Eckardt, *Elder and Younger Brothers: The Encounter of Jews and Christians* (New York: Charles Scribner's Sons, 1967). See the further development of his ideas in *Reclaiming the Jesus of History: Christology Today* (Minneapolis: Fortress Press, 1992), 86–87.

40. Some claim his theory falls in a middle ground between a double- and single-covenant theory. (How appropriate for an Anglican!) See the extended discussion of various theories including Eugene Borowitz's Jewish contribution: *Renewing the Covenant: A Theology for the Postmodern Jew* (Philadelphia: Jewish Publication Society, 1991), summarized in Andrea L. Weiss, "Creative Readings of the Covenant: A Jewish-Christian Approach," *Journal of Ecumenical Studies* 30 (1993): 389–402.

41. These ideas were first presented at the annual meeting of the AAR/SBL in San Francisco on December 29, 1977; see Paul van Buren, "Christ of the Church, Not the Messiah of Israel," in *AAR/SBL Seminar Papers*, 1977, 15–16.

42. This idea appears in his second volume: *Discerning the Way: A theology of the Jewish-Christian Reality* (New York: Seabury Crossroad, 1980) and is most developed in his third volume of the *Theology of the Jewish-Christian Reality*, *Christ in Context* (San Francisco: Harper & Row, 1988).

43. Norbert Lohfink, SJ, *The Covenant Never Revoked: Biblical Reflections on Christian-Jewish Dialogue*, trans. John J. Scullion, SJ (New York: Paulist Press, 1991), 84.

44. Ibid., 85.

45. Ibid., 84.

46. Ibid., 96.

47. Ibid. He goes on to add that "for Jewish-Christian dialogue, I think that it is much more sensible to strike an attitude to the torah and its thinking than to the idea of 'covenant.'" Yet here I believe that Lohfink's reasoning is a bit imprecise because he says that "it would be useful to attend more to the word 'torah,' Torah: 'law,' the 'law of Sinai'" (94) rather than speaking of covenant/new covenant since Jeremiah 31:33 speaks of "new" covenant as only a "new" modality of the same covenant of Sinai. It is precisely *for this reason* that I believe we should retain the use of covenant terminology, but explicate the "newness" of the "new" covenant in nonsupersessionist theologies. The Torah [literally in the Hebrew: "instruction" or "teaching"] is given at Sinai and ratified as a covenant by Moses in a blood ritual (Exod 24:8). Therefore, Torah and covenant cannot be so easily separated as Lohfink seems to think.

48. See pp. 22–24 above.

49. Most Rev. Bruno Forte, archbishop of Chieti-Vasto, "Israel and the Church—The Two Explorers of the Promised Land: Towards a Christian Theology of Judaism," Rome, 4 November 2004 at the Pontifical Gregorian University: www.bc.edu/research/cjl/meta-elements/texts/center/confer ences/Bea_Centre_C–J_Relations_04–05/Forte.htm.

50. Ibid.

51. Ibid.

52. Joseph Cardinal Ratzinger (now Benedict XVI) concludes that "the unconditional nature of the divine covenant has become a definitely two-sided relationship" (*Many Religions—One Covenant: Israel, the Church and the World*, trans. Graham Harrison [San Francisco: Ignatius Press, 1999], 74). See the summary analysis of this book in Mary C. Boys, "The covenant in Contemporary Ecclesial Documents," in *Two Faiths, One Covenant?* ed. Eugene B. Korn and John T. Pawlikowski, OSM (New York: Sheed & Ward, 2005), 86–89. Ratzinger's view of covenant is not far from the image proposed here (see pp. 39–40).

53. This new model was first proposed in a 1982 address to a Religious Leadership Conference in Wisconsin where the dialogue partner was an Orthodox rabbi and it was subsequently published in our seminary journal: Richard C. Lux, "Covenant Interpretations: A New Model for the Christian-Jewish Relationship," *SCHOLA: A Pastoral Review of Sacred Heart School of Theology* 5 (1982): 25–62. The model presented here is in slightly revised form.

54. This is what makes the quest for the Jesus of history such a difficult enterprise with extremely divergent results. As previously mentioned, the church recognizes that there are three distinct phases in understanding Jesus (see above, p. 10 and note 26) and she encourages biblical scholars to pursue their research—wherever it may lead ["The Interpretation of the Bible in the Church," PBC, 1993.] While there are many good studies of these issues by Catholic, Protestant, and Jewish scholars, one of the finest is the work by the Roman Catholic priest, John P. Meier, *A Marginal Jew: Rethinking the Historical Jesus: The Roots of the Problem and the Person*, vol. 1 (New York: Doubleday, 1991); *A Marginal Jew: Rethinking the Historical Jesus: Mentor, Message and Miracle*, vol. 2 (New York: Doubleday, 1994); *A Marginal Jew: Rethinking the Historical Jesus: Companions and Competitors*, vol. 3 (New York: Doubleday, 2001).

55. See Francis I. Andersen and David Noel Freedman, *Hosea*, Anchor Bible, 24 (New York: Doubleday, 1980), 336, 282–84; Hans Walter Wolff, *Hosea*, Hermeneia—A Critical and Historical Commentary on the Bible, trans. Gary Stansell (Philadelphia: Fortress, 1974), and James L. Mays, *Hosea*, Old Testament Library (Philadelphia: Westminster Press, 1969). Also see Brueggemann's work, which deals entirely with covenant and the prophets—particularly Hosea: Walter Brueggemann, *Tradition for Crisis: A Study in Hosea* (Richmond: John Knox Press, 1968).

56. Author's translation.

57. According to the Septuagint, a Greek translation of the Hebrew scriptures probably originating in Alexandria, Egypt, about 250 BCE. See Anthony J. Saldarini, "Septuagint," in the *Harper's Bible Dictionary*, ed.

Paul J. Achtemeier (San Francisco: Harper & Row, 1985), 925. For a more technical article, see Melvin K. H. Peters, "Septuagint," in the *Anchor Bible Dictionary* (New York: Doubleday, 1992) 5:1093–1104.

58. See comment on "enduring love" [lit. *charis* and *aletheia*] in Raymond E. Brown, *The Gospel According to John I–XII*, Anchor Bible, 29 (Garden City: Doubleday, 1966), 14. Also see Schnackenburg's comments on John 1:14 and 1:17 in Rudolf Schnackenburg, *The Gospel According to St. John*, trans. Kevin Smyth (New York: Herder and Herder, 1968), 272–73 and 276–77. Rudolf Bultmann rejects this identification with *hesed* and *emeth* on the basis of other Johannine uses of *charis* and *aletheia* in *The Gospel of John*, trans. G. R. Beasley-Murray (Oxford: Basil Blackwell, 1971), 73–74. Yet the prologue, according to most current interpreters of John, was an earlier composition incorporated into the Gospel, reflecting early Christian-Jewish understandings, and thus not even of the same piece as the rest of John's Gospel. In addition, Brown has, to my mind, satisfactorily refuted this position of Bultmann on linguistic grounds alone without appealing to the complex composition history of John's Gospel. James H. Charlesworth notes the older view of this Gospel as Greek-oriented, nonapostolic, ignorant of the land, and anti-Semitic, and says that a "new view has emerged.... Portions of the Gospel of John may preserve some of the earliest Gospel records. This gospel is in many ways the most Jewish of the Gospels. It is not impossible that in some ways the earliest tradition in it may be related to the apostle John.... It seems, therefore, that the hostile portrayal of the Jews in *John* was occasioned by a harsh social situation: Jews leveling invectives at other Jews. *John* emerges out of a historical situation [of]...some Jews fighting with other Jews" ("Exploring Opportunities for Rethinking Relations Among Jews and Christians," in *Jews and Christians: Exploring the Past, Present, and Future*, ed. J. H. Charlesworth [New York: Crossroad, 1990], 49–50). It is not unreasonable to conclude that the portrait of Jesus in this Gospel is thoroughly Jewish—even vigorously so since John's community, like the author and his community in Matthew, had been thrown out of a synagogue and a community they wished to still be a part of. Lastly, Brown notes "that the Word of God who comes down from heaven in Rev XIX 11–13 is called 'faithful and true [*pistis...alethines*]; which is probably another reflection of the *hesed* and *'emet* motif," Brown, op. cit., 14.

59. Brown, *John I–XII*, 32. This "tenting" is referred to later in Joel 3:17, Zechariah 2:10, and Ezekiel 43:7.

60. Ibid., 33.

61. Ibid., 503.

62. An identification first proposed by Paul van Buren in 1977. See note 41 above.

63. Paul so interprets the lack of success of his "gospel" (and presumably lack of massive Jewish acceptance of the messiahship of Jesus) as God's work of hardening Jewish hearts so that the Gentiles might be brought to the God of the covenant and incorporated into the community of Israel in wholly new ways. This is most likely what Paul means about Jewish rejection of *his* "gospel." It is rejection by most Jews of the "good news" that Paul is preaching to the Gentiles—among other things that admission to Israel is circumcision-free and food-law free (see p. 27 above). This interpretation of the Jewish rejection of "gospel" has been made by Sidney Hall III in *Christian Anti-Semitism and Paul's Theology* (Minneapolis: Fortress, 1993), pp. 126–27 and above, p. 27.

64. This seems to be the meaning of Paul's persecution of the followers of the "Way" (Gal 1:13–14; Phil 3:6; Acts 8:3 and passim). What upsets the rigorously zealous Pharisee, Paul, the follower of Rabbi Shammai, is that a new Halakhah (from *halakh*, "to walk") in the name of Jesus of Nazareth is being preached in Antioch, a new "Way" that does not require circumcision, yet claims that these pagan converts are fully "Jewish," a part of the covenant community of Israel. For Paul this would have been totally unacceptable and meriting persecution—even to the point of trying to eradicate this dissident group of Jews and restore "orthodoxy." See above on p. 28, note 17, on the different types of Christian-Jewish communities and their "evangelical" programs to convert the pagans.

65. It is interesting that Jewish parents give birth to Jewish males who on the eighth day have the requirement of circumcision as the *sign* of their membership in the covenant community of Israel. One could say that the first mitzvah (commandment) incumbent upon a born male Jew is to be circumcised; unlike Christian baptism, circumcision does *not* change the status of a newborn child—it is the acknowledgment, in the flesh, of the child's identity and membership in the covenant community of Israel. On the other hand, Catholic Christian (and all other Christian) parents give birth to "pagan" babies in need of baptism. The new *Catechism* teaches that "through Baptism we are freed from sin and *reborn* [emphasis added] as sons [and daughters] of God; we become members of Christ, are incorporated into the Church and made sharers in her mission: 'Baptism is the sacrament of *regeneration* [emphasis added] through water in the word'" (1213). The language and theology is of rebirth, new birth, regeneration, that is, the move from "paganism," though it sounds harsh to put it this way, to a theism through Jesus, the Christ, the Son of God. One could say that we are "Christians by choice" and not "Christians by birth"; we are not by birth members of the community of believers in God through Christ.

66. Our distinctive Halakhah as followers of Jesus-the-Jew.

3. THE HOLY LAND

1. The following is a development of my article, "Biblical Land Traditions," *The Catholic World* 234 (Jan./Feb. 1991): 4–10.

2. *Catechism of the Catholic Church* (Vatican: Libreria Editrice Vaticana, 2000), 121, which also cites the Vatican Council document, *Dei Verbum*, 14. The Catechism continues, adding that "Christians venerate the Old Testament as true Word of God. The Church has always vigorously opposed the idea of rejecting the Old Testament under the pretext that the New has rendered it void (Marcionism)" (123).

3. Strictly speaking, "Judaism" is the development of Jewish life after the destruction of the Temple in 70 CE. This transformation of Jewish life was accomplished by the Pharisees under the leadership of Johanan ben Zakkai. See Jacob Neusner's popular treatise, *Judaism in the Beginning of Christianity* (Philadelphia: Fortress Press, 1984).

4. See Mircea Eliade, *Cosmos and History: The Myth of the Eternal Return*, trans. Willard R. Trask (New York: Harper Torchbooks, 1959), 12–17, and his *Patterns in Comparative Religion*, trans. Rosemary Sheed (Cleveland: World Publishing Company, c1958, 1963), 367–87.

5. As a secularized "center of the earth," all clocks are calibrated on Greenwich mean time (GMT) in England; in addition, the word *China* means "center of the universe." Examples could be multiplied from the Babylonians, Canaanites, Assyrians, et al.

6. W. Janzen, "Land," *Anchor Bible Dictionary*, ed. David N. Freedman (New York: Doubleday, 1992), 4:146; see complete article, for extensive coverage of the topic, and bibliography, 143–54.

7. For a more comprehensive treatment of the land in the Hebrew scriptures, see "The Land in the Old Testament," in Alain Marchadour and David Neuhaus, *The Land, the Bible, and History* (New York: Fordham University Press, 2007), 9–62.

8. Traditional dating from Martin Noth, *A History of Pentateuchal Traditions*, trans. Bernhard W. Anderson (Englewood Cliffs [NJ]: Prentice-Hall, 1972), 263. See treatment/development of the traditions in the Pentateuch in Noth, and for an excellent, more popular yet sound treatment, see Richard E. Freedman, *Who Wrote the Bible?* 2nd ed. (San Francisco: Harper Collins, 1997), which also contains the history of the development of multiple authors and traditions in the Pentateuch and presents the best modern rationale for the documentary hypothesis. Friedman says that the J narrative "might conceivably have been written as early as the reign of David or Solomon" (86), but he thinks it more likely the J author wrote between 848 and 722; whereas the E narrative was probably composed between 747 and 722 (87, 265). Some other modern authors hold to the traditional dating of a

tenth-century J and a mid-ninth-century E: Michael D. Coogan, *The Old Testament* (New York: Oxford University Press, 2006), 26, and Bernhard W. Anderson, et al., *Understanding the Old Testament*, 5th ed. (Upper Saddle River, NJ: Prentice Hall, 2007), 20, 266. John J. Collins, *Introduction to the Hebrew Bible* (Minneapolis: Fortress Press, 2004), delineates the history of the documentary hypothesis with its dating and the challenges to the traditional point of view, but ventures no opinion of his own (59–64).

9. Although traditionally attributed to E, the story is a redaction of the E and J traditions inasmuch as YHWH occurs in verses 11–14 where Isaac is saved and again in verses 16–18; in the rest of the passage God is referred to as Elohim. See Friedman, *Who Wrote the Bible*, 256–57. In the Jewish tradition this story is called the *Akedah*, the binding of Isaac. See how the various traditions have interpreted this story in Robin Jensen, "How Jews and Christians See Differently [Gen 22:1–18]," *Bible Review* 9, no. 5 (1993): 42–51. In the earliest Muslim tradition, found in the Qur'an, the son is unnamed and for the first three centuries opinion was divided over whether it was Isaac or Ishmael. Present-day Muslims contend it was Ishmael.

10. W. D. Davies, *The Gospel and the Land* (Berkeley: University of California Press, 1974), 18.

11. The covenants with Abraham and David and their interrelation are paralleled in other ancient Near Eastern practices and documents from the second and even third millennium. See "The Covenantal Aspect of the Promise of the Land to Israel," in Moshe Weinfeld, *The Promise of the Land* (Berkeley: University of California Press, 1993).

12. Gerhard von Rad, "There Remains Still a Rest for the People of God: An Investigation of a Biblical Conception," in *The Problem of the Hexateuch and Other Essays*, trans. E. W. Trueman Dicken (New York: McGraw-Hill, 1966), 95.

13. Patrick D. Miller Jr., "The Gift of God: The Deuteronomic Theology of the Land," *Interpretation* 21 (1969): 461.

14. Irrespective of how one interprets the "historical" Abraham and the validity of the antiquity of these traditions/promises, it is clear that the Book of Deuteronomy so understands Abraham in this way. Doubters of Abraham's historicity and antiquity of these traditions include Thomas L. Thompson, *The Historicity of the Patriarchal Narratives: The Quest for the Historical Abraham*, BZAW, 133 (Berlin: Walter de Gruyter, 1974); *The Origin Tradition of Ancient Israel. I. The Literary Formation of Genesis and Exodus 1–23*, JSOT Supp., 55 (Sheffield: JSOT Press, 1987), and John Van Seters, *Abraham in History and Tradition* (New Haven: Yale University Press, 1975). For rejoinders to these positions, see "Face to Face: Biblical Minimalists meet their Challengers," *BAR* 23, no. 4 (July/August 1997): 26–42, 66 (an exchange between Niels Peter Lemche and Thomas

Thompson in disagreement with William Dever and P. Kyle McCarter). The issues are sketched out in the perceptive article by Hershel Shanks, "The Biblical Minimalists: Expunging Ancient Israel's Past," *BR* 13, no. 3 (June 1997): 32–39, 50–52. For a detailed articulation of the issues see William G. Dever, *Who Were the Early Israelites and Where Did They Come From?* (Grand Rapids: Eerdmans, 2003). Dever holds that the ancestors of the "Israelite Peoples" were Canaanites along with some pastoral nomads and small groups of Semitic slaves escaping from Egypt. An excellent source of information on these issues is in the recent book by Kenneth A. Kitchen, *On the Reliability of the Old Testament* (Grand Rapids: Eerdmans, 2003). The views of Thompson and Van Seters remain marginal and unconvincing to most Catholic and Jewish biblical scholars.

15. Many authors (including Miller, "The Gift of God") attempt to apply this Deuteronomic theology to the current conflict between Israelis and Palestinians; while the biblical traditions do have a voice in promoting justice in the land, one cannot make a facile application of continued land tenure to the perceived behavior of present-day antagonists (see n. 17 below).

16. Freedman, *Who Wrote the Bible?* convincingly locates the origin of the written Priestly tradition at the time of the Judean King Hezekiah (715–687 BCE); see 162–73; 210–16.

17. This biblical view is in obvious contradiction to what was just said about the Deuteronomic tradition. As Catholics we hold that all of scripture is inspired, that is, that it is all God's word and speaks to us. We do not hold to a canon within a canon (that is, that certain portions of scripture are more God's word than other parts of scripture), nor that certain parts of the Bible are not (or no longer) God's word—this heresy was condemned long ago. What then are we to make of contradictory statements? Because the scriptures (both Hebrew and Christian) were conditioned by the historical situation of the time, they were God's word for the particular needs and situation of the community. Applying this understanding to these texts, we could say that the promise of the absolute possession of the land probably came in periods when Israel's ownership and possession of the land was threatened or when she was in Exile and needed encouragement, reassurance, and the consolation that their God was still with them and that they would be returned to or preserved in the land. Conversely, threats of deprivation of the land were given by God in times of hubristic certainty of their possession of the land— when Israel is feeling invincible and sure of itself on its own power.

18. Betsy Halpern-Amaru, "Rewriting the Bible: Land and Covenant," in *Post-Biblical Jewish Literature* (Valley Forge: Trinity Press International, 1994), 12.

19. Israel's origins before David are beyond the scope of this treatment. For current discussion, see William G. Dever, "Artifacts, Ecofacts, and Textual Facts," in *Recent Archeological Discoveries and Biblical Research* (Seattle: University of Washington Press, 1990), 1–36, 175–77; "How to Tell a Canaanite from an Israelite," in Hershel Shanks, ed., et al, *The Rise of Ancient Israel* (Washington: Biblical Archeological Society, 1992), 26–85. For a maximalist view, see Provan-Long-Longman, *A Biblical History of Israel* (Louisville: Westminster John Knox Press, 2003) and the opposing minimalist view in Philip R. Davies, *The Origins of Biblical Israel* (New York: T & T Clark, 2007). For a comprehensive collection of essays on all sides of this issue, see V. Philips Long, ed. *Israel's Past in Present Research: Essays on Ancient Israelite Historiography* (Winona Lake, IN: Eisenbrauns, 1999).

20. This is the view of the biblical authors; it does not provide an easy resolution to the right to reside on the land in the postbiblical period.

21. Halpern-Amaru, *Rewriting*, 16.

22. Gog may have been a reference to an historic enemy in Anatolia; even during Ezekiel's lifetime it became a symbol for the attack against Israel by its enemies, whom God would intervene to defeat. See *New Jerome Biblical Commentary* 19:15; 20:89–90.

23. Ottosson, "*erets*" [land], in *Theological Dictionary of the Old Testament*, ed. G. Johannes Botterweck and Helmer Ringgren, trans. John T. Willis (Grand Rapids: Eerdmans, 1977), vol. 1, 402. See entire entry for thorough discussion, 388–405.

24. The prophet Amos, from the Southern Kingdom of Judah, preached to the Northern Kingdom of Israel ca. 760 BCE; however, the end of the book (9:11–15) is generally held to be a later addition by disciples of Amos, redacted during or soon after the Exile in Babylon. See James Mays, *Amos: A Commentary*, Old Testament Library (Philadelphia: Westminster, 1969), 13–14, 163–68; Hans Walter Wolff, *Joel and Amos*, Hermenia, trans. Waldemar Janzen et al. (Philadelphia: Fortress Press, 1977), 350–55, and Francis I. Anderson and David Noel Freedman, *Amos*, Anchor Bible, 24A (New York: Doubleday, 1989), 885–926. For the contrary view that 9:11–15 comes from Amos, see Shalom M. Paul, *Amos*, Hermenia (Minneapolis: Fortress Press, 1991), 288–95.

25. W. D. Davies, *The Territorial Dimension of Judaism* (Berkeley: University of California Press, 1982), 125.

26. Walter Brueggemann, *The Land: Place as Gift, Promise, and Challenge in Biblical Faith*, 2nd ed. (Minneapolis: Fortress Press, 2002), 3.

27. Earl Richard argues for a conflation of two letters to the Thessalonian community (our canonical 1 Thessalonians) with the earliest probably written in 44/45 and the later letter in 49/50, "Early Pauline Thought,"

39–51, in Jouette M. Bassler, ed., *Pauline Theology* (Minneapolis: Fortress Press, 1991). See his commentary, *1 Thessalonians*, Sacra Pagina Commentary Series, ed. Daniel Harrington, SJ (Collegeville, MN: Liturgical Press, 1996). Paul's last writing was his letter to the Roman community while he was in prison in 58 before he was taken to Rome. The seven certainly authentic letters of Paul are: 1 Thessalonians, Galatians, 1–2 Corinthians, Philippians and Romans, probably in this order, with Philemon written (perhaps) in the mid-50s.

28. See the development of the proposal that Paul was a follower of Shammai in Lloyd Gaston, *Paul and the Torah* (Vancouver: University of British Columbia Press, 1987), 28; of course, the most rigorous interpreters of all were the Essenes.

29. It is two chapters later, in Genesis 17, that circumcision is required as a covenant sign in Abraham's flesh and in the flesh of his whole household. It is interesting to note that although Ishmael was also circumcised (Gen 17:26 [P tradition]), indicating that he is in covenant with God, and even though he, too, is given the blessing of progeny, and nationhood, implying territorial possession, the P tradition implies that God's covenant will be "maintained' only with Isaac (Gen 17:21 [P]; 26:12–16 [J]).

30. This is why, in the Christian tradition, Abraham is the model of our faith and our father in the faith: Abraham was bonded (covenanted) with God in an act of faith (Gen 15:6) and not by doing the "deed" of physical circumcision (Gen 17). Since, according to Paul's historical understanding, Abraham's act of faith preceded the act of circumcising, it is not necessary to circumcise Gentiles (since Abraham himself was a Gentile called by God). Although Paul claims that God directly revealed this to him (Gal 1:11–12) he also makes the above scriptural argument for his practice (Gal 3:11–12).

31. Brueggemann, *Land*, 166. Not all agree with this position. W. D. Davies says, "The Gospel substituted for the Torah, Jesus, the Christ, who was indeed born and bred in the Land, but who became the Living Lord.… Thus, once Paul had made the Living Lord rather than the Torah the center in life and in death, once he had seen in Jesus his Torah, he had in principle broken with the land. 'In Christ' Paul was free from the Law and therefore, from the land" (Davies, *The Gospel and the Land*, 219–20).

32. The plurality of Christian-Jewish/Gentile missions is far more complex than most interpreters imagine. See Raymond E. Brown, "Not Jewish Christianity and Gentile Christianity, but Types of Jewish/Gentile Christianity," *CBQ* 45 (1983): 74–79. His theory can be explained briefly as follows: There are four groups of Christian-Jews with their Gentile converts, from the most strict and demanding in their requirements to join this community of followers of Jesus to the most "lax" in their requirements. *Type 1* required full observance of the Mosaic Law, including circumcision; origi-

nated in Jerusalem and found success in Galatia, Philippi, and perhaps elsewhere (see Galatians, esp. ch. 2; Philippians 3 and Acts 15, esp. vss. 1 and 24). This group were opponents of Paul. *Type 2* did *not* require circumcision, but did require some Jewish purity laws and the food laws (see Acts 15:20; Galatians 2:12 on marriage; 1 Corinthians 5:1=Acts 15:20, 29); it originated also in Jerusalem with James (the brother of the Lord as the leader of the community) and Peter as the leader of the Twelve along with John as the "pillars" of the community (Gal 2:9). It was dominant in Antioch [thus Saul/Paul's earlier opposition to the "Way" since they did not require circumcision], Rome, Pontus, Cappadocia, and sections of the Province of Asia (see Galatians 2:7 versus Acts 15:7), the Cephas party in Corinth (see 1 Corinthians 12:12; 9:5); also 1 Peter to Gentile Christians in northern Asia Minor. Note that Peter acquiesced in the food laws and they were enforced at Antioch (Acts 15:23). This type of "evangelical missionary program" was a middle ground between type 1 and type 3. *Type 3* did *not* require circumcision nor the food laws, but probably did require other purity laws, especially regarding marriage (1 Cor 5:1=Acts 15:20, 29). It originated with Paul and his companions who departed from Antioch. After 49 CE Barnabas and John Mark aligned themselves with type 2 and broke with Paul. In the Pauline type 3 Gentile mission, there was *no* break with the cultic practices of Judaism (feasts, Temple, and so on) *nor* were *Christian Jews* who were part of Paul's mission required to abandon the Torah and circumcision. *Type 4* did *not* require circumcision, food laws, or any abiding significance to the Jerusalem Temple. This group spoke only Greek and was thoroughly acculturated to the Greco-Roman world. It probably originated in Jerusalem and spread to Samaria with Philip (Acts 8:4–6) and to the Gentiles (Acts 11:19–20) in Phoenicia, Cyprus, and Antioch. It developed into a more radicalized type of Christianity found in John's Gospel and the Book of Hebrews, where "Judaism" is treated almost as another religion.

33. Paul died in Rome, probably by beheading, which was the form of death for Roman citizens, in the year 62.

34. There were certainly earlier stages of composition of this Gospel, however, and some authors identify its place of origin as Alexandria, Egypt, or perhaps in northern Syria or even in the Galilee. See discussion in John R. Donahue, SJ, and Daniel J. Harrington, SJ, *The Gospel of Mark*, Sacra Pagina 2 (Collegeville, MN: Liturgical Press, 2002), 44–46.

35. Biblical scholars have called this perspective the "Messianic Secret" in Mark's Gospel. See Raymond E. Brown, *An Introduction to the New Testament* (New York: Doubleday, 1997), 153.

36. Although most commentators place the composition of Matthew in Syria, Harrington makes a good case for its composition in Caesarea Maritima or even one of the cities of the Galilee [Sepphoris?]. Daniel J.

Harrington, SJ, *The Gospel of Matthew* (Collegeville, MN: Liturgical Press, 1991), 8–10. For the history of Caesarea and Sepphoris and the roles they played in the Jewish revolt of 66–70 CE and later, see *The Archaeological Encyclopedia of the Holy Land*, eds. Avraham Negev and Shimon Gibson, revised and updated ed. (New York: Continuum, 2003), 102–7, 454–56.

37. It is only the Jesus of Matthew that says he has "come not to abolish [the Torah or the prophets] but to fulfill" (Matt 5:17) and that "until heaven and earth pass away, not the smallest letter or the smallest part of a letter will pass from the law" (Matt 5:18). This Gospel is a sustained polemic against the synagogue "down the block," which probably threw out the Christian-Jews from their midst, and this "tract" was written in defense of their orthodoxy as followers of the Halakhah of Rabbi Jesus. See the excellent commentary on these issues by Harrington, *Matthew*, 17–22, 81, 83–84.

38. Earlier views of the so-called "Council" of Javneh considered there to have been a definite decision and split with the nascent Christian-Jewish sect shortly after 70 CE. Recent works have suggested that this split wasn't complete until after the Bar Kochba revolt (132–135 CE). See Vincent Martin, *A House Divided: The Parting of the Ways between Synagogue and Church* (New York: Paulist Press, 1995). Martha Himmelfarb demonstrates that even in the late fourth century and beyond, there were positive relations between Jews and Christians in Eastern Christianity; see "The Parting of the Ways Reconsidered: Diversity in Judaism and Jewish-Christian Relations in the Roman Empire: 'A Jewish Perspective,'" in *Interwoven Destinies: Jews and Christians Through the Ages*, ed. Eugene J. Fisher (New York: Paulist Press, 1993), 47–61. John G. Gager agrees with Himmelfarb and says that "the hostility that characterizes much of early Christian literature on Judaism does not tell the full story— though it does tell the official one…[that is, it follows] the contours of power and authority within early Christian circles" (p. 71). He continues: "But among early Christians of an ordinary sort, many seem to have experienced no difficulty in combining allegiance to Jesus with respect for Judaism that sometimes took the form of direct participation in the life of the synagogue. Ultimately…inevitably, those in positions of power and authority won out" (p. 72). ("The Parting of the Ways: A View from the Perspective of Early Christianity: 'A Christian Perspective,'" in *Interwoven Destinies*, 62–73.)

39. Nevertheless, Christian-Jewish communities continued to exist well into the second century; see discussion of the Pseudo-Clementines by J. Neville Birdsall, "Problems of the Clementine Literature," in James D. G. Dunn, ed. *Jews and Christians: The Parting of the Way A.D. 70 to 135* (Grand Rapids: Eerdmans, 1999), 347–61.

40. Davies, *Gospel and the Land*, 371.

41. Ibid., 373.

42. It is possible to continue to establish a continuous link with the centrality of the land in Jewish life from the time of the destruction of the Temple in 70 CE until the present. Lawrence A. Hoffman demonstrates how this link continues in Jewish blessings and prayers, especially in the prayers before and after meals; see "Introduction: Land of Blessing and 'Blessings of the Land,'" in *The Land of Israel: Jewish Perspectives*, ed. Lawrence A. Hoffman (Notre Dame: University of Notre Dame Press, 1986), 1–23. Other articles in this volume trace the theme of land from the biblical, Hellenistic, Tannaitic, medieval, and modern periods. Also see the extensive bibliography by Lena Skoog, "Selected Bibliography on the Land and State of Israel," *Immanuel* 22/23 (1989): 215–29 for articles, books, and documents by Christians and Jews on this topic. My particular interest here is the Christian (not Jewish) attachment to the land of Israel; while the theology of the Hebrew scriptures forms part of the Christian confession, my primary focus is our attachment (or lack thereof) to the land from the period of the Christian scriptures to the present.

43. There are many excellent articles and books that treat this subject; see Harry M. Orlinsky, "The Biblical Concept of the Land of Israel: Cornerstone of the Covenant between God and Israel," in Hoffman, *The Land of Israel*, 27–64 [see other articles in this collection]; Martin Buber, *Israel and Palestine: History of an Idea* (London, 1952); Ze'ev W. Falk, "The Notion of Promised Land: Searching for Clarity," *SIDIC* 12:3 (1979): 23–25; Abraham Joshua Heschel, *Israel: An Echo of Eternity* (New York: Farrar, Straus and Giroux, 1967); Dan Bahat, ed., *Twenty Centuries of Jewish Life in the Holy Land: The Forgotten Generations*, 2nd ed. (Jerusalem: The Israel Economist, 1976); Uriel Tal, "Jewish Self-Understanding and the Land and State of Israel," *Union Seminary Quarterly Review* 26 (1971): 351–63.

44. Edward Flannery, *The Anguish of the Jews*, revised and updated (Mahwah, NJ: Paulist Press, 1985), 1–2.

45. Robert L. Wilken, *The Land Called Holy* (New Haven: Yale University Press, 1992), 109.

46. Ibid., citing places of pilgrimage prior to 320 CE in H. Leciercy, "Pèlerinages aux lieux saints," *Dictionnaire d'Archéologie Chrétienne*, 14.1, cols. 68–70.

47. Ibid., 78.

48. Ibid., 81.

49. Ibid.

50. Ibid., 125.

51. "The Jewish Law demanded that every male should make pilgrimage to Jerusalem three times a year (Passover, Feast of Weeks, and Tabernacles; Exod 23:7; Deut 16:16). During the Second Temple period even diaspora

Jews sought to observe it (*Mishnah Aboth* 5.4; *Mishnah Ta'anit* 1:3; Jos. *Wars* 6.9). After the destruction of the Temple in 70 AD pilgrimages to the [Western] Wall became occasions of lamentation. In Islam it is a sacred duty, [once in one's lifetime,] to make the pilgrimage to Mecca (Qur'an 2.196; 3.97)" (Michael Prior, "Pilgrimage to the Holy Land Yesterday and Today," in Michael Prior and William Taylor, eds., *Christians in the Holy Land* [London: World of Islam Trust, 1994], 170).

52. Glen Bowman, "Contemporary Christian Pilgrimage to the Holy Land," in Anthony O'Mahony et al., eds., *The Christian Heritage in the Holy Land* (London: Scorpion Cavendish, 1995), 302–3.

53. That is, the word of God—found in the scriptures, proclaimed to the church, and lived out in our daily lives.

54. *Catechism*, no. 752.

55. As found in the LXX of Daniel 2:28, 29, and 47.

56. Michael G. Lawler, *Symbol and Sacrament: A Contemporary Sacramental Theology* (New York: Paulist Press, 1987), 29.

57. Ibid., 30–31.

58. Ibid., 33.

59. Ibid., 34–45.

60. Ibid., 46.

61. Ibid., 47.

62. Kathleen Hughes, RSCJ, *Saying Amen: A Mystagogy of Sacrament* (Chicago: Liturgy Training Publications, 1999), xx.

63. The golden age of mystagogical preaching is exemplified in the writings of Cyril of Jerusalem, Ambrose of Milan, Theodore of Mopsuestia, John Chrysostom, and sometimes even Augustine. Ibid., 10.

64. Hughes, *Saying Amen*, 9.

65. Ibid., 11.

66. Ibid., 14–15.

67. Ibid., 15.

68. Edward Schillebeeckx, "Transubstantiation, Transfinalization, Transignification," in R. Kevin Seasoltz, OSB, ed., *Living Bread, Saving Cup* (Collegeville, MN: Liturgical Press, 1987) 179–80. Schillebeeckx clarifies his thought in this article, originally delivered in French during the fourth session of Vatican II to fathers of the council at *Domus Mariae* in Rome. Regarding these new theories, Schillebeeckx says that they "do not deviate from the [Tridentine] dogma [of real presence] itself. Rather, they try to present that dogma in existential categories that are at once ontologically profound and more intelligible to the people of our day" (Ibid., 184).

69. Paul VI cites the "Constitution on the Sacred Liturgy," 1:7. Interestingly, all eight types of presence the pope cites are also in the Vatican document on the liturgy, but in a different order. The order he gives in his

encyclical appears to be in ascending order of intensity since of the last he says that the eucharistic presence is in "a manner which surpasses all the others."

70. A slight adaptation of the statement attributed to Cynthia Ozick, "A visitor passes through a place; the place passes through the pilgrim," in Wilken, *Land*, 110.

4. BETWEEN LAND AND STATE: PALESTINIAN PERSPECTIVES

1. Both of whom were Lebanese Christians writing in 1967. See William W. Haddad, "Christian Arab Attitudes toward the Arab-Israeli Conflict," *The Muslim World* 67 (1977):141.

2. Ibid., 142.

3. See Paul Charles Merkley, *Christian Attitudes Towards the State of Israel* (Montreal: McGill-Queens University Press, 2001), 119–20, 148–49.

4. Ibid., 187.

5. Ibid. Italics are in the original.

6. See statements by the Latin patriarch, Michel Sabbah, and writings of Elias Chacour, a Melkite priest, in *We Belong to the Land: The Story of a Palestinian Israeli who lives for Peace and Reconciliation*, HarperSanFrancisco, 1990.

7. See the excellent survey of this long history of Christian residence in Jerusalem and the Holy land by Anthony O'Mahony, "The Christian Communities of Jerusalem and the Holy Land: A Historical and Political Survey," in *The Christian Communities of Jerusalem and the Holy Land: Studies in History, Religion and Politics*, edited by Anthony O'Mahony. Cardiff: University of Wales Press, 2003, 1–37.

8. Jewish and non-Jewish historians claim that most of the Arab population in Israel, the West Bank, and Gaza was a consequence of Jewish immigration and job opportunities, which were the occasion for the movement of Arab peoples from elsewhere in the Middle East to "Palestine." See Joan Peters, *From Time Immemorial: The Origins of the Arab-Jewish Conflict over Palestine* (New York: Harper & Row, 1984), 196–233.

9. Biblical scholars do not support the accuracy of this Palestinian claim. "This scene is basically a Lucan composition, in which Luke makes use of Palestinian tradition, possibly oral, about events that transpired in Jerusalem and mixes it with his own reflection" (Joseph A. Fitzmyer, *The Acts of the Apostles*, Anchor Bible, 31 [New York: Doubleday, 1998], 236–37). Fitzmyer further says that the "added names [Cretans and Arabs] give an expense [expanse ?] not detected in the former names: from the west

(inhabitants of the island of Crete) to the east (people from the Syrian Desert west of Mesopotamia and east of the Orontes and from the peninsula bounded by the Persian Gulf, Indian Ocean, and Red Sea)" (Ibid., 243). Luke Timothy Johnson notes that these peoples listed are "Jews from the Diaspora" who "represent all the lands to which the Jews had been dispersed." These Jews may have been "visiting" for the feast of Shavuot [Pentecost] or had come from all over the world to settle in the city" (*The Acts of the Apostles*, Sacra Pagina, 5 [Collegeville, MN: Liturgical Press, 1992] 47, 43). That at the beginning of the church there was some sort of a large group experience is probably correct (see Gerd Luedemann, *The Acts of the Apostles*, [Amherst, NY: Prometheus Books, 2005], 50). It is fair to conclude that from an early tradition of a powerful experience of the Spirit, probably during the festival of Shavuot, the community of Jesus' followers began to preach to others in fulfillment of Luke's statement that "you will be witnesses…to the ends of the earth" (Acts 1:8). The list of nations (nationalities) is twelve (symbolic of the twelve tribes) and "Cretans and Arabs" was added later to this list. In any event, the Arabs described in this text are Jews who come from the East either as pilgrims for the festival or as residents in Jerusalem. It is therefore historically and theologically tenuous to build a case for continuous Arab (either Christian or non-Christian) presence in Jerusalem (or the land) upon this one biblical reference in Acts.

10. Alan Dershowitz (*The Case for Israel* [Hoboken, NJ: John Wiley and Sons, 2003]) claims the Arab refugee problem "was created by a war initiated by the Arabs" (79), yet, even as a consummate Israeli apologist he nevertheless acknowledges that Israelis bear some responsibility—particularly the Irgun, the paramilitary wing of the revisionist movement headed by Menachem Begin, and Lechi (or the Stern Gang), headed by Yitzhak Shamir, in their massacre of 110 inhabitants of Deir Yassin and the consequences following (81–83). Dershowitz also points out that following the creation of the State of Israel in 1948, the flight/expulsion of 850,000 Jews "from Arab lands was slightly more than the number of Arab refugees from Israel" (88). Though Dershowitz too readily absolves Israel from responsibility, he is correct in his assertion that "[t]here would have been no Arab refugee problem had the Arab states accepted the subsequent U.N. partition. But instead, having rejected Jewish self-determination in 1937, the Arab world rejected it once again in 1948 and attacked Israel in an effort to destroy the new Jewish state, exterminate its Jewish population, and drive the Jews into the sea" (90).

11. Benny Morris, *The Birth of the Palestinian Refugee Problem Revisited* (Cambridge: Cambridge University Press, 2004), map 2 (p. xi), xiv–xviii. He draws together his study in the "Conclusion," 588–600. Also see the perceptive review of Morris (1st edition, 1988), Nur Masalha (*Expulsion of the Palestinians* [Washington: Institute for Palestinian Studies,

1992]) and Walid Khalidi by Ilan Pappe, "Were They Expelled? The History, Historiography and Relevance of the Palestinian Refugee Problem," in *The Palestinian Exodus, 1948–1998*, edited by Ghada Karmi and Eugene Cotran (Reading [UK]: Ithaca Press, 1999), 37–61.

12. Berkeley: University of California Press, 2000. See book jacket.

13. See earlier discussion on the land as holy, pp. 53–60.

14. For Jesus' connection to Jerusalem, especially a reimaging of the last week before his death, see Bargil Pixner, OSB, *With Jesus in Jerusalem: His First and Last Days in Judea* (Rosh Pina [Israel]: Corazin Publishing, 1996).

15. See Father Rafiq Khoury, "The History of Jerusalem: A Christian Perspective," in *The Spiritual Significance of Jerusalem for Jews, Christians and Muslims*, ed. Hans Ucko, (World Council of Churches, 1994), 9–20, and Archbishop Timotheos of Lydda, "Jerusalem's Significance in Scripture and Tradition: A Christian Perspective," 57–66.

16. For the history of this site from the first century CE, including the building of the first church (begun in 326 and dedicated in 335) under the reign of Constantine, see Jerome Murphy-O'Connor, OP, *The Holy Land*, 4th ed., revised and expanded (Oxford: Oxford University Press, 1998), 45–59.

17. David Thomas links Abraham with the Muslim tradition in "Abraham in Islamic Tradition," *Scripture Bulletin* 37 (2007) 1:12–20.

18. John Kaltner, *Ishmael Instructs Isaac: An Introduction to the Qur'an for Bible Readers* (Collegeville, MN: Liturgical Press, 1999), 104. Chapter 3 discusses Abraham in great detail (pp. 87–131; also note Kaltner's comments on the Islamization of the Abraham tradition, pp. 103-6).

19. Dr. Yunis Amr, "The Holy Land in the Islamic Heritage," in *The Holy Land in the Monotheistic Faiths*, ed. Roger Williamson (Uppsala: Life & Peace Institute, 1992), 53.

20. Ibid., 57.

21. See Thomas, "Abraham in Islamic Tradition," 17–18.

22. Kaltner, *Ishmael*, 124.

23. It seems obvious that with three competing religious claims, a way must be found to share this land.

24. "In the seventh century, the Arabs, fanning out northward, eastward and westward from the Arabian Peninsula (today's Saudi Arabia), established an empire extending from Persia to the Atlantic Ocean. Palestine was swept into this empire between 634 and 638 C.E. Under the new rulers, the central portion of the country was made into a separate province called Jund Filastin, with its capital at Ramle (the only city in the Holy Land founded by the Arabs), while the northern part of the country was included in the Jund al-Urdunn (Jordan). Although never an administrative centre,

Jerusalem came to be the third Moslem holy city, after Mecca and Medina"
(Editors of Carta and Moshe Aumann, *Carta's Historical Atlas of Israel*
[Jerusalem: Carta, 1983], 18).

25. Reuven Firestone, "One Holy Land, Three Holy Peoples: Islamic,
Christian, and Jewish Regard for the Holy City," www.umass.edu/jewish/
programs/firestone_talk/ 2002.

26. John Kelsay, "Dar Al-Islam," in the *Encyclopedia of Islam and the
Muslim World*, ed. Richard C. Martin (New York: Macmillan Reference
USA, 2004), 1:169.

27. Ibid.

28. Mohammad-Reza Djalili, "Dar Al-Harb," in *The Oxford
Encyclopedia of the Modern Islamic World*, ed. John L. Esposito (New York:
Oxford University Press, 1995), 1:337.

29. The problem of interpretation is discussed by the respected
Islamic scholar Sherman A. Jackson from the University of Michigan in
"Islam(s) East and West: Pluralism between No-Frills and Designer
Fundamentalism," in *September 11 in History: A Watershed Moment?* ed.
Mary L. Dudziak (Durham: Duke University Press, 2003), 112–35. Sherman
says that the "synergy between Sunnism's doctrine of Prophetic infallibility
and the juridical principle of unanimous consensus (*ijma'*) constituted in
effect classical Islam's 'free speech' provision. As long as an advocate's view
was grounded in authentic and authoritative sources and based on recognized
interpretive methods, no one could deny him the right to express it—regardless of its substance—as long as it did not violate a preexisting unanimous
consensus. Concomitantly, while there might be many views that could justi-
fiably claim to represent an 'Islamic' position, the only views that could
claim to represent *the* 'Islamic' position were those that were backed by
unanimous consensus" (123). Therefore, a rigorous interpretation of *dar al-
islam* and *dar al-harb* does not merit unanimous consent/agreement as to
their claims over the land for Muslims. I owe the references and insight to
discussion with Thomas E. R. Maguire, Center for International Education at
the University of Wisconsin, Milwaukee.

30. See discussion and citations above.

31. For a discussion of the issues since the withdrawal of Israelis from
the Gaza strip in 2005, the victory of Hamas in 2006, and the prospect of a
two-state solution versus a one-state solution, see Rashid Khalidi, *The Iron
Cage: The Story of the Palestinian Struggle for Statehood* (Boston: Beacon
Press, 2006), especially chapter 6, "Stateless in Palestine," 182–217. Khalidi
believes there will be no resolution as long as "there is a continuing refusal to
look honestly at what has happened in this small land over the past century or
so, and especially at how repeatedly forcing the Palestinians into an impossi-

ble corner, into an iron cage, has brought, and ultimately can bring, no lasting good to anyone" (217).

32. This Arabic word means "emigration" and refers to Muhammad's emigration from Mecca to Medina in 622. This took place because of his lack of success in preaching to the inhabitants in Mecca. In Medina, he was quickly successful and the year 622 CE of his *hijra* became the date AH 1 (*anno Hegirae*) in the Muslim calendar. See "Hijra" in *The HarperCollins Dictionary of Religion*, ed. Jonathan Z. Smith (HarperSanFrancisco, 1995), 419.

33. See a description of this journey in Dorothy Drummond, *Holy Land, Whose Land? Modern Dilemma Ancient Roots*, 2nd rev. ed. (Terre Haute [IN]: Fairhurst Press, 2004), 170. At this time, the Temple Mount only contained the ruins of the Second Temple, which was destroyed in 70 CE.

34. A year later, this direction was changed to face Mecca and the Kaaba. Some think this occurred because of the prophet's difficulties with the Jewish community of Medina. Dr. Ghada Talhami, "The History of Jerusalem: A Muslim Perspective," in *The Spiritual Significance of Jerusalem for Jews, Christians and Muslims*, ed. Hans Ucko (World Council of Churches, 1994), 21–22.

35. The name means "the furthermost sanctuary" (from Mecca and Medina). For the history, archaeology, and description of the structures on the Temple Mount (called the Haram esh-Sharif/the Noble Sanctuary in Muslim tradition), see Murphy-O'Connor, *Holy Land*, 80–96.

36. For the detailed building history, see Murphy-O'Connor, *Holy Land*, 94–95.

37. This prohibition included another Jewish holy place, the Tomb of Rachel, in Bethlehem—a site holy to Jews and Muslims. For the Rachel traditions in Judaism, Christianity, and Islam, and a thorough discussion of the site, see Fred Strickert, *Rachael Weeping: Jews, Christians, and Muslims at the Fortress Tomb* (Collegeville, MN: Liturgical Press, 2007).

38. This site has been a source of continual controversy. Most recently (2006–2007) the so-called "Stables of Solomon," which is a large underground area under the Temple Mount used by the Crusaders to stable their warhorses (see Murphy-O'Connor, *Holy Land*, 95–96), has been reconstructed into a very large mosque with concomitant destruction of archaeological evidence. For further discussion of construction on top of the Temple Mount and rebuilding of a ramp from the Western Wall to the Temple Mount, see Hershel Shanks, "Sifting the Temple Mount Dump," *BAR* 31, no. 4 (2005): 14–15; Hershel Shanks, "Israeli Authorities Acquiesce in Destruction of Temple Mount Antiquities," *BAR* 34, no. 3 (2008): 22, and Yuval Baruch, "The Mughrabi Gate Access—The Real Story," www.antiquities.org.il—access "articles."

39. For the history, archaeology, and description, see Murphy-O'Connor, *Holy Land*, 80–96.

40. "In 1967 at the end of the Six-Day War, when Israel has conquered all of Jerusalem, Moshe Dayan, then the country's defense minister, gives authority over the Haram al-Sharif to the Waqf, the Islamic organization responsible for its maintenance. The only condition Dayan sets is that all persons should henceforth have access to the Mount, to which the Waqf agrees" (Drummond, *Holy Land, Whose Land*? 35).

41. See Genesis 23.

42. Opposite the patriarchs lie the tombs of Sarah, Rebecca, and Leah [with Rachel's in Bethlehem]. This site is also holy to Jews and Christians, although nowadays it is not ordinarily a place of Christian pilgrimage.

43. See Hebron in Murphy-O'Connor, *Holy Land*, 273–77.

44. PBUH="Peace be upon him," a blessing uttered by Muslims whenever the name of Muhammad is spoken.

45. Dr. Yunis Amer, "Jerusalem's Significance in Scripture and Tradition: A Muslim Perspective," in Ucko, *The Spiritual Significance*, 68.

46. Palestinians claim that although they have equal standing in law in Israel, in actual practice they are "second-class" citizens.

47. See David Rudge, "Israeli Arabs still feel like second-class citizens," *Jerusalem Post* (March 7, 2004): 3.

5. THE STATE OF ISRAEL

1. This means literally "standing" prayer, which contained eighteen Benedictions. The roots of this prayer were in existence before the time of Jesus and the current formulation dates from the early centuries CE. See the discussion in Jeffery M. Cohen, *Blessed Are You: A Comprehensive Guide to Jewish Prayer* (Northvale [NJ]: Jason Aronson, 1993), 29–40.

2. Slightly revised English translation of the tenth and fourteenth Benediction from the *Prayer Book*, The Commission on Jewish Chaplaincy of the National Jewish Welfare Board, 1958, 57, 61. Compare the traditional English translation and Hebrew in *The Authorised Daily Prayer Book*, rev. ed. by Dr. Joseph H. Hertz (New York: Bloch Publishing Company, 1975), 143, 145–46.

3. Hertz, *The Authorised Daily Prayer Book*, 969, 973, and 975. This prayer probably goes back to the time of the Second Temple since Josephus speaks of it; see discussion in Evelyn Garfiel, *Service of the Heart: A Guide to the Jewish Prayer Book* (Northvale [NJ]: Jason Aronson, 1994 [1958]), 201–11.

4. Dan Cohn-Sherbok, *Israel: The History of an Idea* (London: SPCK, 1992), 1, 148. There are many monumental histories of the Jewish people, including those that trace the rise of the Zionist movement in the nineteenth century; Cohn-Sherbok's is the most readable, brief, popular account that attempts to provide "a succinct historical survey of this…longing for a Jewish homeland" from the time of the patriarchs to the present day. It is not an uncritical survey as he discusses religious and spiritual Zionism, secular Zionism, Anti-Zionism, as well as the intifada and the challenge of justice for the Palestinians.

5. There are many histories of the rise of Zionism, the reactions to it, and the development of this movement for the reestablishment of a Jewish national state in Palestine. For a readable popular treatment see: A. James Rudin, "The Rise of Modern Zionism," in *Israel for Christians: Understanding Modern Israel* (Philadelphia: Fortress Press, 1983), 23–40, and for a more detailed study, see Walter Laqueur, *A History of Zionism: From the French Revolution to the Establishment of the State of Israel* (New York: MJF Books, 1972).

6. M. Lowenthal, ed., *The Diaries of Theodor Herzl* (London: Jewish Publication Society, 1958), 426.

7. Cited by Father Jean Paul Lichtenberg, OP, in his brief monograph *From the First to the Last of the Just: A Study of the History of the Relations Between Jews and Christians Throughout the Centuries* (Jerusalem: Ecumenical Theological Research Fraternity in Israel, 1975), 43, n. 81.

8. The text of the "Fundamental Agreement Between the Holy See and the State of Israel" can be found in Ronald H. Isaacs and Kerry M. Olitzky, eds., *Critical Documents of Jewish History*, A Source Book (Northvale [NJ]: Jason Aronson, 1995), 274–80. On August 16, 1994, the apostolic pro-nuncio, Archbishop Andrea di Montezemolo, presented his credentials to President Chaim Weizmann of the State of Israel and became the first ambassador (apostolic nuncio) of the Vatican to the Jewish State of Israel.

9. I can find no public statement to this effect from the Vatican at the time of the declaration of the reestablishment of the State of Israel in 1948. Negative, though unofficial, statements abound in the "semiofficial" *Civiltà Cattolica*. This journal was founded by the Jesuits in 1850 to defend the religious and political views of the Vatican and is considered to express the views of the Vatican in its articles. Negative views are also consistently found in the official Vatican daily *L'Osservatore Romano*. See the extensive discussion by Sister Charlotte Klein in her two articles: "Vatican and Zionism, 1897–1967," *Christian Attitudes on Jews and Judaism*, nos. 36–37 (1974), 11–16, and "Vatican View of Jewry, 1939–1962, in the Mirror of *Civiltà Cattolica*," *Christian Attitudes on Jews and Judaism*, no. 43 (1976),

12–16. Klein thoroughly documents the hostile and rejectionist view of the Vatican toward Herzl, Zionism, Jewish issues, and the State of Israel. It's not until 1964 that any positive change takes place, which she attributes to Vatican II, Cardinal Bea, many American bishops, and Pope John XXIII — see pp. 15–16.

10. Interview in *Parade* magazine on April 3, 1994; excerpts from Pope John Paul II, *Spiritual Pilgrimage*, 187.

11. "...the Church keeps ever before her mind the words of the apostle Paul about his kinsmen: 'they are Israelites, and to them belong the sonship, the glory, the covenants, the giving of the law, the worship, and the promises; to them belong the patriarchs, and of their race according to the flesh, is the Christ' (Rom 9:4–5)." *Nostra Aetate*, no. 4 in *Vatican Council II: The Conciliar and Post Conciliar Documents*, ed. Austin Flannery, OP. 1981 edition (Northport [NY]:Costello Publishing Co., 1975), 740.

12. Pope John Paul II, *Spiritual Pilgrimage*, 187–88.

13. "Encyclical of our Holy Father Pope Pius XII on Palestine" [*In Multiplicibus Curis*], *CBQ* 11 (1949): 89.

14. See map of proposed boundaries in Martin Gilbert, *The Dent Atlas of the Arab-Israeli Conflict*, 6th ed. (London: Dent, 1993), 36.

15. *Civiltà Cattolica* commentary as reported in Klein, "Vatican and Zionism," 14.

16. Ibid., 15–16.

17. Anthony Kenny, *Catholics, Jews and the State of Israel* (New York: Paulist Press, 1993).

18. See my comments earlier on the current state of the church's teaching on the Jewish people in fourteen different areas beginning on p. 7; number 7 treats the State of Israel, p. 9.

19. Dr. Meir Mendes, "The Catholic Church, Judaism and the State of Israel," *Christian Jewish Relations*, 21, no. 2 (1988): 28.

20. Apostolic Letter of John Paul II (*Redemptionis Anno*), in *Spiritual Pilgrimage*, 35.

21. Ibid., 36.

22. Ibid.

23. Ibid.

24. Merkley traces the development leading to the eventual diplomatic recognition of the State of Israel by the Holy See (Vatican City State); see Paul Charles Merkley, *Christian Attitudes towards the State of Israel* (Montreal: McGill-Queen's University Press, 2001), 151–54.

25. Kenny, *Israel*, 116–17.

26. Background report, "Israel-Vatican relations: A long, slow thaw," by Haim Shapiro in *The Jerusalem Post*, Tuesday, February 4, 1997.

27. It seems apparent that the rapid signing after the first formal announcement was made to forestall any possible organized public protest by those still opposing the diplomatic recognition of Israel by the Vatican— notably among some Palestinian Christians (both Roman Catholic and others) as well as possible protests from other Western and Arab Christians in the Middle East.

28. *Christians and Israel*, 3, no. 1 (Winter 1993/1994): 4.

29. Ibid.

30. Ibid., 8.

31. The Vatican City State is a pale shadow of the nineteenth-century Papal States and in size even smaller (number of acres=109) than the tiny Principality of Monaco (number of acres = 320), yet in influence it could, in many ways, be considered a "superpower"; Israel, on the other hand most resembles other nation states in the United Nations, yet it, too, has significance transcending its apparent size and "might."

32. See above, p. 9.

33. From the time of the Crusader capture of Jerusalem in 1099, there has been tension between the Latin Church and the Eastern (Orthodox) Church. Nowadays the "status quo" refers to "the arrangements existing in 1852 [= the decree (*firman*) issued by the Ottoman government known today as the "Status Quo," see Bailey, *Who Are the Christians*, 91] which correspond to the Status Quo of 1757 as to the rights and privileges of the Christian communities officiating in the Holy Places [which] have to be most meticulously observed, and what each rite practiced at that time in the way of public worship, decorations of altars and shrines, use of lamps, candelabra, tapestry and pictures, and in the exercise of the most minute acts of ownership and usage has to remain unaltered. Moreover, the Status Quo applies also to the nature of the officiants" (Lincoln G. A. Cust, *The Status Quo in the Holy Places* [Jerusalem: Ariel Publishing, 1980 (facsimile edition of 1929)], 11). The holy places affected by the Status Quo are (1) the Holy Sepulcher with all its dependencies, (2) the Deir al Sultan [a convent adjacent to the Church of the Holy Sepulcher], (2) the Sanctuary of the Ascension [on the Mount of Olives], (4) the Tomb of the Virgin [near Gethsemane], and (5) the Church of the Nativity [in Bethlehem]. Two Jewish sites are also included in the Status Quo agreement, namely, the Western Wall and Rachel's Tomb [near Bethlehem].

34. Fundamental Agreement, article 11, par. 2.

35. As of June 2, 2003, the ambassador to the Vatican is Oded Ben Hur.

36. Official translation of the ambassador's address, which was given in Spanish, in the Vatican's *Information Service*, no. 88 (1995/1): 39.

37. Ibid., 40.

38. Ibid., 38–39, for the complete response.

39. *Information Service*, no. 91 (1996/I–II): 56.

40. A networking organization, founded on January 16, 1991, the eve of the Gulf War, to "promote greater mutual understanding among people of different faith communities" in Israel. Their 1996–1997 *Guide to Interreligious and Intercultural Activities in Israel* (published by ICCI, Jerusalem 91078, Israel) lists sixty-one different member organizations. As of 2005 their Web site, www.icci.co.il/, lists seventy member organizations.

41. Rabbi Ronald Kronish, "The Implications of the Peace Agreements for Interreligious/Intercultural Relations in Israel," *SIDIC* 29, nos. 2–3 (1996): 35.

42. The other co-sponsors were: The Rabbi Marc H. Tanenbaum Foundation, Foundation to Advance Interfaith Trust and Harmony (FAITH), Israel Jewish Council for Interreligious Relations (IJCIR), and in cooperation with the ministry of foreign affairs of the State of Israel.

43. Dr. Ron Kronish and Emily Michelson, "A Summary of ICCI's Recent Symposium in Jerusalem," *Insight Israel* #3 (2/26/97) from the ICCI (see web address above n. 40), an e-mail subscription service of ICCI, p. 2. Cardinal Cassidy's talk, "The Next Issues in Jewish-Catholic Relations," can be found in *Origins* 26 (1997): 665, 667–70.

44. From the author's notes of the conference and audio tapes.

45. His talk, "Jewish-Catholic Relations After the Fundamental Agreement," is published in *Origins* 26 (1997): 671–74.

46. In private discussion with the author and partly in the discussion period after the talks by Winer and Brunett. Not to my knowledge in any published form by him.

47. "Founded in 1966 by a group of theologians and clergy living in Israel, it was established to draw personnel together into a theological fraternity; to help the Christian Church to understand itself in the new situation; to deepen the Christian relationship with Jews, Judaism and Israel" (*Guide*, 30).

48. Drawn from the article by Petra Heldt and Malcolm Lowe, "Theological Significance of the Rebirth of the State of Israel: Different Christian Attitudes," *Immanuel* 22/23 (1989): 133–45, and the report of an Israel Colloquium Program at Hebrew University ("Christians in the Middle East") by Rev. Petra Heldt in *Christians and Israel* 2, no. 4 (Autumn 1993): 4–5. For a more extended discussion, see Paul Charles Merkley, *Christian Attitudes Towards the State of Israel* (Montreal: McGill-Queen's University Press, 2001). Most of this book treats attitudes of Protestants—especially Evangelicals and Christian Zionists. There is a brief chapter on "Roman Catholic Attitudes in Transition" (134–60).

49. For detailed comments on the non-Chalcedonian Churches, see Thordson, *Christians*, 29–43.

50. Heldt, "Theological Significance," 134.

51. The ICEJ was founded "in 1980 to demonstrate worldwide Christian support for Israel and for Jerusalem as its eternal capital.... It is a center where Christians from all over the world can gain a correct biblical understanding of Israel and learn to be rightly related to the nation" (*Guide*, 40). Its first director was the Dutch Christian, Jan Willem van der Hoeven. In November 2000, Reverend Malcolm Hedding was appointed executive director. For further information see www.icej.org/.

52. See additional comments on Protestant churches, Heldt, "Theological Significance," 137–42.

53. *The MECC: A Introduction to the Middle East Council of Churches*, 1st ed. (Limassol [Cyprus]: MECC Communications, 1995), 6.

54. Ibid., 11. Yet there is no chair listed for this program, see p. 41.

55. John T. Pawlikowski, OSM, "The Vatican-Israeli Accords: Their Implications for Catholic Faith and Teaching," *PACE* 24 (November 1994): 20.

56. On both grounds of the Hebrew scriptures and the Christian scriptures (including an understanding of the Incarnation), I believe Father Pawlikowski misses the point of holiness. Holiness (*Kadosh*) refers to a setting apart for a special purpose or task, for example, God desires a people "holy" to him. The theological notion of a priestly people applied to both Israel and in Christian thought refers to a special task or purpose of the people (*mutans mutandis*, to the land of Israel). As the rabbis taught that all the Earth was holy (created by God, linked to him, and set apart for his purpose), the holiest land on Earth was Israel, and the holiest part of Israel was the holy city of Jerusalem, the holiest part of Jerusalem was the Temple Mount, and the holiest part of the Temple Mount was the Holy of Holies itself! This tradition articulates a theology of divine presence, that is, of degrees of awareness and intensity of presence. See below for a Catholic articulation of this theology. In any event, Pawlikowski is mistaken in his understanding of the leveling out of holiness, which in effect makes nothing holy rather than equalizing holiness!

57. Pawlikowski, "Vatican-Israel Accords," 20.

58. *Providence Journal Bulletin* (Providence, RI), April 26, 1996, as cited on www.nclci.org/articles/art-flan-ethos.htm.

59. "A Christian View of Israel," *United Synagogue Review* (Fall 1971): 10.

60. "The Challenges We Jointly Face: A Catholic View," *Face to Face* 12 (Fall, 1985): 48.

61. J. Christiaan Beker has brought this into sharp focus in *Paul's Apocalyptic Gospel* (Philadelphia: Fortress Press, 1982) and in *The Triumph of God* (Minneapolis: Fortress Press, 1990).

62. Some have argued that this fervent expectation of the Second Coming waned toward the end of Paul's ministry, yet James D. G. Dunn says that "there is a striking consistency in imminence of expectation throughout the undisputed letters of Paul. Paul's sense of 'eager expectation' of the final denouement is as fresh in the later letters as in the early (Gal 5:5; 1 Cor 1:7; Rom 8:19, 23, 25; Phil 3:20).... Similarly with the assertions in Rom 13:11–12 that 'now is our salvation nearer than when we [first] believed' and that 'the night is far advanced, the day is at hand'" (*The Theology of Paul the Apostle* [Grand Rapids: Eerdmans, 1998], 311).

63. Jesus says in Mark 8:34 (// Mt 16:24) that one must take up the cross and follow him—a one-time event in expectation of the end-time; whereas Jesus says in Luke 9:23 that one must *daily* take up the cross and follow him. In the last book written in the Christian scriptures (ca. 130 CE), 2 Peter 3:3–4, 8–10 refutes those who scoff at the Second Coming because of its long delay. This event has not yet occurred because God is patient with those who need to repent; Jesus' return will surely occur in God's own good time.

64. For the quality of the messianic age see Micah 4:1–5 // Isaiah 2:2–4; 9:5–6; 11; Zechariah 9:9–10.

65. "Any time is a potential time for the coming of Mashiach. This does not mean, however, that at the appropriate time he will suddenly emerge from Heaven to appear on earth. On the contrary: Mashiach is already on earth, a human being of great saintly status (a *tzadik*) appearing and existing in every generation. 'In every generation is born a progeny of Judah fit to be Israel's Mashiach!'" (Jacob Immanuel Schochet, *Mashiach: The Principle of Mashiach and the Messianic Era in Jewish Law and Tradition*, 3rd ed. [New York: S.I.E., 1992], 38–39).

66. "When the Messianic idea appears as a living force in the world of Judaism—especially in that of medieval Judaism, which seems so totally interwoven with the realm of the *Halakhah*—it always occurs in the closest connection with apocalypticism" (Gershom Scholem, *The Messianic Idea in Judaism* [New York: Schocken Books, 1971], 4). Chapter 1, "Toward an Understanding of the Messianic idea in Judaism" (1–36), is a particularly good overview of this concept in Judaism.

67. TANAKH is an acronym formed from the initial letter of the three divisions of the Hebrew scriptures/Hebrew Bible: **T**orah (teaching or instruction=the first five books), **N**eviim (prophets, including not only what Christians call the major and minor prophets but also including Joshua, Judges, Samuel, and Kings), and lastly the **K**ethuvim (the remainder of the Bible including psalms and wisdom literature).

68. See the documentation in chapter 1 (above), especially the Statement on Catholic-Jewish Relations by the U.S. National Conference of Catholic Bishops, November 20, 1975.

69. Ibid.

70. Rabbi David Hartman has been called "Israel's paramount religious philosopher" in a profile, "Sage in a Land of Anger," *Time* magazine, April 30, 1990, 90–91.

71. A good summary of his position is found in the chapter, "The Challenge of Modern Israel to Traditional Judaism," in *Conflicting Visions: Spiritual Possibilities of Modern Israel* (New York: Schocken Books, 1990), 31–53. This thesis was first presented in *Modern Judaism* 7, no. 3 (October 1987): 229–52.

72. The author was present at Hartman's lecture at the Tantur Ecumenical Institute, Jerusalem, "New Directions and Challenges for Religious Zionism," March 6, 1997 (from tape).

73. What this means is found in the passage in the Babylonian Talmud (Eruvin 13b) as Rabbi Hartman recounts the story and the interpretation drawn from it: "The rival schools of Hillel and Shammai were so much in disagreement that the Torah threatened to become two Torahs, with the community divided totally. This dispute ended only when a heavenly voice was heard, saying 'These and these are the words of the living God, but the *Halakhah* is according to Hillel.' Either would be acceptable, so why did God prefer Hillel? The Talmud answers: because when he used to speak in the house of learning, he would always begin by mentioning Shammai's position first. He was so 'kindly and modest' that when he spoke to his students, he told them first the contrary view and argued to its plausibility, and only then he presented his own opinion. He never taught Torah pretending to possess the unique truth, but admitting that two opinions might have plausibility and meaning. So let us also belong to teachers who taught a way of commitment to Judaism and the love of God, while maintaining the unsettling assertion that 'these and these are the words of the living God'" ("Judaism Encounters Christianity Anew," in *Visions of the Other: Jewish and Christian Theologians Assess the Dialogue*, ed. Eugene J. Fisher [New York: Paulist, 1994], 80).

74. Hartman, *Conflicting Visions*, 39–40.

75. Ibid., 41.

76. This refers to the Haredim (pl.), which literally means "reverently fearful," from the Hebrew *hared*, "fearful, trembling, pious"; commonly used of the ultra-Orthodox Jews. Israeli estimates place their number between 250,000 and 300,000. To varying degrees they all support the state and take part in Israeli institutions; only the radical Hasidic sect, the Satmar, bitterly and hatefully oppose the state. In the Mea Shearim section of

Jerusalem, the ultra-Orthodox area, one can still find such slogans attacking Zionism and the state as "Nazi" type institutions. These extreme views are held by only a very small portion of the ultra-Orthodox. For a thorough discussion see the *Encyclopaedia Judaica*, ed. Cecil Roth (Jerusalem: Keter Publishing, 1972) 15: 908–10.

77. Hartman, *Conflicting Visions*, 48–49.

78. These are the two small leather boxes containing four passages from the scriptures (Exod 13:1–10, 11–16; Deut 6:4–9; 11:13–21). "In accordance with Deut 6:8, they are worn by adult male Jews, bound by leather straps to the arm and the head. Their purpose is to remind the wearer to keep the law" (Cohn-Sherbok, *The Blackwell Dictionary of Judaica* [Oxford: Blackwell Publishers, 1992], 537). The New Testament incorrectly refers to tefillin as "phylacteries" (Matt 23:5), which means "amulet" in Greek.

79. Hartman, "Judaism Encounters Christianity Anew," 77-78.

80. Answer period at talk at Tantur, see n. 70.

81. Hartman is not clear in his writing whether Zionism and the hope for reestablishing a State of Israel had this covenantal dimension from its origin, even though it may not have been so expressed by early Zionist leaders. Or whether this covenantal view has been developing over a long period and has now come clearly to light.

82. *Lumen Gentium*, no. 8 in *Vatican Council II: The Conciliar and Post Conciliar Documents*, edited by Austin Flannery, OP, (Northport [NY]: Costello, 1981), 357.

83. Ibid.

84. Richard P. McBrien, *Catholicism*, revised and updated (San Francisco: Harper Collins, 1994), 670. The correctness of this interpretation is brought out in the discussion that took place at an International Theological Conference at the University of Notre Dame, March 20–26, 1966, in an exchange on no. 8 of *Lumen Gentium*: Thomas F. Stransky, CSP (Secretariat for the Promotion of Christian Unity) said, "I think what Professor [William] Wolf [Episcopal Theological School] was getting at was perhaps not understood by Canon Moeller [Louvain University]. This is perhaps the most important one-word change in Vatican Council II—*subsists in*. The reason officially given was that *de facto* there does exist outside the visible boundaries of the Catholic Church *elementa bona sanctificationis*. I think this is a crucial issue for a theology of the Christian divisions, the relationship not only of individuals, but of non-Roman Catholic Christian communities, to the Roman Catholic Church, and vice versa. Much of it is based, I think, on this distinction between *est* and *subsistit in*. In fact, we do not have all of the Christian elements of sanctification existing within the Catholic Church. And what does this mean when we talk about where is, not subsists but where is the one, holy, catholic and apostolic Church professed

by the creed." Following a further clarification of Canon Moeller's thought, Yves M. J. Congar, OP (editor, *Unam Sanctam*), says, "What I want to say has already been partly said by Father Stransky. It appears to me that Canon Moeller has explained 'subsists in' as if it were a question of the mystical body and union of Christ, whereas *it is essentially a matter of the [Roman Catholic] Church as a society* [emphasis added]. And it seems to me that the intention of 'subsists in,' as was said at the Council, is not to unchurch the other churches, not to disqualify other churches as churches. That is why this expression was repeated, at least by way of the allusion, at the beginning of the Declaration on Religious Freedom" (John H. Miller, CSC, ed., *Vatican II: An Interfaith Appraisal* [Notre Dame: University of Notre Dame Press, 1966], 179–80.

85. Cardinal Johannes Willebrands, "Vatican II's Ecclesiology of Communion," *Origins* 17, no. 2 (May 28, 1987): 31.

86. Ibid., 32.

87. "Statement on Catholic-Jewish Relations," National Conference of Catholic Bishops, November 20, 1975.

6. ISSUES, REFLECTIONS, AND CONCLUSIONS

1. The Noahide laws are traditionally enumerated as: the prohibitions of idolatry, blasphemy, bloodshed, sexual sins, theft, and eating from a living animal, as well as the injunction to establish a legal system. They are derived from the commands addressed to Adam (Gen 2:16) and to Noah (Gen 9:4–7). Since they are addressed to the biblical progenitors of all humankind, they are regarded as universal.

2. Although the number of Noahide laws has fluctuated, the fact of their existence and the promise of a place in the world to come for the righteous Gentiles is not in question during the first century of the Christian era. For a more detailed discussion, see, Steven S. Schwarzschild and Saul Berman, "Noahide Laws," in *Encyclopedia Judaica* (Jerusalem: Macmillian, 1971), vol. 12, 1189–91.

3. This term is used by Luke in Acts 10:2, 22, 35; 13:16, 26. See the discussion of "Righteous Gentiles" and the "God-fearers" in Terence L. Donaldson, *Paul and the Gentiles: Remapping the Apostle's Convictional World* (Minneapolis: Fortress Press, 1997), 65–69; Joseph A. Fitzmyer, SJ, *The Acts of the Apostles*, AB, 31 (New York: Doubleday, 1998), 446–52, and for the cultural context see Ben Witherington III, *The Acts of the Apostles: A Socio-Rhetorical Commentary* (Grand Rapids: Eerdmans, 1998), 341–44. Even the usually very skeptical Gerd Luedemann accepts the existence of "godfearer" during the Second Temple period—if not earlier. See his *Early*

Christianity according to the Traditions in Acts: A Commentary, trans. John Bowden (Minneapolis: Fortress, 1989), 155–56.

4. See discussion below on *Dabru Emet* in note 14.

5. Franz Rosenzweig, *The Star of Redemption*, trans. 2nd ed. of 1930 by William W. Hallo (New York: Holt, Rinehart and Winston, 1971). Norbert M. Samuelson attempts to present the simple meaning of Rosenzweig's philosophically complex thought in *A User's Guide to Franz Rosenzweig's Star of Redemption* (Surrey [England]: Curzon Press, 1999). See chapter 2, "The Rays, or the Eternal Way," 274–331, which gives a clear view of Judaism and Christianity and their interrelatedness.

6. Jeremy Worthen demonstrates that this is an erroneous view in "Beginning Without End: Christianity in Franz Rosenzweig's *Star of Redemption*," *Journal of Ecumenical Studies* 39 (2002): 340–62.

7. Ibid., 349.

8. Ibid.

9. Michael S. Kogan, "Toward a Jewish Theology of Christianity," *JES* 32 (1995): 92. Kogan first explored the possibility of a mutual affirmation of Jews and Christians in "Jews and Christians: Taking the Next Step," *JES* 26 (1989): 703–13. In this article, he puts his finger on the critical problem for Christians: "how to be faithful to the New Testament command to witness for Christ to all peoples and to convert all nations, while, at the same time, affirming the ongoing validity of the covenant between God and Israel viz. Abraham and Moses. Can the church have it both ways?" (p. 705). Philip A. Cunningham has proposed a nuanced theological view upholding Christ's universally salvific mission without requiring Jewish conversion to Christianity either now or in the end-time. See "A Covenantal Christology" in the new peer-reviewed e-journal of the Council of Centers on Jewish-Christian Relations, published by the Center for Christian-Jewish learning at Boston College. Go to www.bc.edu/research/cjl/ and access *Studies in Christian-Jewish Relations* 1 (2005–2006), 41–52, note p. 48, and conclusions pp. 51–52.

10. Ibid.

11. Ibid., 98, 101.

12. Ibid., 152.

13. Ibid., 96.

14. The title *Dabru Emet* comes from Zechariah 8:16: "These then are the things you should do: *Speak the truth* to one another; let there be honesty and peace in the judgments at your gates." The full document can be found at www.bc.edu/research/cjl… and in the collection of essays on the affirmations of *Dabru Emet*: *Christianity in Jewish Terms*, eds. Tikva Frymer-Kensky, David Novak, et al. (Boulder [CO]: Westview Press, 2000); the document is found on pp. xvii–xx. An interesting collection of papers from

the conference "Jews and Christians: People of God" at Augsburg College, Minneapolis, Minnesota, June 10–12, 2001, concerning issues in *Dabru Emet* has been published as *Jews and Christians: People of God*, ed. Carl E. Braaten and Robert W. Jenson (Grand Rapids: Eerdmans, 2003). Except for the insightful response by Rabbi Barry Cytron (192–96), the three papers at the end of the volume from Christian scholars from a symposium dealing with *Dabru Emet* (183–92) either missed the central points of *Dabru Emet* or were partisan and polemical. An excellent resource guide and study text for *Dabru Emet* has been edited by David F. Sandmel, Rosann M. Catalano, and Christopher M. Leighton, *Irreconcilable Differences? A Learning Resource for Jews and Christians* (Boulder [CO], Westview Press, 2001).

15. See Jacob Neusner's popular treatise, *Judaism in the Beginning of Christianity* (Philadelphia: Fortress Press, 1984).

16. Braaten, *Jews and Christians*, 181. The complete text of *Dabru Emet* is found on pages 179–82.

17. Pope John Paul II, Letter, "Pilgrimage to Places Linked to the History of Salvation," in *Origins* 29 (1999): 126.

18. Ibid., 125.

19. Ibid.

20. An account of this pilgrimage with the texts of all the pope's talks and commentary by a Christian and Jewish scholar can be found in *John Paul II in the Holy Land: In His Own Words*, with Christian and Jewish Perspectives by Yehezkel Landau and Michael McGarry, CSP, edited by Lawrence Boadt, CSP, and Kevin di Camillo (New York: Paulist Press, 2005).

21. Ibid., 127.

22. St. Bede (673–735 CE) was a biblical scholar and the "Father of English History" (*Oxford Dictionary of the Christian Church*, 148). Ibid., 84.

23. Alexander Schmemann, *For the Life of the World: Sacraments and Orthodoxy* (Crestwood [NY]: St. Vladimir's Seminary Press, 2000), 20. I owe this reference to Dr. Mark Schwehn, a scholar colleague in residence with me at the Collegeville Institute for Ecumenical & Cultural Research.

24. Alexander Schmemann, *Introduction to Liturgical Theology*, trans. Asheleigh E. Moorhouse (Crestwood [NY]: St. Vladimir's Seminary Press, 1986), 117.

25. Stephen C. Doyle, OFM, *The Pilgrim's New Guide to the Holy Land*, 2nd ed. (Collegeville, MN: Liturgical Press, 1999), 13. Doyle's book only includes the holy places and gives almost no notice to other sites, for example, Qumran, Masada, the Herodion, and Caesarea. Contrast Doyle's book with the archaeological and historical guide books of Jerome Murphy-O'Connor (*The Holy Land: An Oxford Archaeological Guide from Earliest Times to 1700*, 4th ed. [New York: Oxford University Press, 1998]) and G. S.

P. Freeman-Grenville (*The Holy Land: A Pilgrim's Guide to Israel, Jordan and the Sinai* [Jerusalem: Carta, 1996]), which are excellent treatises covering every conceivable site, but give not a word of prayer or religious meditation.

26. Ibid., 14.

27. Ibid., 16.

28. Bruce Feiler, *Walking the Bible* (New York: William Morrow, 2001).

29. Ibid., 10–11.

30. Ibid., 11–12.

31. Mark Twain, *The Innocents Abroad* or *The new Pilgrims' Progress* (Hartford: American Publishing Company, 1882, c1869).

32. Bruce Feiler, *Abraham* (New York: William Marrow, 2002), 10.

33. Ibid., 215–16.

34. Bruce Feiler, *Where God Was Born* (New York: William Morrow, 2005). Whereas Feiler spent one year trekking "across the Middle East, from Turkey to Jordan, and explored the first five books of the Bible," (3), for his third book he journeyed "to the flash points in the new world war over God—Israel, Iraq, and Iran—and [brought] along my Bible. And I [began] my quest with the second half of the Hebrew bible, at the moment when the children of Israel…face their harshest challenge. 'Conquer the Promised Land,' God says to Joshua, Moses' successor, at the start of the book of the Prophets"[=beginning with the Book of Joshua, for the Catholic description of the books] (4).

35. Ibid., 376.

36. Feiler, *Walking*, 421.

37. As Paul says, "…yet I live, no longer I, but Christ lives in me" (Gal 2:20).

38. Feiler, *Walking*, 422–23.

39. Thomas Cahill, *How the Irish Saved Civilization* (New York: Nan A. Talese, Doubleday, 1995).

40. Thomas Cahill, *The Gifts of the Jews* (New York: Nan A. Talese, Doubleday, 1998).

41. Thomas Cahill, *Desire of the Everlasting Hills: The World before and after Jesus* (New York: Nan A. Talese, Doubleday, 1999), 8.

42. See his two excellent books, Elias Chacour with David Hazard, *Blood Brothers* (Grand Rapids: Chosen Books, 1984), and Elias Chacour with Mary E. Jensen, *We Belong to the Land: The story of a Palestinian Israeli who lives for Peace and Reconciliation* (San Francisco: Harper, 1990).

43. Chacour, *We Belong to the Land*, 196.

44. See the history, liturgy, and an interview with the Melkite patriarch, His Beatitude Gregorius III Laham, in Thordson, *Christians*, 48–52 and Bailey, *Who Are Christians?* 86–89.

45. Biram was the birth village and ancestral home of Chacour's family that was tragically destroyed in the war of 1948 and that Elias has been fighting to restore through the Israeli courts and peaceable actions. This is the primary focus of his first book, *Blood Brothers*.

46. The village where Chacour lives and pastors a Melkite Church there in the Galilee.

47. Chacour, *We Belong to the Land*, 8.

48. Much more could and should be said about the implications and consequences of identifying the Roman Catholic Church and the State of Israel as two manifestations of covenantal institutions of God. There are many books tracing the Arab-Israeli histories, wars, controversies, theological views, and histories of failed and successful negotiations between the parties. All of this must be left to a later book that the author hopes to write. For now, it is sufficient to set out the theoretical possibility of viewing the church and Israel as both covenantal institutions instituted and blessed by God.

Bibliography

Ali, Michael Nazir. "Christians in the Holy Land." In *Christians in the Holy Land*, edited by Michael Prior and William Taylor, 161–68. London: World of Islam Trust, 1994.

Amr, Dr. Yunis. "The Holy Land in the Islamic Heritage." In *The Holy Land in the Monotheistic faiths*, edited by Roger Williamson, 51–63. Uppsala: Life & Peace Institute, 1992.

———. "Jerusalem's Significance in Scripture and Tradition: A Muslim Perspective." In *The Spiritual Significance of Jerusalem for Jews, Christians and Muslims*, edited by Hans Ucko, 67–72. World Council of Churches, 1994.

Anderson, Francis I., and David Noel Freedman. *Amos*. Anchor Bible, 24A. New York: Doubleday, 1989.

———. *Hosea*. Anchor Bible, 24. New York: Doubleday, 1980.

"Anti-Semiticism." In *HarperCollins Dictionary of Religion*, edited by Jonathan Z. Smith, 53–54. SanFrancisco: HarperCollins, 1995.

Ateek, Naim. "Who is the Church? A Christian Theology for the Holy Land." In *The Christian Heritage in the Holy Land*, edited by Anthony O'Mahony, with Goran Gunner and Kevork Hintlian, 311–20. London: Scorpion Cavendish, 1995.

Aumann, Moshe, and Carta editors. *Carta's Historical Atlas of Israel*. Jerusalem: Carta, 1983.

The Authorized Daily Prayer Book. Revised edition by Dr. Joseph H. Hertz. New York: Bloch Publishing Company, 1975.

Bahat, Dan, ed. *Twenty Centuries of Jewish Life in the Holy Land: The Forgotten Generations*. 2nd edition. Jerusalem: The Israel Economist, 1976.

Bailey, Betty Jane, and J. Martin Bailey. *Who Are the Christians in the Middle East*? Grand Rapids: Eerdmans, 2003.

Beker, J. Christiaan. *Paul's Apocalyptic Gospel*. Philadelphia: Fortress Press, 1982.

———. *The Triumph of God*. Minneapolis: Fortress Press, 1990.

Bemporad, Rabbi Jack. "The Universal Cathechism's (*sic*) Teaching on the Jews and Judaism in the Context of the Documents Stemming from Vatican II and the Statements of Pope John Paul II." In *The Catholic*

Catechism on Jews and Judaism, Institute Paper, 15–32. South Orange, NJ: Institute of Judaeo-Christian Studies, 1996.

Benedict XVI, Pope. Address to the International Jewish Committee on Interreligious Consultations, June 9, 2005. http://www.bc.edu/research/cjl/meta-elements/texts/cjrelations/resources/documents/catholic/Benedict_XVI/IJCIC_9June05.htm.

Bishop, Claire Huchet. "Introduction to Jules Isaac." In Jules Isaac, *The Teaching of Contempt: The Christian Roots of Anti-Semitism*. Translated by Helen Weaver, 3–15. New York: Holt, Rinehart and Winston, 1964.

Blenkinsopp, Joseph. *The Pentateuch: An Introduction to the First Five Books of the Bible*. New York: Doubleday, 1992.

Blumenthal, David. "Antisemitism (Jewish View)." In *A Dictionary of the Jewish-Christian Dialogue*, expanded edition, edited by Leon Klenicki and Geoffrey Wigoder, 9–12. Mahwah, NJ: Paulist Press, 1995.

Boadt, Lawrence, and Kevin di Camillo, eds. *John Paul II in the Holy Land with Christian and Jewish Perspectives by Yehezkel Landau and Michael McGarry, CSP*. New York: Paulist Press, 2005.

Borowitz, Eugene. *Renewing the Covenant: A Theology for the Postmodern Jew*. Philadelphia: Jewish Publication Society, 1991.

Bowman, Glenn. "Contemporary Christian Pilgrimage to the Holy Land." In *The Christian Heritage in the Holy Land*, edited by Anthony O'Mahony with Goran Gunner and Kevorki Hintlian, 288–310. London: Scorpion Cavendish, 1995.

Boys, Mary C. "The Covenant in Contemporary Ecclesial Documents." In *Two Faiths, One Covenant?* edited by Eugene B. Korn and John T. Pawlikowski, OSM, 81–110. New York: Rowman & Littlefield Publishers, 2005.

————. "How Shall We Christians Understand Jews and Judaism? Questions about the New Catechism." *Theology Today* 53 (1995): 165–67.

————. "A More Faithful Portrait of Judaism: An Imperative for Christian Educators." In *Within Context: Essays on Jews and Judaism in the New Testament*, edited by David P. Efroymson, Eugene J. Fisher, and Leon Klenicki, 1–20. Mahwah, NJ: Paulist Press, 1993.

Braaten, Carl E., and Robert W. Jenson. *Jews and Christians: People of God*. Grand Rapids: Eerdmans, 2003.

Brown, Raymond E. *The Gospel According to John I–XII*. Anchor Bible, 29. Garden City: Doubleday, 1966.

————. *An Introduction to the New Testament*. New York: Doubleday, 1997.

————. "Not Jewish Christianity and Gentile Christianity but Types of Jewish/Gentile Christianity." *CBQ* 45 (1983): 74–79.

————. Joseph A. Fitzmyer, and Roland E. Murphy, eds. *The New Jerome Biblical Commentary.* Englewood Cliffs, NJ: Prentice-Hall, 1990.

Brueggemann, Walter. *The Land: Place as Gift, Promise, and Challenge in Biblical Faith.* 2nd edition. Minneapolis: Fortress Press, 2002.

————. *Tradition for Crisis: A Study in Hosea.* Richmond: John Knox Press, 1968.

Buber, Martin. *Israel and Palestine: History of an Idea.* Translated by Stenley Godman. London: East and West Library, 1952.

Bultmann, Rudolf. *The Gospel of John.* Translated by G. R. Beasley-Murray. Oxford: Basil Blackwell, 1971.

Buren, Paul van. *Christ in Context.* Part 3 of *A Theology of the Jewish-Christian Reality.* San Francisco: Harper & Row, 1988.

————. "Christ of the Church, Not the Messiah of Israel." *AAR/SBL Seminar Papers.* 1977, 15–16.

————. *A Christian Theology of the People Israel.* Part 2 of *A Theology of the Jewish-Christian Reality.* New York: Seabury, 1983.

"Caesarea" and "Sepphoris." In *The Archaeological Encyclopedia of the Holy Land,* edited by Avraham Negev and Shimon Gibson, 102–7, 454–56. Revised and updated. New York: Continuum, 2003.

Cahill, Thomas. *Desire of the Everlasting Hills: The World before and after Jesus.* New York: Nan A. Talese, Doubleday, 1999.

————. *The Gifts of the Jews.* New York: Nan A. Talese, Doubleday, 1998.

————. *How the Irish Saved Civilization.* New York: Nan A. Talese, Doubleday, 1995.

Cassidy, Idris Cardinal. "The Next Issues in Jewish-Catholic Relations." *Origins* 26 (1997): 665, 667–70.

Catechism of the Catholic Church. Liberia Editrice Vaticana. Liguori, MO: Liguori Publications, 1994.

Catechism of the Catholic Church. Modifications from the Editio Typica. Washington: United States Catholic Conference, 1998.

Chacour, Elias, with David Hazard. *Blood Brothers.* Grand Rapids: Chosen Books, 1984.

————, with Mary E. Jensen. *We Belong to the Land: The Story of a Palestinian Israeli Who Lives for Peace and Reconciliation.* San Francisco: Harper, 1990.

Charlesworth, James H. "Exploring Opportunities for Rethinking Relations among Jews and Christians." In *Jews and Christians: Exploring the Past, Present, and Future,* edited by James H. Charlesworth, 35–39. New York: Crossroad, 1990.

Cohen, Jeffery M. *Blessed Are You: A Comprehensive Guide to Jewish Prayer*. Northvale, NJ: Jason Aronson, 1993.

Cohn-Sherbok, Dan. *The Blackwell Dictionary of Judaica*. Oxford: Blackwell Publishers, 1992.

―――――. *The Crucified Jew: Twenty Centuries of Christian Anti-Semitism*. San Francisco: Harper Collins, 1992.

―――――. *Israel: The History of an Idea*. London: SPCK, 1992.

Commission for Religious Relations with the Jews. "We Remember: A Reflection on the 'Shoah.'" *Origins* 27 (1998): 669, 671–75.

Cook, Joan E., SC. "The New PBC Document: Continuity, Discontinuity, and Progression Revisited." Paper delivered at the Catholic Biblical Association meeting in San Francisco on August 5, 2003. http://www. bc.edu/texts/cjrelations/resources/articles/cook.htm.

Cross, F. L., ed. *The Oxford Dictionary of the Christian Church*. London: Oxford University Press, 1966.

Cunningham, Philip A. "Covenantal Christology." *Studies in Christian-Jewish Relations* 1 (2005–2006): 41–52. An e-journal of the Council of Centers on Jewish-Christian Relations: http://escholarship.bc.edu/csjr/vol1/iss1/6/.

―――――. *Education for Shalom: Religion Textbooks and the Enhancement of the Catholic and Jewish Relationship*. Collegeville, MN: Liturgical Press, 1995.

―――――. *Jewish Apostle to the Gentiles: Paul as he Saw Himself*. Mystic, CT: Twenty-Third Publications, 1986.

Cust, Lincoln G. A. *The Status Quo in the Holy Places*. Jerusalem: Ariel Publishing, 1980 [facsimile edition of 1929].

Davies, W. D. *The Gospel and the Land*. Berkeley: University of California Press, 1974.

―――――. *The Territorial Dimension of Judaism*. Berkeley: University of California Press, 1982.

Dershowitz, Alan. *The Case for Israel*. Hoboken, NJ: John Wiley and Sons, 2003.

Dever, William G. "Artifacts, Ecofacts, and Textual Facts." In *Recent Archaeological Discoveries and Biblical Research*, 1–36, 175–77. Seattle: University of Washington Press, 1990.

―――――. "How to Tell a Canaanite from an Israelite." In *The Rise of Ancient Israel*, edited by Hershel Shanks, 26–85. Washington: Biblical Archaeology Society, 1992.

―――――. "Is This Man a Biblical Archaeologist?" *BAR* 22, no. 4 (July/August, 1996):30–39, 62–64.

Djalili, Mohammad-Reza. "Dar Al-Harb." In *The Oxford Encyclopedia of the Modern Islamic World*, edited by John L. Esposito, 1:337. New York: Oxford University Press, 1995.

Donahue, John R., and Daniel J. Harrington. *The Gospel of Mark*. Collegeville, MN: Liturgical Press, 2002.

Donaldson, Terence L. *Paul and the Gentiles: Remapping the Apostle's Conviction World*. Minneapolis: Fortress Press, 1997.

Doyle, Stephen C. *The Pilgrim's New Guide to the Holy Land*. 2nd edition. Collegeville, MN: Liturgical Press, 1999.

Drummond, Dorothy. *Holy Land, Whose Land? Modern Dilemma Ancient Roots*. 2nd revised edition. Terre Haute, IN: Fairhurst Press, 2004.

Dunn, James D. G. *Romans*. 2 vols. Dallas: Word Books, 1988.

————. *The Theology of Paul the Apostle*. Grand Rapids: Eerdmans, 1998.

Eckardt, A. Roy. *Elder and Younger Brothers: The Encounter of Jews and Christians*. New York: Charles Scribner's Sons, 1967.

————. *Reclaiming the Jesus of History: Christology Today*. Minneapolis: Fortress Press, 1992.

Eliade, Mircea. *Cosmos and History: The Myth of the Eternal Return*. Translated by Willard R. Trask. New York: Harper Torchbooks, 1959.

Falls, Ze'ev W. "The Notion of Promised Land: Searching for Clarity." *SIDIC* 12, no. 3 (1979): 23–25.

Feiler, Bruce. *Abraham*. New York: William Morrow, 2002.

————. *Walking the Bible*. New York: William Morrow, 2001.

————. *Where God Was Born*. New York: William Morrow, 2005.

Firestone, Reuven. "One Holy Land, Three Holy Peoples: Islamic, Christian, and Jewish Regard for the Holy City." 2002. www.umass.edu/jewish/programs/firestone_talk/.

Fisher, Eugene J. "The Catechism and 'Our Elder Brothers in the Faith.'" *Explorations* 10, no. 5 (1996): 5.

————. "Catholics and Jews Confront the Holocaust and Each Other." *America* 181 (September 11, 1999): 9–14.

————. "The Development of a Tradition." *SIDIC* 19, no. 2 (1986): 20–23.

————. "Epilogue." In *Interwoven Destinies: Jews and Christians Through the Ages*, edited by Eugene J. Fisher, 143–46. Mahwah, NJ: Paulist Press, 1993.

————. "Reflections on the Catechism of the Catholic Church." *Interfaith Focus* 1, no. 2 (1994): 10–21.

————. "Reflections on the Catechism of the Catholic church." *SIDIC* 27, no. 2 (1994): 2–8.

————. "Update on Catholic Education on Jews and Judaism." *SIDIC* 27, no. 3 (1994): 24–30.

————. "A Word for Continuity: A Response to Joann Spillman." *JES* 35 (1998): 85–87.

Fitzmyer, Joseph A. *The Acts of the Apostles*. Anchor Bible, 31. New York: Doubleday, 1998.

Flannery, Edward. *The Anguish of the Jews*. Revised and updated. Mahwah, NJ: Paulist Press, 1985.

————. "The Challenges We Jointly Face: A Catholic View." *Face to Face* 12 (Fall 1985): 43–48.

————. "A Christian View of Israel." *United Synagogue Review* (Fall 1971): 10–11, 30.

————. "Christian Zionist Ethos Should Be Revived." *Providence Journal Bulletin* (Providence, RI) April 26, 1996. http://nclci.org/articles/art-flan-ethos.htm.

Forte, Most Rev. Bruno. "Israel and the Church—The Two Explorers of the Promised Land: Towards a Christian Theology of Judaism." Address at the Pontifical Gregorian University, Rome, 4 November 2004. http://www.bc.edu/research/cjl/meta-elements/texts/center/conferences/Bea_Centre_C-JRelations_04-05/Forte.htm.

Freedman, Richard E. *Who Wrote the Bible?* 2nd edition. San Francisco: Harper Collins, 1997.

Freeman-Grenville, G. S. P. *The Holy Land: A Pilgrim's Guide to Israel, Jordan and the Sinai*. Jerusalem: Carta, 1996.

Frymer-Kensky, Tikva, and David Novak, Peter Ochs, David Fox Sandmel, and Michael A. Signer. *Christianity in Jewish Terms*. Boulder, CO: Westview Press, 2000.

Fumagalli, Pier Francesco. "The Church and the Jewish People—Twenty-Five Years after the Second Vatican Council (1963–1965)." *SIDIC* 25, no. 2 (1992): 19.

Gager, John G. "The Parting of the Ways: A View from the Perspective of Early Christianity: 'A Christian Perspective.'" In *Interwoven Destinies: Jews and Christians Through the Ages*, edited by Eugene J. Fisher, 62–73. New York: Paulist Press, 1993.

————. *Reinventing Paul*. New York: Oxford University Press, 2000.

Garfiel, Evelyn. *Service of the Heart: A Guide to the Jewish Prayer Book*. Northvale, NJ: Jason Aronson, 1958/1994.

Gaston, Lloyd. "Paul and the Torah." In *Antisemitism and the Foundations of Christianity*, edited by Alan T. Davies, 48–71. New York: Paulist Press, 1979.

Gilbert, Martin. *The Dent Atlas of the Arab-Israeli Conflict*. 6th edition. London: Dent, 1993.

Gnuse, Robert. "Israelite Settlement of Canaan: A Peaceful Internal Process—Part 1and 2." *BTB* 21 (1991): 56–66, 109–17.

Goldstein, Jonathan A. *II Maccabees*. Anchor Bible, 41A. New York: Doubleday, 1984.

Haddad, William W. "Christian Arab Attitudes toward the Arab-Israeli Conflict." *The Muslim World* 67, no. 2 (1977): 127–45.

Hall, Sidney G. III. *Christian Anti-Semitism and Paul's Theology*. Minneapolis: Fortress Press, 1993.

Halpern-Amaru, Betsy. *Rewriting the Bible: Land and Covenant in Post-Biblical Jewish Literature*. Valley Forge, PA: Trinity Press International, 1994.

Harrington, Daniel J. *The Gospel of Matthew*. Sacra Pagina, 1. Collegeville, MN: Liturgical Press, 1991.

———. "A New Paradigm for Paul." *America* 157 (1987): 290–93.

———. "Paul and Judaism: 5 Puzzles." *Bible Review* 9, no. 2 (April 1993):19–25, 52.

———. "Paul the Jew." *The Catholic World* 235 (March/April 1992): 68–73.

———. *Romans: The Good News According to Paul*. Hyde Park, NY: New City Press, 1998.

Hartman, Rabbi David. "The Challenge of Modern Israel to Traditional Judaism." In *Conflicting Visions: Spiritual Possibilities of Modern Israel*, 31–53. New York: Schocken Books, 1990.

———. "Judaism Encounters Christianity Anew." In *Visions of the Other: Jewish and Christian Theologians Assess the Dialogue*, edited by Eugene J. Fisher, 67–80. New York: Paulist Press, 1994.

Hayes, Zachary. "Eschatology." In *The Modern Catholic Encyclopedia*, edited by Michael Glazier and Monika K. Hellwig, 274–76. Revised and expanded edition. Collegeville, MN: Liturgical Press, 2004.

Heldt, Petra. "Christians in the Middle East." *Christians and Israel* 2, no. 4 (Autumn 1993): 4–5.

——— and Malcolm Lowe. "Theological Significance of the rebirth of the State of Israel: Different Christian Attitudes." *Immanuel* 2/23 (1989): 133–45.

Hellwig, Monika. "Christian Theology and the Covenant of Israel." *JES* 7 (1970): 37–51.

———. "From the Jesus Story to the Christ of Dogma." In *Antisemitism and the Foundations of Christianity*, edited by Alan T. Davies, 118–36. New York: Paulist Press, 1979.

Heschel, Abraham Joshua. *Israel: An Echo of Eternity*. New York: Farrar, Straus and Giroux, 1967.

"Hijra." In *The HarperCollins Dictionary of Religion*, edited by Jonathan Z. Smith, 419. San Francisco: HarperSanFrancisco, 1995.

Hilberg, Raul. *The Destruction of the European Jews*. Chicago: Quadrangle Books, 1961.

Himmelfarb, Martha. "The Parting of the Ways Reconsidered: Diversity in Judaism and Jewish-Christian Relations in the Roman Empire: 'A Jewish Perspective.'" In *Interwoven Destinies: Jews and Christians Through the Ages*, edited by Eugene J. Fisher, 47–61. New York: Paulist Press, 1993.

Hoffman, Lawrence A. "Introduction: Land of Blessing and 'Blessings of the Land.'" In *The Land of Israel: Jewish Perspectives*, edited by Lawrence A. Hoffman, 1–23. Notre Dame: University of Notre Dame Press, 1986.

Holwerda, David E. *Jesus & Israel: One Covenant or Two?* Grand Rapids: Eerdmans,1995.

Hughes, Kathleen. *Saying Amen: A Mystagogy of Sacrament*. Chicago: Liturgy Training Publications, 1999.

International Catholic-Jewish Liaison Committee Meeting at Vatican. "Joint Communique [Document on the '*Shoah*,' March 26, 1998]." *Origins* 27 (April 9, 1998): 701, 703–4.

Interreligious Coordinating Council in Israel. *Guide to Interreligious and Intercultural Activities in Israel*. Jerusalem: ICCI, 2001.

Isaacs, Ronald H., and Kerry M. Olitzky, eds. *Critical Documents of Jewish History: A Source Book*. Northvale, NJ: Jason Aronson, 1995.

Jackson, Sherman A. "Islam(s) East and West: Pluralism between No-Frills and Designer Fundamentalism." In *September 11 in History: A watershed Moment?* edited by Mary L. Dudziak, 112–35. Durham, NC: Duke University Press, 2003.

Janzen, Waldemar W. "Land." In *Anchor Bible Dictionary*, edited by David Noel Freedman, 4:146. New York: Doubleday, 1992.

Jensen, Robin. "How Jews and Christians See Differently [Gen 22:1–18]." *Bible Review* 9, no. 5 (1993): 42–51.

John Paul II. "Address of Pope John Paul II during a meeting with the Central Council of the Jews in Germany on 23 June 1996 in Berlin." *SIDIC* 29, nos. 2–3 (1996): 54–56.

———. "Pilgrimage to Places Linked to the History of Salvation." *Origins* 29 (July 15, 1999): 125–28.

———. *Redemptionis Anno* ("In the year of Redemption"), Apostolic Letter, Good Friday, April 1984. *Origins* 14, no. 2 (May 24, 1984): 31–32.

———. "The Roots of Anti-Judaism." *Origins* 27 (November 13, 1997): 365.

———. *Spiritual Pilgrimage: Texts on Jews and Judaism, 1979–1995*, with commentary and introduction by Eugene J. Fisher and Leon Klenicki, eds. New York: Crossroad Publishing Company, 1995.

―――. *Tertio Millennio Adveniente* ("Coming of the Third Millennium") *Origins* 24, no. 24 (November 24, 1994): 401, 403–16.

Johnson, Luke Timothy. *The Acts of the Apostles.* Sacra Pagina, 5. Collegeville, MN: Liturgical Press, 1992.

Kaltner, John. *Ishmael Instructs Isaac: An Introduction to the Qur'an for Bible Readers.* Collegeville, MN: Liturgical Press, 1999.

Keeler, William Cardinal, and Eugene J. Fisher. "Implications of the Document on the '*Shoah.*'" *Origins* 27 (March 26, 1998): 675.

Kelsay, John. "Dar Al-Islam." In the *Encyclopedia of Islam and the Muslim World*, edited by Richard C. Martin, 1:169. New York: Macmillan Reference USA, 2004.

Kenny, Anthony. *Catholics, Jews and the State of Israel.* Mahwah, NJ: Paulist Press, 1993.

Khalidi, Rashid. *The Iron Cage: The Story of the Palestinian Struggle for Statehood.* Boston: Beacon Press, 2006.

Khoury, Father Rafiz. "The History of Jerusalem: A Christian perspective." In *The Spiritual Significance of Jerusalem for Jews, Christians and Muslims*, edited by Hans Ucko, 9–20. World Council of Churches, 1994.

Kitchen, Kenneth A. *On the Reliability of the Old Testament.* Grand Rapids: Eerdmans, 2003.

Klein, Charlotte. "Vatican and Zionism, 1897–1967." *Christian Attitudes on Jews and Judaism*, nos. 36–37 (1974): 11–16.

―――. "Vatican View of Jewry, 1939–1962, in the Mirror of *Civiltà Cattolica.*" *Christian Attitudes on Jews and Judaism*, no. 43 (1976): 12–16.

Kogan, Michael S. "Jews and Christians: Taking the Next Step." *JES* 26 (1989): 703–13.

―――. "Toward a Jewish Theology of Christianity." *JES* 32 (1996): 89–106, 152.

Kronish, Rabbi Ronald. "The Implications of the Peace Agreements for Interreligious/Intercultural Relations in Israel." *SIDIC* 29, nos. 2–3 (1996): 30–35.

――― and Emily Michaelson. "A Summary of ICCI's Recent Symposium in Jerusalem." *Insight Israel*, no. 3 (February 26, 1997).

Laqueur, Walter. *A History of Zionism: From the French Revolution to the Establishment of the State of Israel.* New York: MJF Books, 1972.

Laurentin, Rene, and Joseph Neuner. *Declaration on the Relation of the Church to Non-Christian Religions of Vatican Council II.* Glen Rock, NJ: Paulist Press, 1966, 17–77.

Lawler, Michael G. *Symbol and Sacrament: A Contemporary Sacramental Theology*. New York/Mahwah, NJ: Paulist Press, 1987.

Lemche, Niels Peter, Thomas Thompson, William Dever, and P. Kyle McCarter. "Face to Face: Biblical Minimalists Meet Their Challengers," by Hershel Shanks. *BAR* 23, no. 4 (July/August 1997): 26–42.

Levine, Amy-Jill. "The Jewish People and Their Sacred Scriptures in the Christian Bible: A Jewish Reading of the Document." *The Bible Today* 32 (2003): 167–72.

──────. "Roland Murphy, The Pontifical Biblical Commission, Jews, and the Bible." *BTB* 33 (2003): 104–13.

Lichtenberg, Jean Paul. *From the First to the Last of the Just: A Study of the History of The Relations Between Jews and Christians Throughout the Centuries*. Jerusalem: Ecumenical Theological Research Fraternity in Israel, 1975.

Lohfink, Norbert. *The Covenant Never Revoked: Biblical Reflections on Christian-Jewish Dialogue*. Translated by John J. Scullion. New York: Paulist Press, 1991.

Lowenthal, M., ed. *The Diaries of Theodor Herzl*. London; Jewish Publication Society, 1958.

Luedemann, Gerd. *The Acts of the Apostles*. Amherst, NY: Prometheus Books, 2005.

──────. *Early Christianity according to the Traditions in Acts: A Commentary*. Translated by John Bowden. Minneapolis: Fortress Press, 1989.

Lux, Richard C. "Biblical Land Traditions." *The Catholic World* 234 (Jan./Feb. 1991): 4–10.

──────. "Covenant Interpretations: A New Model for the Christian-Jewish Relationship." *SCHOLA: A Pastoral Review of Sacred Heart School of Theology* 5 (1982): 25–62.

──────. "The Two State Solution: Pope Benedict XVI and Israel/Palestine." *The Catholic World* 243, no. 1453 (July/August 2009), http://www.thecatholicworld.com.

McBrien, Richard P. *Catholicism*. Revised and updated. San Francisco: HarperCollins, 1994.

McGarry, Michael. "Antisemitism (Christian View)." In *A Dictionary of the Jewish-Christian Dialogue*, edited by Leon Klenicki and Geoffrey Wigoder, 12–14. Expanded edition. Mahwah, NJ: Paulist Press, 1995.

Marthaler, Bernard L., ed. *Introducing the Catechism of the Catholic Church: Traditional Themes and Contemporary Issues*. Mahwah, NJ: Paulist Press, 1994.

Martin, Vincent. *A House Divided: The Parting of the Ways between Synagogue and Church*. New York: Paulist Press, 1995.

Masalha, Nur. *Expulsion of the Palestinians*. Washington: Institute of Palestinian Studies, 1992.

Mays, James A. *Amos: A Commentary*. Philadelphia: Westminster Press, 1969.

———. *Hosea: A Commentary*. Philadelphia: Westminster Press, 1969.

Meier, John P. *A Marginal Jew: Rethinking the Historical Jesus: Companions and Competitors*. Vol. 3. New York: Doubleday, 2001.

———. *A Marginal Jew: Rethinking the Historical Jesus: Mentor, Message and Miracle*. Vol. 2. New York; Doubleday, 1994.

———. *A Marginal Jew: Rethinking the Historical Jesus: The Roots of the Problem and the Person*. Vol. 1. New York: Doubleday, 1991.

Melloni, Alberto. "Nostra Aetate and the Discovery of the Sacrament of Otherness." Lecture delivered at the Pontifical Gregorian University in Rome, November 9, 2004. http://www.bc.edu/research/cjl/meta-elements/texts/conferences/Bea_centre_C-J_Relations_04-05/melloni.htm.

Mendes, Meir. "The Catholic Church, Judaism and the State of Israel." *Christian-Jewish Relations* 21, no.2 (1988): 28.

Merkley, Paul Charles. *Christian Attitudes Towards the State of Israel*. Montreal: McGill-Queen's University Press, 2001.

Middle East Council of Churches. *The MECC: An Introduction to the Middle East Council of Churches*. Limassol [Cyprus]: MECC Communications, 1995.

Miller, Charles H. "Translation Errors in the Pontifical Biblical Commission's 'The Jewish People and Their Sacred Scriptures in the Christian Bible.'" *BTB* 36 (2005): 34–39.

Miller, John H., ed. *Vatican II: An Interfaith Appraisal*. Notre Dame: University of Notre Dame Press, 1966.

Miller, Patrick D. Jr. "The Gift of God: The Deuteronomic Theology of the Land." *Interpretation* 23 (1969): 451–65.

Morris, Benny. *The Birth of the Palestinian Refugee Problem Revisited*. Cambridge: Cambridge University Press, 2004.

Murphy-O'Connor, Jerome. *The Holy Land: An Oxford Archaeological Guide from Earliest Times to 1700*. 4th edition. New York: Oxford University Press, 1998.

National Conference of Catholic Bishops. "Statement on Catholic-Jewish Relations (November 20, 1975)." In *Stepping Stones to Further Jewish-Christian Relations: An Unabridged Collection of Christian Documents*, edited by Helga Croner, 29–34. New York: Stimulus Books, 1977.

Neusner, Jacob. *Judaism in the Beginning of Christianity*. Philadelphia: Fortress Press, 1984.

Nicholls, William. *Christian Antisemitism: A History of Hate*. Northvale, NJ: Jason Aronson,1993.

Niditch, Susan. "Jericho and Achan (Joshua 6—7)." In *War in the Hebrew Bible*, 58–61. New York: Oxford University Press, 1993.

Noth, Martin. *A History of Pentateuchal Traditions*. Translated by Bernard W. Anderson. Englewood Cliffs, NJ: Prentice-Hall, 1972.

O'Connor, John Cardinal. "A Step Forward in an Ongoing Dialogue." *Origins* 27 (March 26, 1998): 676.

O'Hare, Padraic. "The Reform of Christian Religious Education: The End of 'The Teaching of Contempt.'" *Interfaith Focus* 1, no. 2 (1994): 1–2.

O'Mahony, Anthony. "The Christian Communities of Jerusalem and the Holy Land: A Historical and Political Survey." In *The Christian Communities of Jerusalem and the Holy Land: Studies in History, Religion and Politics*, edited by Anthony O'Mahony, 1–37. Cardiff: University of Wales Press, 2003.

Orlinsky, Harry M. "The Biblical Concept of the Land of Israel: Cornerstone of the Covenant between God and Israel." In *The Land of Israel: Jewish Perspectives*, edited by Lawrence A. Hoffman, 27–64. Notre Dame: University of Notre Dame Press, 1986.

Ottoson, Magnus. "*'erets* (land)." In *Theological Dictionary of the Old Testament*, edited by G. Johannes Boterweck and Helmer Ringgren, 1:388–405. Translated by John T. Willis. Grand Rapids: Eerdmans, 1977.

Pappe, Ilan "Were They Expelled? The History, Historiography and Relevance of the Palestinian Refugee Problem." In *The Palestinian Exodus, 1948–1998*, edited by Ghada Karmi and Eugene Cotran, 37–61. Reading [UK]: Ithaca Press, 1999.

Parkes, James. *Judaism and Christianity*. Chicago: University of Chicago Press, 1948.

Paul, Shalom M. *Amos*. Minneapolis: Fortress Press, 1991.

Paul VI. *Ecclesiam Suam* ("Paths of the Church"). Encyclical, August 6, 1964. In *The Papal Encyclicals, 1958–1981*, edited by Claudia Carlen Ihm, 135–60. Wilmington [NC]: McGrath Publishing Company, 1981.

———. *Mysterium Fidei* ("The Mystery of Faith"). Encyclical, September 3, 1965. In *The Papal Encyclicals, 1958–1981*, edited by Claudia Carlen Ihm, 165–77. Wilmington [NC]: McGrath Publishing Company, 1981.

Pawlikowski, John T. "The Historicizing of the Eschatological: The Spiritualizing of the Eschatological: Some Reflections." In *Antisemitism and the Foundations of Christianity*, edited by Alan T. Davies, 151–66. New York: Paulist Press, 1979.

———. "Single or Double Covenant? Contemporary Perspectives." In *Peace in Deed: Essays in Honor of Harry James Cargas*, edited by

Zev Garber and Richard Libowitz, 147–62. Atlanta: Scholars Press, 1998.

————. "The Vatican-Israel Accords: Their Implications for Catholic Faith and Teaching." *PACE* 24 (November, 1994): 15–21.

————. "We Remember: A Constructive Critique." (2000) http://www. nclci.org/Articles/art-remember.htm.

————. *What Are They Saying about Christian-Jewish Relations?* New York: Paulist Press, 1980.

Peters, Joan. *From Time Immemorial: The Origins of the Arab-Jewish Conflict over Palestine.* New York: Harper & Row, 1984.

Peters, Melvin K. H. "Septuagint." In *Anchor Bible Dictionary*, edited by David Noel Freedman, 5:1093–1104. New York: Doubleday, 1992.

Pius XII. "Encyclical of Our Holy Father Pope Pius XII on Palestine [*In Multiplicibus Curis*]." *CBQ* 11 (1949): 89–90.

Pixner, Bargil, OSB. *With Jesus in Jerusalem: His First and Last Days in Judea.* Rosh Pina [Israel]: Corazin Publishing, 1996.

Pontifical Biblical Commission. "Instruction on the Historical Truth of the Gospel." In *A Christological Catechism: New Testament Answers*, Joseph A. Fitzmyer, 131–42. New York: Paulist Press, 1982.

The Prayer Book. The Commission on Jewish Chaplaincy of the National Jewish Welfare Board, 1958.

Prior, Michael. "Pilgrimage to the Holy Land Yesterday and Today." In *Christians in the Holy Land*, edited by Michael Prior and William Taylor, 169–99. London: World of Islam Trust, 1994.

Rad, Gerhard von. *The Problem of the Hexateuch and Other Essays.* Translated by E. W. Trueman. New York: McGraw-Hill, 1966.

Ratzinger, Joseph Cardinal. *Many Religions—One Covenant: Israel, the Church and the World.* Translated by Graham Harrison. San Francisco: Ignatius Press, 1999.

Richard, Earl. "Early Pauline Thought." In *Pauline Theology*, edited by Jouette M. Bassler, 39–51. Minneapolis: Fortress Press, 1991.

————. *First and Second Thessalonians.* Sacra Pagina, 11. Collegeville, MN: Liturgical Press, 1996.

Rosenzweig, Franz. *The Star of Redemption.* Translation of the 2nd edition of 1930 by William Hallo. New York: Holt, Rinehart, Winston, 1971.

Rudin, A. James. "The Rise of Modern Zionism." In *Israel for Christians: Understanding Modern Israel*, 23–40. Philadelphia: Fortress Press, 1983.

Ruether, Rosemary Radford. *Faith and Fratricide: The Theological Roots of Anti-Semitism.* New York: Seabury Press, 1974.

Rylaarsdam, J. Coert. "Jewish-Christian Relationship: The Two Covenants and the Dilemmas of Christology." *JES* 9 (1992): 249–70.

Saldarini, Anthony J. "Septuagint." In *The HarperCollins Bible Dictionary*, edited by Paul J. Achtemeier, 996. San Francisco: Harper & Row, 1996.

Samuelson, Norbert M. *A User's Guide to Franz Rosenzweig's Star of Redemption*. Surrey [England]: Curzon Press, 1999.

Sanders, E. P. *Paul and Palestinian Judaism*. Philadelphia: Fortress Press, 1977.

————. *Paul, the Law and the Jewish People*. Philadelphia: Fortress Press, 1983.

Sandmel, David F., Rosann M. Catalano, and Christopher M. Leighton, eds. *Irreconcilable Differences? A Learning Resource for Jews and Christians*. Boulder [CO]: Westview Press, 2001.

Schiffman, Lawrence H. *Who Was a Jew? Rabbinic and Halakhic Perspectives on the Jewish-Christian Schism*. Hoboken, NJ: KTAV Publishing House, 1985.

Schillebeeckx, Edward. "Transubstantiation, Transfinalization, Transignification." In *Living Bread, Saving Cup*, edited by R. Kevin Seasoltz, OSB, 175–89. Collegeville, MN: Liturgical Press, 1987.

Schmemann, Alexander. *For the Life of the World: Sacraments and Orthodoxy*. Crestwood [NY]: St. Vladimir's Seminary Press, 2000.

————. *Introduction to Liturgical Theology*. Translated by Asheleigh E. Moorhouse. Crestwood [NY]: St. Vladimir's Seminary Press, 1986.

Schnackenburg. Rudolf. *The Gospel According to St. John*. Translated by Kevin Smyth. New York: Herder and Herder, 1968.

Schochet. Jacob Immanuel. *Mashiach, The Principle of Mashiach and the Messianic Era in Jewish Law and Tradition*. 3rd edition. New York: S.I.E., 1992.

Scholem, Gershom. *The Messianic Idea in Judaism*. New York: Schocken Books, 1971.

Schwarzschild, Steven S., and Saul Berman. "Noachide Laws." In *Encyclopedia Judaica*, edited by Cecil Roth, 12:1189–91. Jerusalem: Keter, 1971.

Seters, John van. *Abraham in History and Tradition*. New Haven: Yale University Press, 1975.

Shanks, Hershel. "The Biblical Minimalists: Expunging Ancient Israel's Past." *BR* 13, no. 3 (June 1997): 50–52.

Shapiro, Haim. "Israel-Vatican Relations: A Long, Slow Thaw." *The Jerusalem Post*, February 4, 1997.

Signer, Michael A. "One Covenant or Two: Can We Sing a New Song?" In *Reinterpreting Revelation and Tradition*, edited by John T. Pawlikowski and Hayim Goren Perelmuter, 3–23. Franklin [WI]: Sheed & Ward, 2000.

Skoog, Lena. "Selected Bibliography on the Land and State of Israel." *Immanuel* 22/23 (1989): 215–29.

Spillman, Joann. "The Image of Covenant in Christian Understandings of Judaism." *JES* 35 (1998): 63–84.

Stendahl, Krister. *Final Account: Paul's Letter to the Romans*. Minneapolis: Fortress Press, 1995.

———. *Paul Among Jews and Gentiles*. Philadelphia: Fortress Press, 1976.

Stransky, Thomas F. "The Genesis of Nostra Aetate." *America* 193, no. 12 (2005): 8–12.

———. "Holy Diplomacy: Making the Impossible Possible." In *Unanswered Questions: Theological Views of Jewish-Catholic Relations*, edited by Roger Brooks, 51–69. Notre Dame: University of Notre Dame Press, 1988.

Strickert, Fred. *Rachael Weeping: Jews, Christians, and Muslims at the Fortress Tomb*. Collegeville, MN: Liturgical Press, 2007.

Tal, Uriel. "Jewish Self-Understanding and the Land and State of Israel." *Union Seminary Quarterly Review* 26 (1971): 351–63.

Talhami, Dr. Ghada. "The History of Jerusalem: A Muslim Perspective." In *The Spiritual Significance of Jerusalem for Jews, Christians and Muslims*, edited by Hans Ucko, 21–30. World Council of Churches, 1994.

Thomas, David. "Abraham in Islamic Tradition." *Scripture Bulletin* 37, no. 1 (2007): 12–20.

Thompson, Thomas L. *The Historicity of the Patriarchal Narratives: The Quest for the Historical Abraham*. BZAW, 133. Berlin: Walter de Gruyter, 1974.

———. *The Origin Tradition of Ancient Israel. 1. The Literary Formation of Genesis and Exodus 1–23*. JSOT Supp., 55. Sheffield: JSOT Press, 1987.

Thordson, Maria. *Christians 2,000 A.D. Men and Women in the Land of Christ: A Living Church History*. Jerusalem: Emerezian Establishment, 1996.

Timotheos of Lydda, archbishop "Jerusalem's Significance in Scripture and Tradition: A Christian Perspective." In *The Spiritual Significance of Jerusalem for Jews, Christians and Muslims*, edited by Hans Ucko, 57–66. World Council of Churches, 1994.

Twain, Mark. *The Innocents Abroad or The New Pilgrims' Progress*. Hartford: American Publishing Company, 1882 [c1869].

Vatican Commission for Religious Relations with the Jews. "Guidelines and Suggestions For Implementing the Conciliar Declaration 'Nostra Aetate.'" In *In Our Time: The Flowering of Jewish-Catholic Dialogue*, edited by Dr. Eugene J. Fisher and Rabbi Leon Klenicki, 29–37. Mahwah, NJ: Paulist Press, 1990.

Weis, Andrea L. "Creative Readings of the Covenant: A Jewish-Christian Approach." *JES* 30 (1993): 389–402.

Wilken, Robert L. *The Land Called Holy*. New Haven: Yale University Press, 1992.

Willebrands, Johannes Cardinal. *Church and Jewish People: New Considerations*. Mahwah, NJ: Paulist Press, 1992.

———. "Vatican II's Ecclesiology of Communion." *Origins* 17, no. 2 (May 28, 1987): 27–33.

Winer, Rabbi Mark. "Jewish-Catholic Relations After the fundamental Agreement." *Origins* 26 (1997): 671-674.

Witherington, Ben III. *The Acts of the Apostles: A Socio-Rhetorical Commentary*. Grand Rapids: Eerdmans, 1998.

Wolff, Hans Walter. *Joel and Amos*. Translated by Waldemar Janzen, S. Dean McBride Jr., and Charles A. Muenchow, edited by S. Dean McBride Jr. Philadelphia: Fortress Press, 1977.

———. *Hosea*. Translated by Gary Stansell, edited by S. Dean McBride Jr. Philadelphia: Fortress Press, 1974.

Worthen, Jeremy. "Beginning Without End: Christianity in Franz Rosenzweig's Star of Redemption." *JES* 39 (2002): 340–62.

Wright, John H. "eschatology, universal." In *The HarperCollins Encyclopedia of Catholicism*, edited by Richard P. McBrien, 476–77. San Francisco: HarperCollins, 1995.

Wyschogrod, Michael. "The Torah as Law in Judaism." *SIDIC* 19, no. 3 (1986): 8–13.

Ziesler, John. *Paul's Letter to the Romans*. Philadelphia: Trinity Press International, 1989.

Index

Other Volumes in This Series

Helga Croner, compiler, *Stepping Stones to Further Jewish-Christian Relations: An Unabridged Collection of Christian Documents* (A Stimulus Book, 1977).

Helga Croner and Leon Klenicki, editors, *Issues in the Jewish-Christian Dialogue: Jewish Perspectives on Covenant, Mission and Witness* (A Stimulus Book, 1979).

Helga Croner, Leon Klenicki, and Lawrence Boadt, CSP, editors, *Biblical Studies: Meeting Ground of Jews and Christians* (A Stimulus Book, 1980).

Clemens Thoma, *A Christian Theology of Judaism* (A Stimulus Book, 1980).

Helga Croner and Martin A. Cohen, editors, *Christian Mission/Jewish Mission* (A Stimulus Book, 1982).

John T. Pawlikowski, OSM, *Christ in the Light of the Christian-Jewish Dialogue* (A Stimulus Book, 1982).

Leon Klenicki and Gabe Huck, editors, *Spirituality and Prayer: Jewish and Christian Understandings* (A Stimulus Book, 1983).

Helga Croner, compiler, *More Stepping Stones to Jewish-Christian Relations: An Unabridged Collection of Christian Documents 1975–1983* (A Stimulus Book, 1985).

Edward Flannery, *The Anguish of the Jews* (A Stimulus Book, 1985).

Clemens Thoma and Michael Wyschogrod, editors, *Understanding Scripture: Explorations of Jewish and Christian Traditions of Interpretation* (A Stimulus Book, 1987).

Bernard J. Lee, SM, *The Galilean Jewishness of Jesus: Retrieving the Jewish Origins of Christianity,* Conversation on the Road Not Taken, Vol. 1 (A Stimulus Book, 1988).

Clemens Thoma and Michael Wyschogrod, editors, *Parable and Story in Judaism and Christianity* (A Stimulus Book, 1989).

Eugene J. Fisher and Leon Klenicki, editors, *In Our Time: The Flowering of Jewish-Catholic Dialogue* (A Stimulus Book, 1990).

David Burrell and Yehezkel Landau, editors, *Voices from Jerusalem* (A Stimulus Book, 1991).

Leon Klenicki, editor, *Toward A Theological Encounter* (A Stimulus Book, 1991).

John Rousmaniere, *A Bridge to Dialogue: The Story of Jewish-Christian Relations,* edited by James A. Carpenter and Leon Klenicki (A Stimulus Book, 1991).

Michael E. Lodahl, *Shekhinah/Spirit* (A Stimulus Book, 1992).

George M. Smiga, *Pain and Polemic: Anti-Judaism in the Gospels* (A Stimulus Book, 1992).

Eugene J. Fisher, editor, *Interwoven Destinies: Jews and Christians Through the Ages* (A Stimulus Book, 1993).

Anthony Kenny, *Catholics, Jews and the State of Israel* (A Stimulus Book, 1993).

Bernard J. Lee, SM, *Jesus and the Metaphors of God: The Christs of the New Testament,* Conversation on the Road Not Taken, Vol. 2 (A Stimulus Book, 1993).

Eugene J. Fisher, editor, *Visions of the Other: Jewish and Christian Theologians Assess the Dialogue* (A Stimulus Book, 1995).

Leon Klenicki and Geoffrey Wigoder, editors, *A Dictionary of the Jewish-Christian Dialogue,* Expanded Edition (A Stimulus Book, 1995).

Vincent Martin, *A House Divided: The Parting of the Ways between Synagogue and Church* (A Stimulus Book, 1995).

Philip A. Cunningham and Arthur F. Starr, editors, *Sharing Shalom: A Process for Local Interfaith Dialogue Between Christians and Jews* (A Stimulus Book, 1998).

Frank E. Eakin, Jr., *What Price Prejudice? Christian Antisemitism in America* (A Stimulus Book, 1998).

Ekkehard Schuster and Reinhold Boschert-Kimmig, *Hope Against Hope: Johann Baptist Metz and Elie Wiesel Speak Out on the Holocaust* (A Stimulus Book, 1999).

Mary C. Boys, *Has God Only One Blessing? Judaism as a Source of Christian Understanding* (A Stimulus Book, 2000).

Avery Dulles, SJ, and Leon Klenicki, editors, *The Holocaust, Never to Be Forgotten: Reflections on the Holy See's Document* We Remember (A Stimulus Book, 2000).

Johannes Reuchlin, *Recommendation Whether to Confiscate, Destroy and Burn All Jewish Books: A Classic Treatise against Anti-Semitism,* translated, edited, and with an introduction by Peter Wortsman (A Stimulus Book, 2000).

Philip A. Cunningham, *A Story of Shalom: The Calling of Christians and Jews by a Covenanting God* (A Stimulus Book, 2001).

Philip A. Cunningham, *Sharing the Scriptures,* The Word Set Free, Vol. 1 (A Stimulus Book, 2003).

Dina Wardi, *Auschwitz: Contemporary Jewish and Christian Encounters* (A Stimulus Book, 2003).

Michael Lotker, *A Christian's Guide to Judaism* (A Stimulus Book, 2004).

Lawrence Boadt and Kevin di Camillo, editors, *John Paul II in the Holy Land: In His Own Words: With Christian and Jewish Perspectives by Yehezkel Landau and Michael McGarry, CSP* (A Stimulus Book, 2005).

James K. Aitken and Edward Kessler, editors, *Challenges in Jewish-Christian Relations* (A Stimulus Book, 2006).

George M. Smiga, *The Gospel of John Set Free* (A Stimulus Book, 2008).

Daniel J. Harrington, SJ, *The Synoptic Gospels Set Free* (A Stimulus Book, 2009).

STIMULUS BOOKS are developed by the Stimulus Foundation, a not-for-profit organization, and are published by Paulist Press. The Foundation wishes to further the publication of scholarly books on Jewish and Christian topics that are of importance to Judaism and Christianity.

The Stimulus Foundation was established by an erstwhile refugee from Nazi Germany who intends to contribute with these publications to the improvement of communication between Jews and Christians.

Books for publication in this Series will be selected by a committee of the Foundation, and offers of manuscripts and works in progress should be addressed to:

The Stimulus Foundation
c/o Paulist Press
997 Macarthur Boulevard
Mahwah, NJ 07430
www.paulistpress.com